# The Spirits of '76
## A Catholic Inquiry

Donald J. D'Elia

CHRISTENDOM PUBLICATIONS
Christendom College Press
Route 3, Box 87
Front Royal, Virginia 22630

L.C. Classification Number: E221.D25
ISBN: 0-931888-10-7

*To the Memory of My Father,*

*Lt. Col. Anthony B. D'Elia, Jr (1903-1973),*

*Soldier of Mercy*

The publication of this book was made possible in part through the support of the Christendom Publishing Group. Members are listed below:

Mr. Wil Van Achthoven
All Saints Religious Art and Books
Anonymous
Anonymous
Mr. & Mrs. John and Opal Baye
Mr. Joseph C. Berzanskis
Mr. John F. Bradley
Mr. George Bridgman
Mr. & Mrs. Robert Brindle
Mrs. Martha Brown
Paul A. Busam, M.D.
Mr. Robert M. Caley
Mr. Thomas Calvo
Mr. Charles M. Campbell
Miss Priscilla Carmody
Mr. Herb Cary
Joseph C. Caserrelli, Esq.
Mrs. Virginia J. Chipp
Mrs. S. J. Conner
Rev. Edward J. Connolly
Mr. John W. W. Cooper
Mr. & Mrs. Chris N. Cuddeback
Mr. Robert J. Cynkar
Mrs. Ellen L. Dalby
The Dateno Family
Mr. B. P. Davidson
Rev. Herman J. Deimel
Mrs. George de Lorimier
Rev. Robert J. Dempsey
Mr. Joseph L. DeStefano
Rev. Daniel B. Dixon
Mr. Thomas C. Domeika
Mr. Francis Donahue
Mr. & Mrs. Leon W. Doty
Mr. Thomas J. Dowdall
Mr. Edward A. Dreis
Mr. John H. Duffy
Rev. J. A. Duraczynski
Mrs. Clarence Ebert
Mr. D. N. Ehart
Sister Ellen, S.J.W.
Mr. William W. Elliott
Rev. George S. Endal, S. J.
Mr. Francis G. Fanning

Mr. & Mrs. Victor Fernandez
Miss Margaret C. Fitzgerald
Mr. Eugene P. Foeckler, Sr.
Mr. John F. Foell
Mr. J. P. Frank, Jr.
Mrs. Claudette Fredricksen
Mrs. Adele Fricke
Mr. Edward Patrick Garrigan
Mr. Richard L. Gerhards
Gysgt. R. P. Gideon
Mr. Patrick Guinan
Rev. A. A. Halbach
Mr. Robert E. Hanna
Mrs. Mary J. Hart
Mr. Frank E. Hauck
Mr. David Havlicek
Rev. Brian J. Hawker
Mrs. Francis Heaverlo
Rev. Herman L. Heide
Rev. Hugh P. Henneberry, S.S.J.
Rev. Albert J. Herbert, S.M.
Arthur Hopkins, M.D.
Mr. & Mrs. André Huck
Mrs. Doris L. Huff
Edgar Hull, M.D.
Rev. Jeffrey A. Ingham
Mr. Herman Jadloski
Mr. & Mrs. Dave Jaszkowiak
Mr. Marley Francis Jones
Mr. Edward E. Judge
Mr. & Mrs. Albert Kais
Mrs. Betty Kelly
Rev. Michael J. Kelly
Mr. & Mrs. Frank Knoell
Mr. John R. Knoll
Mr. William C. Koneazny
James W. Lassiter, M.D.
Miss Thérèse Lawrence
Rev. Harry J. Lewis
Very Rev. Victor O. Lorenz
Mrs. Carolyn C. MacDonald
Mrs. Katherine I. MacDonald
Mr. George F. Manhardt
Mr. Thomas Manning

(continued on page 6)

*4*

# CONTENTS

(Members of the Christendom Publishing Group, cont. from p. 4)

Mrs. Jeanette Maschmann
N. Anthony Mastropietro, M.D.
Mr. Thomas J. May
Mrs. W. C. McCarthy
Rev. William R. McCarthy
John A. McCarty, Esq.
Mr. James McConnell
Mr. Robert McConville
Mr. Robert E. McCullough, M.D.
Mr. Joseph D. McDaid
Mr. & Mrs. Dennis P. McEneany
Rev. P. J. McHugh
Mr. Thomas A. McLaughlin
Mr. J. R. McMahon
Mr. Robert Cruise McManus
Mrs. Kenneth McNichol
Rev. Edward J. Melvin, C.M.
Mr. Larry G. Miezio
Mr. Larry Miggins
Mr. Michael P. Millner
Mr. Joseph Monahan
Rev. Hugh Monmonier
Mr. James B. Mooney (St. Gerard
    Foundation)
Mrs. Gertrude G. Moore
Col. Chester H. Morneau
Mrs. Stella Morrison
Mr. Nicholas J. Mulhall
Mr. Frank Newlin
Mr. Joseph F. O'Brien
Mr. & Mrs. Tim O'Donnell
Mr. John F. O'Shaughnessy, Jr.
Mr. Lawrence P. O'Shaughnessy
Mrs. Veronica M. Oravec
Mrs. John F. Parker
Rev. Laszlo Pavel
Robert N. Pelaez, M.D.
Mr. & Mrs. Joseph and Mary Peek
Mr. Alfred H. Pekarek
Robert N. Palaez, M.D.
Mr. & Mrs. William H. Power, Jr.
Mr. Stuart Quinlan
Dr. William E. Rabil
Rev. T. A. Rattler, O.S.A.
Mr. & Mrs. Joseph E. Rau
Rev. Robert A. Reed

Mrs. John F. Reid
Mr. & Mrs. John J. Reuter
Mrs. John B. Reynolds
Dr. Charles E. Rice
Bro. Philip Romano, O.F.M. Cap.
Mr. Bernard J. Ruby
Mr. G. Salazar
Mr. Richard W. Sassman
Mr. & Mrs. George Scanlon
Mrs. Marian C. Schatzman
Miss Constance M. Scheetz
Mrs. Margaret Scheetz
Mrs. Francis R. Schirra
Mrs. Clargene Schmidt
Mrs. Job A. Schumacher
Mr. & Mrs. Ralph Schutzman
Mr. Frank P. Scrivener
Dr. John B. Shea
John R. Sheehan, M.D.
Mrs. Anne Sherman
Mr. W. R. Sherwin
Mr. Richard M. Sinclair, Jr.
Capt. Arthur Sippo
Mrs. Walter Skorupski
Mr. S. C. Sloane
Mrs. Mary Smerski
Mr. Vincent C. Smith
Mrs. William Smith
Mrs. Ann Spalding
Mr. Edward S. Szymanski
Mr. Raymond F. Tesi
Rev. Clyde Tillman
Mr. Dominic Torlone
Rev. Frederick J. Vaughn
Mr. William C. Vinet, Jr.
Rev. George T. Voiland
Mr. & Mrs. David and Marie Walkey
Honorable Vernon A. Walters
Mr. Fulton John Waterloo
Mr. Ralph A. Wellings
Mr. John R. Wilhelmy
Mrs. Mary Williams
Mrs. Mary Wimmenauer
Mr. Michael C. Winn
Mr. Walter D. Young
James F. Zimmer, M.D.

# Preface

In teaching American history over the last twenty years, I have often wanted to probe more deeply into the lives and thought of the Founding Fathers in order to see what manner of men they really were. My first book, *Benjamin Rush: Philosopher of the American Revolution*, was a full-length biography of one of them, although it was more narrative than analytical and critical, only suggesting those larger questions that I have tried to answer in the following essays. These questions are the kind that I, as an historian in the post-modern age, think necessary to ask of Rush, Thomas Jefferson, John Adams, Charles Carroll, Alexander Hamilton, George Washington, and Benjamin Franklin. But this is not to deny that there are other useful perspectives from which to view these men; and it is my hope that this small volume will encourage further research and writing along different lines, all converging someday on the whole truth about the Founding Fathers and the American Revolution.

Four of the essays below were first published in *Faith and Reason* and I would like to thank its editor, Dr. Jeffrey A. Mirus, who helped in so many ways but especially in contributing ideas to the chapter on Rush. The remaining chapters likewise appear in the order of their composition, for the reason that this arrangement best shows the development of my own thinking over the last three years as I have tried to understand these complicated men.

The writings the Founding Fathers left are more than ample for historical purposes: their silence, however—what they thought and said but never committed to the record—is lost and beyond recovery. And this silence, I realize—like the dog in the Sherlock Holmes story which by not barking helped solve the mystery—may be more vital to any true understanding of their lives and thought than all their literary remains. Nevertheless, they have left us a written testament, and our duty to explain it as best we can is clear. My own judgments, which are at times perhaps severe, must in the end be those of only one fallible man who will himself someday be judged. The motives of men, recognized now as often buried deep in the soul, are known ultimately only to God. But to please honest John Adams, I am willing as an historian to take the oath of Thuanus, to swear before God and man that I am telling the truth to the best of my ability.

I am grateful to President and Mrs. Warren H. Carroll of Christendom College, Dr. Frederick Wilhelmsen, L. Brent Bozell of the Society for the Christian Commonwealth, and Mr. and Mrs. William Koneazny, friends who have been a constant inspiration to me. Their ideas and those of Rev. Robert J. Levis, Ph.D., have influenced my thinking in many ways. The librarians of the Sojourner Truth Library, State University College at New Paltz, and the Bibliotheque de L'Universite de Besancon, were generous in helping provide the necessary research materials. A sabbatic leave from the State University College at New Paltz afforded me the precious time in which to complete this work.

The Founding Fathers, who shared a great respect for the family, would understand my love for my wife, Margaret, and my children, Keith, Gregory, Nancy, and Anthony, without whom this book could not have been written.

D. J. D'Elia
Besançon
April 6, 1979

# 1.
# The Relevance
# of Thomas Jefferson

Among the Founding Fathers of the American nation there appears to be none more deserving of the title of "modern man" than the Virginian, Thomas Jefferson, author of the Declaration of Independence and third President of the United States. His tall, God-like figure looms over the American past, his name continues to be celebrated in endless books and after-dinner speeches, and his democratic authority must be invoked by every aspiring statesman and grasping politician. Indeed, Jefferson's relevance for modern man has led to a veritable cult whose shrine on the banks of the Potomac draws worshippers from all over the world.

Often it happens in history and life itself, that a good but naive man's principles have been mercilessly exposed by time to reveal logical implications which he would have condemned in his own lifetime. Such, we shall argue, was notably the case with Thomas Jefferson who, bereft of the Church's wisdom and maternal protection, fell victim to false principles long ago unmasked by Revelation and true philosophy. These false principles, known collectively as liberalism, were made by Jefferson into a kind of religion, as we shall see; and in using the prestige of the presidency to advance this secular religion, Jefferson unwittingly proved himself to be the first of a long line of abusers of the highest office of the land. For the Jeffersonian mentality, despite all good intentions, leads inexorably to moral nihilism and the abortionist Supreme Court of the 1970's.

Jefferson was born in 1743, the son of Peter Jefferson, a Virginian surveyor without pretensions to wealth or title. After studying Latin and Greek with Anglican priests in Albemarle county, who apparently failed to teach him the rudiments of a Christian faith, Jefferson entered the College of William and Mary where he remained a student until his graduation in 1762. It was in Williamsburg that the intelligent and highly impressionable young man came under the decisive influence of the only lay member of the faculty, Dr. William Small, professor of mathematics and natural philosophy. Small had recently come over from Scotland to teach at the Anglican college, and had brought with him many of the leading ideas of the Scottish Enlightenment, ideas which challenged religious orthodoxy and promoted the empirical philosophy of Francis Bacon (1561-1626) and John Locke (1632-1704).[1]

In his autobiography, Jefferson later wrote that Dr. Small's influence on him was so great as to have "probably fixed the destinies of my life." The Scottish *philosophe* was "a man profound in most of the useful branches of science, with a happy talent of communication, correct and gentlemanly manners, and an enlarged and liberal mind. He, most happily for me, became soon attached to me, and made me his daily companion when not engaged in the school; and from his conversation I got my first views of the expansion of science and of the system of things in which we are placed."[2]

That "system of things," as we have intimated, was the narrow one of modern philosophy, to wit, that of English empiricism, or better, Sensism. According to John Locke, its most famous exponent, Sensism taught that true knowledge consists only of the facts of sense experience (seeing, hearing, etc), that, therefore, natural reason—as understood by Aristotle, St. Thomas Aquinas, and the great majority of Western thinkers—is incapable of arriving at knowledge and truth, which come after and directly from experience *per se*. It was a philosophy as erroneous and destructive as that of René Descartes (1596-1650), the other major thinker of the Enlightenment, whose "Exaggerated Intellectualism" overemphasized natural reason and altogether rejected sense experience. Paradoxically, both the Sensism of Locke and the *a priori* rationalism (innatism) of Descartes, while seemingly opposite in the extreme, amount to a radical idealism that denies the mind's ability to transcend its own ideas.[3] But Thomas Jefferson, like most Enlightenment *philosophes*, was not rigorously analytical enough to see this. A derivative and eclectic thinker, he was to appropriate ideas from both the Lockean and Cartesian tradition and elaborate his thinking within this world view or "system of things."

Dr. Small also taught ethics at the College of William and Mary, and it is easy to infer from what we know about Small's other views— and Jefferson's—that it was not Christian ethics in any recognizable sense. Small probably had abandoned Revelation, if he had ever considered it in a mature way, and Jefferson, as we shall see, seems never to have appreciated its very possibility. The same may be said for metaphysics in general. Neither Dr. Small nor Governor Francis Fauquier, F. R. S. and Newtonian philosopher, his friend and another mentor of young Jefferson, were given to metaphysical discussions. Jefferson tells us in his autobiography that he was often a dinner guest at Gov. Fauquier's mansion where, with Fauquier, Small, and George Wythe, professor of classics, he "heard more good sense, more rational and philosophical conversations, than in all my life besides."[4] It was doubtless the example of these Virginia *philosophes*, Small and Wythe, the latter a fellow Signer of the Declaration of Independence and an intimate lifelong friend, that Jefferson came to worship his "trinity of genius," Francis Bacon, Sir Isaac Newton, and John Locke.[5]

None of these Enlightenment thinkers, whom Jefferson saw as personifying his naive faith in empirical science, could offer him that deeper view of man as spiritual person. They were modern, Protestant writers whose understanding of the philosophy and civilization of the Middle Ages was tenuous at best. So far was John Locke from the medieval Catholic appreciation of man as made in the image of God, as a spiritual person with all its consequences for private and social life, that his empiricism led him in his political and ethical theory to reduce man to a kind of atom in mere combination with others (social compact theory); led him, accordingly, to neglect a serious analysis of the concept of the common good, and to suggest a crude hedonistic utilitarianism.[6] All of these typically Enlightenment errors and superficialities were repeated by Jefferson and Locke's other American students, undermining the very edifice of the new nation that they were to build. However, the

Englishman's positive contribution of a natural rights doctrine in his *Second Treatise of Government* perhaps compensated for these grave weaknesses of thought at least in the short run.

Locke's spell over Jefferson was so complete, especially in writing the Declaration of Independence, that, when he was accused of plagiarizing from the *Treatise*, he vindicated himself by admitting that the ideas were so much a part of him as to be second nature. And, indeed, so they were, along with other of Locke's characteristic doctrines. "We hold these truths to be self-evident," Jefferson had written,

> that all men are created equal, that they are endowed by their Creator with certain unalienable Rights, that among these are Life, Liberty, and the pursuit of Happiness. That to secure these rights, Governments are instituted among Men, deriving their just powers from the consent of the governed, That whenever any Form of Government becomes destructive of these ends, it is the Right of the People to alter or to abolish it, and to institute new Government, laying its foundation on such principles and organizing its powers in such form, as to them shall seem most likely to effect their Safety and Happiness.[7]

The Declaration, in essence, was a transcript of Locke's partisan 17th century Whig political theory; only Locke's timeless normative concept of natural and moral law, which Jefferson and his colleagues likewise accepted, raised the American charter above past historical circumstances.[8]

Locke's—and Jefferson's—hedonistic utilitarianism is presupposed in the Declaration, as are social and political atomism, all of them manifestations of that Protestant individualism which was elaborated and radicalized by Jefferson into the first principle of his thought. Just as Locke's Sensism in his *Essay Concerning Human Understanding* (1690), his nominalistic teaching that knowledge is merely the perception of the agreement or disagreement of ideas (sensations), developed logically into the skepticism of David Hume, so Locke's social and political nominalism led to the radical individualism of Jefferson and his modern followers.

The Epicurean phrase, "the pursuit of Happiness," which Jefferson substituted in the Declaration of Independence for Locke's "property" in the triad, "life, liberty, and property," illustrates this well. Man had a natural right to happiness, to pursue happiness, and correlative to this right, Jefferson believed, was man's absolute freedom of conscience as the means necessary to achieve happiness, i.e. personal gratification. True, he intimated throughout his early writings that this freedom of conscience was subject to objective natural and moral law, but there is no doubt that ultimately Jefferson radically absolutized reason, the individual's own reason, as normative. With Protagoras, his logic was bound to hold that man is the measure of all things. He frankly said as much in his writings on religion, which unlike much of his political rhetoric reveal his true character as a thinker. "I never will, by any word or act, bow to the shrine of intolerance, or admit a right of inquiry into the religious opinions of others," Jefferson wrote in 1813. "On the contrary, we are bound, you, I, and everyone, *to make common cause, even with error itself, to maintain the common right of freedom of conscience*"(my italics).[9] Each of us "must act according to the dictates of his own reason."[10] Not the right use of the faculty of reason, which the more respectable Enlightenment philosophers taught, but simply willy nilly the use of reason, was Jefferson's ultimate statement on religion and everything else. "We should all then, like the Quakers, live without an order of priests, moralize for ourselves, follow the oracle of conscience, and say nothing about what no man can understand, nor therefore believe; for I suppose belief to be the assent of the mind to an intelligible proposition."[11]

Thomas Jefferson Randolph claimed that his grandfather would not even discuss religion with his own family, lest he influence their religious "opinions" which they must work out for themselves. "It was a subject each was bound to study assiduously for himself, unbiased by the opinions of others—it was a matter solely of conscience; after thorough investigation, they were responsible for the righteousness, but not the rightfulness of their opinions; that the expression of his opinion might influence theirs, and he would not give it."[12] One must be free to do one's thing, Jefferson believed, since there was no God's thing, no Church, no Revelation.

Jefferson's modern, negative conception of freedom was of course the basis for this solipsism. We are all too familiar today with this absolutizing of private judgment, this heresy of man's first parents—"You shall be as gods."[13] It clearly inverts the natural order, of first being and then judgment, of truth as a condition of freedom.[14] "And you shall know the truth, and the truth shall make you free."[15] Jefferson, deprived of the truths of Revelation by an 18th century bourgeois culture which opposed faith to reason, body to soul, and truth to freedom, could not see this, as millions today cannot. "Your own reason," he told his nephew, Peter Carr, "is the only oracle given you by heaven, and you are answerable, not for the rightness, but uprightness of the decision."[16]

None of his "trinity of genius," Bacon, Locke, and Newton, had gone so far as to deny Revelation and isolate man in subjectivism. For all the dangerous implications of their Sensism, they were 17th century thinkers who still placed the norm of truth in the object. Jefferson, like his much greater contemporaries, David Hume and Immanuel Kant, was simply developing the logical consequences of British empiricism and Cartesian innatism in an idealism which located the norm of truth in the subject. He was not, of course, aware of this logical and historical development of thought: of the steady reduction of object to subject (which continues in our own day). Freedom of conscience, reason, and consciousness were so thrown together in his own superficial mind, lacking as he did a faculty of logical definition, that soon, despite his ostensible appeal to reason, Jefferson was in reality taking the idealistic position that individual consciousness alone determines the object.

"The error seems not sufficiently eradicated," Jefferson wrote in his *Notes on Virginia* (1785),

> that the operations of the mind, as well as the acts of the body, are subject to the coercion of laws. But our rulers can have no authority over such natural rights, only as we have submitted to them. The rights of conscience we never submitted, we could not submit. We are answerable for them to our God. The legitimate powers of government extend to such acts only as are injurious to others. But it does me no injury for my neighbor to say there are twenty gods, or no God. It neither picks my pocket nor breaks my leg.[17]

This famous quotation, which goes to the heart of Jefferson's position, puts one in mind of William James's "Will to Believe," and doubtless comes from the same voluntaristic (Protestant) tradition. We are struck, too, by Jefferson's inconsistency here in not recognizing that religious ideas, like all ideas, have consequences. Elsewhere, he emphasizes this and even judges a man's religion by his life.[18] For clearly it does matter if one's neighbor is a satanist; it does make a difference to you if he

believes that God exists and forbids abortion. Jefferson's own voluntaristic religious ideas had profound consequences for himself, his state,
and the new nation, especially in his authorship of the Virginia Statute
for Religious Freedom which was enacted into law by the Virginia
assembly in 1786 and became the model for the First Amendment to
the U. S. Constitution.

As is evidenced above in the quotation from the *Notes on Virginia*,
Jefferson viewed the Virginia Statute for Religious Freedom as the
religious complement to that social and political philosophy which he
had articulated ten years before in the Declaration of Independence. He
was a lawyer by training and mentality, we should remember, and,
moreover, like other Enlightenment thinkers—Helvétius, for example—he
exaggerated the role of law in improving men according to his own liberal
values. Thus, he profoundly believed to the very end of his life, as his
carefully written epitaph shows, that he had guaranteed at law and for
all time man's natural rights to life, political and religious liberty, and
the pursuit of happiness.[19] And once again, Jefferson's master teacher
in this, his life work, was John Locke, whose *Essay Concerning Human
Understanding* and political and religious writings supported the extreme
individualism of the Protestant tradition. And neither thinker, of course,
rose above Locke's famous definition of a "church" as merely a volun-
tary society of men, a reductionistic conception held by Jefferson in the
*Statute*.

> Well aware that Almighty God hath created the mind free; that all at-
> tempt to influence it by temporal punishments or burthens, or by civil
> incapacitations, tend only to beget habits of hypocrisy and meanness,
> and are a departure from the plan of the Holy Author of our religion,
> who, being Lord both of body and mind, yet chose not to propagate
> it by coercions on either, as was in his Almighty power to do,

Jefferson stated in his preamble to the Virginia law and went on to reflect
the influence of Locke's empiricist epistemology and his arguments from
the nominalistic *Reasonableness of Christianity* and the *Letter of
Toleration*.[20] But there were really significant differences between the
two men too. Locke affirmed the existence of Revelation and denied in
the strongest terms that Christianity was only natural religion. He
recognized Jesus as the Messiah and his fulfillment of Old Testament

prophecies and working of miracles. And Locke, unlike Jefferson, saw true morality as having more than a merely natural basis.[21] Here again, the student deduced from his teacher's Sensism, his empiricist theory of knowledge, the conclusion that extra-sensory (extra-mental) realities like Revelation and supernatural morality could not exist, and that Locke was inconsistent with his own principles in holding to them. The practical-minded American could, however, accept his master's religious liberalism, with its aversion to priests and dogmas.

Jefferson's nominalistic conception of man as a "law unto himself" in religious matters, and the consequences of this belief for religious orthodoxy, make up a good part of his writings over the years. Everything he ever wrote on Christianity was vitiated by his puerile understanding of the claims of Revelation and the Incarnation. Deep mysteries like the Trinity, Creation, Original Sin, the Immaculate Conception, the Atonement, the Resurrection, and the Real Presence of Christ he scorned as priestly frauds.[22] They were empirically unverifiable, to use the modern expression of positivists. "Rejecting all organs of information, therefore, but my senses," he arrogantly observed to John Adams late in life,

> I rid myself of the pyrrhonisms with which an indulgence in specula-
> tions hyperphysical and antiphysical, so uselessly occupy and disquiet
> the mind. A single sense may indeed be sometimes deceived, but rarely;
> and never all our senses together, with their faculty of reasoning. They
> evidence realities, and there are enough of these for all the purposes
> of life, without plunging into the fathomless abyss of dreams and phan-
> tasms. I am satisfied, and sufficiently occupied with the things which
> are, without tormenting or troubling myself about those which may
> indeed be, but of which I have no evidence.[23]

Take one world at a time, was the way like-minded Mark Twain was to put it years later, and with equal superficiality.

Jefferson's attitude towards the Bible was well described in his let-
ter to his nephew, Peter Carr, whose education he was supervising after the death of the boy's parents. Once again betraying the destructive influence of Locke and especially Hume, who drew out the latent skep-
ticism in Locke's work, Jefferson urged the young man to take "nature" (sensible reality) as his only guide. "Read the Bible, then, as you would read Livy or Tacitus. The facts which are within the ordinary course of nature, you will believe on the authority of the writer, as you do those

of the same kind in Livy and Tacitus." But a so-called inspired writer's claim of a miracle, he goes on to say, requires that the boy's own reason decide whether "its falsehood would be more improbable than a change in the laws of nature, in the case he relates. For example, in the book of Joshua, we are told, the sun stood still several hours. Were we to read that fact in Livy or Tacitus, we should class it with their showers of blood, speaking of statues, beasts, etc." Nephew Peter was

> astronomer enough to know how contrary it is to the law of nature that a body revolving on its axis, as the earth does, should have stopped, should not, by that sudden stoppage, have prostrated animals, trees, buildings, and should after a certain time have resumed its revolution, and that without a second general prostration. Is this arrest of the earth's motion, or the evidence which affirms it, most within the law of probabilities?[24]

The same reasoning, Jefferson argued, the same appeal to the objective laws of nature (whose existence is notoriously inconsistent with Hume's and Jefferson's exaggerated Sensism) demonstrated that Jesus was only a man, if a great one.[25] Convinced of this by his naive "higher criticism," and dismissing almost two millennia of judgment and learning as irrelevant to the conclusion of his own "oracle" of reason, Jefferson turned to the "simplifying of the Christian philosophy" and its reconstruction as natural religion consonant with modern science. As for those speculative questions about, say, the nature of life after death, which he believed lay beyond reason in the unknown, "I have for many years," he wrote in 1801, "ceased to read or to think concerning them, and have reposed my head on that pillow of ignorance which a benevolent Creator has made soft for us, knowing how much we should be forced to use it."[26]

Jefferson's "oracle" of reason answered enough questions about Christianity, however, to purge it of what he considered corruptions and superstitions and to reconstruct it on a "rational" basis. No sooner had he been elected President of the United States than he began privately to reform Christianity according to his own ideas. The formal project consisted of two exercises: "an estimate of the merit of the doctrines of Jesus, compared with those of others," as Jefferson himself put it, and a selection of those passages of the New Testament concerning the life and morals of Jesus which the new Chief Executive of the United States approved as probable in the light of natural reason. In this work, which Jefferson thought to be of the highest scholarship, he took for his inspiration Martin Luther and the other Reformers of the 16th century; and there is no question that he viewed his revolutionizing of Christianity as the other side of his political mission to liberate America from Old World tyranny. The "metaphysical insanities of Athanasius, of Loyola, and of Calvin" had no place in the new, progressive religion of republican America.[27] That religion was "rational Christianity" or Unitarianism, and Jefferson was its prophet.[28] But even here Jefferson's extreme nominalism was the final norm: "As the Creator has made no two forces alike, so no two minds, and probably no two creeds."[29]

In April of 1803 Jefferson sent Dr. Benjamin Rush, his friend and co-signer of the Declaration of Independence, an outline or syllabus of "the comparative merit of Christianity." He had promised Rush, who was a more mature Christian thinker, his controversial views on the subject.

> They are the result of a life of inquiry and reflection, [he wrote in the covering letter] and very different from that anti-Christian system imputed to me by those who know nothing of my opinions. To the corruptions of Christianity I am indeed opposed; but not to the genuine precepts of Jesus himself. I am a Christian, in the only sense in which he wished any one to be; sincerely attached to his doctrines, in preference to all others; ascribing to himself every *human* excellence; and believing he never claimed any other.[30]

The other moral doctrines which Jefferson compared with those of Christianity were those of the Jews and of Epicurus, Socrates, Pythagoras, Epictetus, and other Stoic and Epicurean philosophers. Jesus, like Socrates and all men who try "to enlighten and reform mankind," was doomed to fall "an early victim to the jealousy and combination of the altar and the throne, "but even in his short life he carried ethics beyond the mere externalism of the Jews and ancient philosophers and "pushed his scrutinies into the heart of man; erected his tribunal in the region of his thoughts, and purified the waters at the fountain head."[31] Like Socrates too, Jefferson believed, Jesus had his false disciples, his Platos. "Of this band of dupes and imposters, Paul was the great Coryphaeus, and first corruptor of the doctrines of Jesus."[32]

But it was Plato who was most responsible for caricaturing the simple moral teachings of Jesus. It was he who, "dealing out mysticisms incomprehensible to the human mind, has been deified by certain sects usurping the name of Christians; because, in his foggy conceptions, they found a basis of impenetrable darkness whereon to rear fabrications as delirious, of their own invention."[33] And that was not all. Jefferson's arrogant Sensism knew no bounds. "We must dismiss the Platonists and Plotinists, the Stagyrites and Gamalielites, the Eclectics, the Gnostics and Scholastics, their essences and emanations, their Logos and Demiurgos, Aeons and Daemons, male and female, with a long train of etc., etc., etc., or, shall I say at once, of nonsense."[34] Orthodox Christianity was priest-ridden, Platonized Christianity, Jefferson wrote again and again.

It was true, Jefferson conceded, that Jesus, while admirable in his moral doctrine, was in error as to his alledged spiritualism, if that was really what he meant by saying that, "God is a spirit." More likely, it was Jesus' metaphysical followers, the "spiritualizing" Platonists, who introduced this "heresy of *immaterialism*" into the Christian church.[35] Jesus himself never denied that matter was all that existed.[36] He may even have been an empiricist and materialist like Epicurus, Locke, and Jefferson, who believed, in the words of the latter, that "to talk of *immaterial* existences is to talk of *nothings*. To say that the human souls, angels, God, are immaterial, is to say, they are *nothings*, or that there is no God, no angels, no soul. I cannot reason otherwise."[37] Here Jefferson was reflecting, too, the influence of lesser modern thinkers, especially the French sensationalists, P.J.G. Cabanis 1757-1808) and Destutt de Tracy (1754-1836), who drew the necessary materialistic conclusion from Locke's Sensism.[38]

In addition to his "estimate of the merit of the doctrines of Jesus," and as a consequence of it, Jefferson set about revising—demythologizing would be the modern word—the New Testament. He began the project while in the White House, but finished it only after his retirement to Monticello. "I have performed this operation for my own use," he wrote John Adams in 1813, "by cutting verse by verse out of the printed book, and arranging the matter which is evidently his, and which is easily distinguishable as diamonds in a dunghill. The result is an octavo of forty-six pages, of pure and unsophisticated doctrines, such as were professed and acted on by the *unlettered* Apostles, the Apostolic Fathers, and the Christians of the first century.''[39] It marked, he hoped, the beginning of ''euthanasia for Platonic Christianity, and its restoration to the primitive simplicity of its founder.''[40] The mutilated text that Jefferson finally produced after his scissors-and-paste exercise would make a study in itself, and offers a striking example of how to trivialize one's own thinking along with the Word of God. Shorn of every evidence of transcendence, Jefferson's Bible characteristically ends with Jesus's death and entombment.[41] The Resurrection, after all, was unscientific because it was beyond the realm of positive sense experience.

Jefferson did not relent in his crusade against Platonizing Christians even in the final years of his life. Indeed, his founding of the University of Virginia, in 1819, was conceived as a means of promoting his Enlightenment philosophy of reason and science against the forces of reaction. These were being led by the old enemies of Jefferson and the rights of man, the Presbyterians, the Jesuits, and other Platonized followers of that ''fanatic Athanasius,'' who opposed ''freedom of religious opinion and its external divorce from the civil authority.''[42] Their creeds and formulas, their ''hocus-pocus phantasm of a God like another Cerberus, with one body and three heads'' were ''the bane and ruin of the Christian church, its own fatal invention, which, through so many ages, made of Christendom a slaughter-house, and at this day divides it into casts of inextinguishable hatred to one another.''[43]

America must be saved from ''the fire and faggots of Calvin and his victim Servetus.'' And it would be saved, Jefferson was certain, by that very materialistic and anti-trinitarian doctrine for which Servetus was martyred: Unitarianism. ''The diffusion of instruction, to which there is now so growing an attention,'' he confided to his friend, Thomas Cooper, his choice for a professorship at the University of Virginia, ''will be the remote remedy to this fever of fanaticism; while the more proximate one will be the progress of Unitarianism. That this will, ere long, be the religion of the majority from north to south, I have no doubt.''[44]

It was, apparently, with these views that Thomas Jefferson, the third President of the United States, went to his death on July 4, 1826, the fiftieth anniversary of the Declaration of Independence. We have no evidence that he ever thought otherwise. Just before he died, he composed his epitaph, listing his authorship of the Declaration, of the Virginia Statute for Religious Freedom, and his founding of the University of Virginia as his greatest achievements. His nephew, Thomas Jefferson Randolph, said that the eighty-seven year old patriot had nothing to confess on his death bed.[45] Dr. Robley Dunglinson, Jefferson's friend and attending physician, testified, after his patient's death, that he had "never heard an observation that savored, in the slightest degree, of impiety."[46]

Yet, Jefferson's false principles in philosophy and religion and his private scurrilities must be an affront to real Christians. This truth is beyond opinion, despite Jefferson's transparent sincerity. The man who had "sworn upon the altar of God, eternal hostility against every form of tyranny over the mind of man"[47] was himself the victim of the most dangerous tyranny of all: ignorance of the Word of God. For Jefferson could not declare himself independent of God's truth.

## NOTES

[1] Thomas Jefferson's "Autobiography" in H. A. Washington (ed.), *Writings of Thomas Jefferson* (9 v., Washington, D. C., 1853) *1*: p. 2. Hereafter cited as *Writings*.

[2] *Ibid;* Jefferson to Mr. Louis H. Girardin, January 15, 1815, ibid. *6*: p. 411. Thomas Jefferson hereafter cited as TJ.

[3] See Father Michael J. Mahony's brilliant analysis of the *History of Modern Thought; The English, Irish and Scotch Schools* (New York: Fordham University Press, 1933), esp. pp. 11, 76. An earlier work of genius is Jacques Maritain, *Three Reformers: Luther, Descartes, Rousseau* (New York: Thomas Y. Cromwell Co., 1970).

[4] *Writings 1:* p. 2.

[5] TJ to Benjamin Rush, January 16, 1811, *Writings 5:* p. 599. See D. J. D'Elia, "Jefferson, Rush, and the Limits of Philosophical Friendship," *Proceedings of the American Philosophical Society 117* (October, 1973): pp. 333-343.

[6] Frederick Copleston, S.J., *A History of Philosophy* (8 v., Westminster, Maryland: The Newman Press) *5: Hobbes to Hume*, pp. 127, 139; See Russel Kirk (ed.), John Locke, *An Essay Concerning Human Understanding* (Chicago, Ill.: Henry Regnery, 1956), preface, pp v-xii. Fr. John Courtney Murray's controversial thesis in *We Hold These Truths; Catholic Reflections on the American Proposition* (N.Y.: Sheed & Ward, 1960) should not detract from his excellent treatment of natural law and incisive commentary on modernity. See TJ to Thomas Law, June 13, 1814, Saul K. Padover (ed.), *The Complete Jefferson; Containing His Major Writings, Published and Unpublished, Except His Letters* (Freeport, N. Y.: Books for Libraries Press, 1969), p. 1034.

[7] *Idem., Thomas Jefferson and the Foundations of American Freedom* (Princeton, N. J.: D. Van Nostrand Co., 1965), p. 85.

[8]Copleston, p. 138.

[9]TJ to Edward Dowse, April 19, 1803, in Norman Cousins (ed.), "*In God We Trust*": *The Religious Beliefs and Ideas of the American Founding Fathers* (New York: Harper & Brothers, 1958), p. 167. This includes a useful collection of Jefferson's writings on religion.

[10]TJ to Samuel Miller, January 23, 1808, *ibid.*, p. 137.

[11]TJ to John Adams, August 22, 1813, *ibid.*, p. 237

[12]Henry S. Randall, *The Life of Thomas Jefferson* (3 v., New York, 1858) *3*: p. 672, cited in George H. Knowles's helpful but uncritical "The Religious Ideas of Thomas Jefferson," *Mississippi Valley Historical Review 30* (September, 1943): pp. 187-204.

[13]Mahony, p. 159.

[14]See Stephen D. Schwarz, 'Who's to Judge?' A Reply to Ethical Relativism," *Faith & Reason 2* (Spring, 1976): p. 42.

[15]John 8:32, and Christopher Derrick's commentary on this verse at the Manhattan Institute Conference, March 18-20, 1977.

[16]Cousins, p. 129.

[17]Padover, *The Complete Jefferson*, p. 675.

[18]TJ to Mrs. Samuel H. Smith, August 6, 1816, *ibid.*, p. 955.

[19]Padover, *Thomas Jefferson*, p. 40.

[20]Cousins, p. 125. Also see TJ's "Notes on Religion," Padover, *The Complete Jefferson*, pp. 937-946.

[21]*The Reasonableness of Christianity*, edited by I.T. Ramsey (Stanford: Stanford University Press, 1974), pp. 60-61, *et passim*.

[22]TJ to William Short, October 31, 1819, Cousins, p. 149, *et passim*.

[23]August 15, 1820, *ibid.*, p. 286.

[24]August 10, 1787, *ibid.*, p. 128.

[25]TJ to Benjamin Rush, April 21, 1803, *ibid.*, p. 168.

[26]TJ to Isaac Story, December 5, 1801, *ibid.*, p. 133.

[27]TJ to Jared Sparks, November 4, 1820, *ibid.*, p. 156.

[28]TJ to Timothy Pickering, February 27, 1821, *ibid.*, p. 157.

[29]*Ibid.*

[30]TJ to Benjamin Rush, April 21, 1803, *ibid.*, p. 168.

[31]"Syllabus," *ibid.*, pp. 170-171.

[32]TJ to William Short, April 13, 1820, *ibid.*, p. 150. Jefferson's principal theological authority for these and other ideas seems to have been Dr. Joseph Priestley (1733-1804), renowned chemist and Unitarian thinker, whose *Scorates and Jesus Compared* appeared in 1803 and whose *The Doctrines of Heathen Philosophy Compared with Those of Revelation* (1804) was written at the suggestion of Jefferson, John F. Fulton, "Joseph Priestley, " *Dictionary of American Biography 8*: pp. 223-226. A more general, but equally decisive influence on Jefferson was that of the English freethinker, Conyers Middleton (1683-1750). See Leslie Stephen, *History of English Thought in the Eighteenth Century* (2 vols., London, 1876). IX, 75.

[33]TJ to William Short, October 31, 1819, Cousins, p, 149.

[34]TJ to John Adams, October 13, 1813, *ibid.*, p. 242.

[35]TJ to John Adams, August 15, 1820, *ibid.*, p. 286; TJ to Thomas Cooper, August 14, 1820, *ibid.*, p. 132.

[36]TJ to John Adams, August 15, 1820, *ibid.*, p. 286.

[37]*Ibid.*

[38]D'Elia, "Jefferson, Rush, and Limits of Philosophical Friendship," pp. 340-342. Important, too, in TJ's thinking at this time was the Scottish "common-sense" philosopher, Dugald Stewart (1753-1828), see Adrienne Koch, *The Philosophy of Thomas Jefferson* (Chicago, 1964), *et. passim.*

[39]TJ to John Adams, October 13, 1813, Cousins, p. 242.

[40]*Ibid.*, p. 243.

[41]"The Life and Morals of Jesus of Nazareth," *ibid.*, p. 216.

[42]TJ to James Smith, December 8, 1822, *ibid.*, p. 159.

[43]*Ibid.*; TJ to Thomas Whittemore, June 5, 1822, *ibid.*, p. 158.

[44]TJ to Thomas Cooper, November 2, 1822, pp. 163-164; TJ to Benjamin Waterhouse, July 19, 1822, *ibid.*, p. 162. "I can never join Calvin in addressing *his* God. He was indeed an atheist, which I can never be; or rather his religion was daemonism. If ever man worshipped a false God, he did. The being described in five points, is not the God whom you and I acknowledge and adore, the creator and benevolent governor of the world; but a daemon of malignant spirit. It would be more pardonable to believe in no God at all, then to blaspheme him by the atrocious attributes of Calvin," TJ to John Adams, April 11, 1823, *ibid.*, p. 289.

[45]Knowles, "The Religious Ideas of Thomas Jefferson," pp. 203-204.

[46]Quoted in Knowles, *ibid.*

[47]TJ to Benjamin Rush, September 23, 1800, *Writings 4*: p. 336.

# 2.
# Benjamin Rush:
# A Christian Revolutionary?

It is well known among closer students of history, whether professional or lay, that modern secular culture is achieving dramatic results
in abolishing the past as a critical factor in man's consciousness.[1] But,
despite the criticisms of Jefferson in the preceding chapter, there is simply
no arguing from the historical record that the violent departure from the
natural law characteristic of our own time[2] is compatible in any way,
however cleverly redefined, with the values of most of the Founding
Fathers. Madison, Washington, Rush, Charles Carroll of Carrollton, and
scores of other patriots of the American Revolution testify, without exception, to the objective reality of natural law and those "unalienable
Rights" which it is government's purpose to serve.

That the American nation was founded on natural law, as the Declaration of Independence makes clear, is something which legitimate history
ought to take seriously. Even if the Declaration had said nothing about
the natural rights of Life, Liberty, and the Pursuit of Happiness, and
all the other charters of our Revolution were equally silent on this great
theme—which is demonstrably not the case—the truth would remain that
the Fathers of this country knew in their sanity that commonwealths must
be built on fundamental law. This was obvious to them as it had been
to the overwhelming majority of the world's people, East and West; the
Law was "written in their hearts."[3] More often than not, as was
customary with the Founding Fathers, they took for granted in their
writings and speeches "certain unalienable Rights" that no one in his

right mind would question. Tyrannous government, they knew, needed to be reminded and chastised for its insolence; hence, the absolute, articulately worded Declaration of Independence. This point that governmental law must follow natural law is illustrated even more strikingly in the argument over the need for a written Bill of Rights, where its critics maintained with remarkable prescience that natural and positive law should not be confounded, lest the ever ambitious state enroach upon the former. They were right, of course, in fearing that their descendants, robbed of the common and true past, would be seduced into paying too generous a coin of tribute to Caesar.

Not only, in this pre-Kantian age, did the American patriot's own reason teach him that government was his servant in these matters that touched the infinite worth and dignity of the human person. His mental framework and convictions were formed historically, in the widest sense, as well as ontologically. It is true that he was Protestant or post-Protestant, except for signer Charles Carroll of Carrollton and a few other Catholic leaders, but a Jefferson or an Adams was still, for all that, very much a son of the Catholic West in certain basic attitudes. The Virginian admittedly succumbed to the fashionable naturalism of the Enlightenment, apparently never realizing the anti-intellectualism of his position; and crotchety John Adams, equally sincere and intelligent, but in his early life accepting the fact of Revelation, seems to have kept his crude and invincibly ignorant understanding of Catholicism to the end. Yet, both men, whatever the degree of their post-Protestantism, were typical of the Revolutionary leadership in recognizing and seeking to apply in their age time-honored Christian social principles. St. Thomas's "Good is to be done and sought for, evil is to be avoided"[4] was the wisdom they accepted.

Given this unique character of the American Founding Fathers, we would expect to find some good and some bad—but all instructive—in a serious consideration of the political traditions they established. With respect to Thomas Jefferson, a number of flaws were noted. But in order to maximize the positive, it is helpful to focus here on Dr. Benjamin Rush (1746-1813), another Protestant signer of the Declaration of Independence, who was unique in being professedly Christian in every way about his understanding of the American Revolution. Rush's Christocentric philosophy of the American Revolution may be viewed

as a kind of *summa* of the times, indeed the most comprehensive doctrine from any Founding Father on the meaning of the independence of
the United States in the economy of salvation.[5] A close analysis of the
development of Rush's theory will reveal both the strengths and
weaknesses of the early American vision of the political order.

Like all of the colonial leaders who resisted the British government's
totalitarian ambitions in 1776, Rush was well educated at home and in
school and college in the historical values of Christendom, values which
he and his teachers could only derive from secondary Protestant
authorities. Professor James J. Walsh clearly demonstrates in his book
*The Education of the Founding Fathers* that the College of New Jersey
(now Princeton), where Rush graduated, Harvard, Yale, the College of
Philadelphia (now University of Pennsylvania), William and Mary,
King's College (now Columbia), Queens College (now Rutgers), and
the other colonial colleges required work of their students very much
like that of the medieval Catholic universities. Graduating seniors had
to defend their theses publicly at commencements, following the tradition of Scholasticism, and the titles and contents of these papers were
little different from those debated, say, at the University of Paris in the
thirteenth century.[6] The sacred freedom and immortality of the person,
his rights and duties under natural law, and the claims of Revelation were
medieval and enduring truths that Rush and every other Founding Father
learned, in greater or lesser degree, in the colleges and schools of Christian America. Rush elaborated his own views in a letter to Jefferson:

> I have always considered Christianity as the strong ground of
> republicanism. The spirit is opposed, not only to the splendor, but even
> to the very forms of monarchy, and many of its precepts have for their
> objects republican liberty and equality as well as simplicity, integrity,
> and economy in government. It is only necessary for republicanism
> to ally itself to the Christian religion to overturn all the corrupted
> political and religious institutions in the world.[7]

We may momentarily pass over the veiled reference to Catholicism (and
Anglicanism) here to further establish Rush's belief that the new
American public order was built on Christian principles. In arguing that
the Bible should be used to teach Christianity in the public schools, he

wrote:

> A Christian cannot fail of being a republican. The history of the creation of man, and of the relation of our species to each other by birth, which is recorded in the Old Testament, is the best refutation that can be given to the divine right of kings, and the strongest argument that can be used in favor of the original and natural equality of all mankind. A Christian, I say again, cannot fail of being a republican, for every precept of the Gospel inculcates those degrees of humility, self-denial, and brotherly kindness, which are directly opposed to the pride of monarchy and the pageantry of a court.[8]

While it is true that Rush may have confused legitimate monarchy with divine right monarchy, he clearly recognized that the "divine right of kings or states"—totalitarianism is what Rush and the other founders of the American nation would call it today—violated God's law. Everyone who knew history, knew this.

These and other truths about the nature and dignity of man, deriving ultimately from classical and medieval times, were 'self-evident' to the Signers of the Declaration of Independence and remain so to men and women of right thinking. Rush, Adams, Jefferson, Madison, and the Revolutionary leadership in general, consciously or otherwise knowing the office and limitations of reason, had no doubt about man's natural Rights to Life, Liberty, and the Pursuit of Happiness, even if they naively credited minor Protestant thinkers like Richard Hooker, John Milton, and John Locke rather than St. Thomas, Cardinal Bellarmine, and Suarez. "Reason and religion have the same objects," Rush asserted with that decisiveness characteristic of the Founders. "They are in no one instance opposed to each other. On the contrary, reason is nothing but imperfect religion, and religion is nothing but perfect reason."[9] How could Rush and the others, born and reared in a culture already declining into post-Protestantism, appreciate the anti-historical character of the Protestant Revolution? But the point is that the Founding Father's past as Western men had not been abolished, as is fast becoming the case with ours. Theirs had not been abolished, only changed and rendered superficial in its dimensions by their ancestor's defection from the church, the Mother of history. They knew the 'self-evident' truths and built a nation on them, even if they did not know the ultimate historical sources and continuities. They believed that God watched over their city, and that was enough.

The curriculum at Princeton included logic, ethics, rhetoric, classical languages, Hebrew, natural philosophy, and metaphysics, subjects from the trivium and quadrivium of the Middle Ages. Logic and ethics were emphasized, and a young man came away from instruction with confidence in the nature and extent of his reasoning faculty and belief in absolute values. In the 1750's, 60's and 70's, when the Revolutionary generation was educated, the onslaught of Kantian subjectivism had not yet begun and men were sure of their ability rationally to arrive at truth. The corrosion of the Western mind had, in fact, started long ago, but Protestant America and its institutions enjoyed in relative isolation a kind of diluted synthesis of reason and Revelation which, in contrast to the ferment of doubt in Europe, was never seriously challenged until after the American Revolution, and then by a few Enlightenment *philosophes* like Jefferson, Thomas Paine, Elihu Palmer, and Ethan Allen.[10] Moreover, most of the academies and colleges had been established as seminaries for the preparation and training of ministers, and they possessed an ethos which excluded skepticism in any recognizably modern form. Realism was unquestioned, but it was still a moderate or 'common sense' realism.[11] The young minds formed in this liberal arts tradition were quick to see the invasion of their natural and civil rights when the time came. There was nothing muddled about their logic, their apprehension of reality. The best of them always tried to bring their facts under the governance of principles and, scorning what would later be called moral relativism, grasped right from wrong with a precision of understanding. Indeed, in a true sense, American independence was won not on the playing fields but in the lecture halls of the Colonial colleges. And it is this blending of faith and reason in a strongly metaphysical atmosphere which accounts for much of the good, especially in theory, behind the original American dream.

The degree to which faith and reason were combined in the thinking of the professors who taught Rush—and most if not all of the other college men who made up half of the delegates to the Continental Congress—may be illustrated in Rev. Samuel Davies (1721-1761), president of the College of New Jersey and Rush's most influential teacher. Before coming to Princeton, Davies had played a leading role in the revival of Christianity known as the Great Awakening which swept the Colonies at mid-century and helped cause the American Revolution in ways that historians are just beginning to understand.[12] A brilliant, largely self-educated classicist and orator, Davies had attended an evangelical Presbyterian seminary or "School of the Prophets" in Pennsylvania, where he had been taught that reason and Revelation complemented each other in an organic synthesis of truth. At Princeton, which was modeled on Davies' Alma Mater, Rush and other young patriots were inculcated with the perennial truth that man is made in the image of God and accordingly possesses infinite worth and natural rights and duties.

Davies exhorted his students in *Religion and Public Spirit,* a commencement address of 1760, to be "proper Agents" of God charged with "an indispensable Obligation" to be like David, " the *Servant of God and his Generation.*"[13] "He suffered, he fought, he reigned, he prophesied, he sung, he performed every Thing, to serve his Generation, according to the Will of God."[14] Each of them, Davies said with profound Christian sincerity, must be formed of true religion and true public spirit, "the truly good and useful Man; a proper Member of human Society; and even of the grand Community of Angels and Saints." He continued:

> Public Spirit and Benevolence without Religion is but a warm Affection for the Subjects, to the Neglect of their Sovereign; or a Partiality for the Children in Contempt of their Father, who is infinitely more worthy of Love. And Religion without Public Spirit and Benevolence is but a sullen, selfish, sour and malignant Humour for devotion, unworthy that sacred Name. "For if a Man love not his Brother, whom he hath seen, how can he love God whom he hath not seen?"[15]

Rush and his fellow-students must be apostles of love.

This ideal of Christendom, and his role as an apostle in its realization, together explain Benjamin Rush's part in the American Revolution. The fact that Rush was as a Protestanct cut off from a living and specific interpreter of the principles upon which Christendom must be based likewise explains the weaknesses in Rush's approach. It must first be said that both as a member of Congress and as a volunteer physician at the Battle of Princeton, he was inspired by President Davies's dream of a new Christian order of love. "I am and have been several years before the memorable 1776 a republican in principle," he wrote of his Christian theory of the American Revolution,

not only because I conceive republican governments are most confor-
mable to reason but to revelation likewise. The pride of monarchy and
the servility of that state which induces in all its subjects are alike contrary to the humility and dignity of the Christian character. It is the
Spirit of the Gospel (though unacknowledged) which is now rooting
monarchy out of the world. Truth in this case is springing up from
that earth which helped the woman. . . . How truly worthy of a God
who styles himself Love is that religion which is opposed to everything
which disturbs or violates the order and happiness of society, whether
that society consists in the relation of individuals or of nations to each
other. . . . I anticipate with a joy which I cannot describe the speedy
end of the misery of the Africans, of the tyranny of kings. . . . Connected with the same events, I anticipate the end of war and such a
superlative tenderness for human life as will exterminate capital
punishments from all our systems of legislation. In the meanwhile let
us not be idle with such prospects before our eyes. *Heaven works by
instruments, and even supernatural prophecies are fulfilled by natural
means. It is possible we may not live to witness the approaching
regeneration of our world, but the more active we are in bringing it
about, the more fitted we shall be for that world where justice and
benevolence eternally prevail.* (emphasis added)[16]

The American Revolution, to this Signer of the Declaration of Independence, was nothing less than the divine opportunity for man to
reconstruct the world on Christian principles. "At present we wish 'liberty to the whole world',," Rush noted to a friend. "But the next touch
of the celestial magnet upon the human heart will direct it into wishes
for the *salvation of all mankind.*"[17] And in his ecumenical address of
1788 to all Christian ministers, including Roman Catholic priests, he
pleaded for their leadership as agents of social charity:

> America has taught the nations of Europe by her example to be free,
> and it is to be hoped she will soon teach them to govern themselves.
> Let her advance one step further—and teach mankind that it is possi-
> ble for Christians of different denominations to love each other and
> to unite in the advancement of their common interests. By the gradual
> operation of such natural means, the kingdoms of this world are pro-
> bably to become the kingdoms of the Prince of Righteousness and
> Peace.[18]

Americans were predestined in God's salvific plan to be the first of the
world's people to live in a premillennial state of grace and brotherly love.

The reign of natural law and rights, victorious over British totalitarianism and celebrated in the Declaration of Independence, would soon give way to the Messianic Kingdom. History, whole in its mysterious Christian character and unperverted by secularizing mentalities, was being fulfilled.

Regrettably for Rush, it was precisely in the specific application of Christianity to American institutions that the general principles of the natural law were no longer a sufficient guide. For Rush, unable to authoritatively identify that church which unfolds the kingdom of God on earth, confused God's kingdom with the American state. The "Spirit of the Gospel," Rush believed, had produced the miracle of the Federal Constitution. "I do not believe that the Constitution was the offspring of inspiration, but I am as perfectly satisfied that the Union of the States, in its *form* and *adoption*, is as much the work of a Divine Providence as any of the miracles recorded in the Old and New Testaments were the effects of a divine power."[19] The Federal and State Constitutions were, as republican forms of government, "the best repositories of the Gospel: I therefore suppose they are intended as preludes to a glorious manifestation of its power and influence upon the hearts of men."[20] "Justice has descended from heaven to dwell in our land, and ample restitution has at last been made to human nature by our new Constitution for all the injuries she has sustained in the old world from arbitrary government, false religions, and unlawful commerce."[21] Again, we pass over the reference to Catholicism, despite its significance here, in order to clarify Rush's views. For as he put it, "The language of these free and equal governments seems to be like that of John the Baptist of old. 'Prepare ye the way of the Lord—make his paths strait'."[22] Christ, the Lord of history, the " 'life of the world,' 'the prince of life,' and 'life' itself, in the New Testament"[23] was liberating man once and for all from violence of every kind; and the new Federal Constitution, Rush believed, guaranteed man's right to participate in divine life and freedom.[24]

Rush's Christocentric theory of the American Revolution was, as we have noted, much more explicit and systematic than that of the other Fathers. And, of course, there is no denying that with some of the Revolutionary leadership a tenaciously held belief in natural law had become detached from its historical source in Christ. Even with Rush himself in his middle years, it is clear that the *Zeitgeist* of the eighteenth-century Enlightenment was dangerously close to obscuring whatever remained of Catholic Truth in the Modern world. As has been suggested, republican constitutions—like his King James Bible—were in effect divinized, even though wisdom and Rush's contemporary and favorite poet, Alexander Pope, warned, "For forms of government let fools contest; Whate'er is best adminster'd is best."[26] Politics was assigned an unwarranted primacy in his vague doctrine of "Christian republicanism," foreshadowing nineteenth-century Marxism's politicizing of reality. A heady millennialism, defiant of centuries of cautioning by St. Augustine and others, was ingratiated into the whole as a thinly disguised variant of the Enlightenment's bourgeois historicism and progressivism. And America, not Christ and His Church, threatened to usurp the role of Liberator of mankind in an easily recognized messianism.[27]

It was precisely this eschatological chauvinism—this confusion of America with the kingdom of God—that prevented Rush, even in his most idealistic moments, from following his Master's advice to "Seek ye therefore first the kingdom of God and his justice."[28] There was no distinction between first and second in his mind when it came to God's kingdom and America, Republicanism and the Church. Thus his magnificent efforts to change the world, by his own confession, foundered in temporalism and, ultimately, ended in bitter disillusionment with all kinds of revolutionary activism. "Since the year 1790," Rush wrote at the close of the century,

> I have taken no part in the disputes or parties of our country. My retirement from political pursuits and labors was founded upon a conviction that all I had done, or could do for my country would be fruitless, and that things would assume the same course in America, that they had done in Europe, and from similar causes, and that disorder would reign everywhere until the coming of the Messiah. This disorder is perhaps necessary to form a contrast to his divine and peaceful government. 'Offences must come.' Tyranny, anarchy, war, debt, standing armies &c are the natural consequences of liberty and power uncontrolled by the spirit of Christianity. They must therefore exist, perhaps to furnish an opportunity of a display of divine power in destroying them. . . . I have abstracted my attention from the operations of human governments, and directed it wholly to that kingdom in which there shall be absolute monarchy with perfect freedom, uncontrolled power, with universal justice, perpetual safety without fleets and armies, unparalleled splendor supported without taxes or a national debt, and general equality of rights without disrespect for superiors. This

kingdom I believe will be administered in person by our Saviour upon
our globe.[29]

It is this last despair that any good can be done in the public order
that reveals the full import of the shortcomings of Rush's earlier optimistic position. It also fully explains Rush's hints that Catholicism was
a corrupt religion, similar in the nature of its corruption to monarchy.
For Rush never came to grips with any principle of authority on this
earth. In his initial identification of the kingdom of God with American
Republicanism, he had expected all good to arise spontaneously from
mankind as a whole. The Constitution itself had replaced a long-rejected
hierarchy as the chief vehicle of grace. This alone was thought sufficient to activate the operations of the natural law Rush cherished in his
heart. The absurdity of this position became obvious by events, and Rush
then set aside all political ambition to wait for the coming of a kingdom
characterized, as he said, by the absolute monarchy of God. It is a pity
that he could find no reflection of this heavenly order in the world of
time. He failed to see any connection between authority wielded by God
and authority wielded by men. In consequence, he could give natural
law neither its divine moorings nor its specific human application.

Had Rush recognized that papal authority was precisely the missing
link between divine law and human stewardship, he would have avoided both his confusion of republicanism with the kingdom of God and
his later despair of ever building Christendom. For Rush would have
then discovered an external and inviolable principle of human and divine
authority against which he might have very specifically judged even the
directions of the American state. In the central authority of Christ's own
Church, Rush would have found the means to preserve and act on his
understanding of the natural law. As it was, this Founding Father,
bewildered by the failure of his first dream, was forced to abandon his
former legitimate hope of applying natural law to nature. But even in
his confusion he at least settled on half of the truth. He recognized rightly
not that nothing positive can be done here below, but that perfect peace
and harmony can come only at the Parousia—that there is no paradise
to be built on earth by men, and no political form to guarantee its success. Rush finally began to distinguish the spiritual from the temporal
kindgom.

And so, having exhausted an honest but superficial doctrine of·the American Revolution, one essentially more Enlightenment than Christian, Benjamin Rush advanced in his later years beyond what the less Christian Founding Fathers could hope to see. He glimpsed an eternal Christendom resembling in some ways what Pope Paul VI has called in our day the dawning "civilization of love."[30] This, at least, was truly a Christocentric commentary on the American Revolution, born of experience itself.

## NOTES

[1]*Cf.* John A. Lukacs, *Historical Consciousness; or, the Remembered Past* (New York: Harper & Row, 1968); and Frederick D. Wilhelmsen, *The Paradoxical Structure of Existence* (Dallas: University of Dallas Press, 1970), esp. ch. VIII.

[2]I refer especially to the rise of legal positivism, seen most clearly in public acceptance of abortion. See Edward J. Melvin, C.M., *A Nation Built on God* (Huntington, Indiana: Our Sunday Visitor, Inc., 1975), *passim*.

[3]*Rom.* 2:14-15; C.S. Lewis, *The Abolition of Man* (New York: The MacMillan Co., 1965), *passim*.

[4]*Summa theol.,* I-II, q. 94, a.2; Cletus Dirksen, C.P.P.S., *Catholic Social Principles* (St. Louis, Mo.: B. Herder Book Co., 1961), ch. 5, *passim;* A. P.d'Entreves, *Natural Law: An Introduction to Legal Philosophy* (London: Hutchinson University Library, 1951), *passim*.

[5]D.J. D'Elia, *Benjamin Rush: Philosopher of the American Revolution* (Philadelphia: The American Philosophical Society, 1974) *(Transactions,* new ser., v. 64, part 5), *passim*.

[6]James J. Walsh, *Education of the Founding Fathers of the Republic; Scholasticism in the Colonial Colleges; a Neglected Chapter in the History of American Education* (New York: Fordham Unversity Press, 1935), *passim*.

[7]August 22, 1800, Lyman H. Butterfield, ed., *Letters of Benjamin Rush,* 2 vols. (Philadelphia: The American Philosophical Society, 1951), II, 820-821; Rush to John Adams, July 21, 1789, *ibid.*, I, 523.

[8]*Of the Mode of Education Proper in a Republic* in *Essays, Literary, Moral and Philosophical* (2nd ed., Philadelphia, 1806), pp. 8-9; D.J. D'Elia, *The Republican Theology of Benjamin Rush* in *Pennsylvania History* XXXIII (April, 1966), pp. 187-203.

[9]*Considerations on the Injustice and Impolity of Punishing Murder by Death* (Philadelphia, 1972), pp. 12-13; d'Entreves, *passim*.

[10]On Jefferson, see D.J. D'Elia, *Jefferson, Rush, and the Limits of Philosophical Friendship* in *Proceedings of the American Philosophical Society,* XCVII, No. 5 (October, 1973) pp. 333-343; Ethan Allen's *Reason the Only Oracle of Man* appeared in 1784, Paine's *Age of Reason* in 1794-96, and Elihu Palmer's *Principles of Nature* in 1797. The seminal work, of course, is Msgr.

Romano Guardini's *The End of the Modern World*, edited with an introduction by Frederick D. Wilhelmsen (Chicago: Henry Regnery Co., 1968).

[11]See, *e.g.*, Francis L. Broderick, *Pulpit, Physics, and Politics: The Curriculum of the College of New Jersey, 1746-1794* in *William & Mary Quarterly*, 3rd ser., VI (January, 1949), pp. 52, 57, *et. passim*. On the widely accepted *Scottish Philosophy of Common Sense*, S.A. Grave's book by that title is well worth consulting (Oxford: Oxford U. Press, 1960). Excellent on the philosophic background in general is Guardini's study and Etienne Gilson and Thomas Langan, *Modern Philosophy: Descartes to Kant* vol. III of Etienne Gilson, ed., *A History of Modern Philosophy* (New York: Random House, 1963).

[12]William B. Sprague, *Annals of the American Pulpit; or Commemorative Notices of Distinguished American Clergymen of Various Denominations, from the Early Settlement of the Country to the Close of the Year Eighteen Hundred and Fifty-Five* (9 vols., New York, 1857-1869) III, pp. 140-146. See, *e.g.*, Alan Heimert, *Religion and the American Mind: From the Great Awakening to the Revolution* (Cambridge, Mass.: Harvard University Press, 1966), *passim*.

[13]*Religion and Public Spirit, A Valedictory Address to the Senior Class, Delivered in Nassau Hall*, September 21, 1760, (New York) 1761, pp. 3-5.

[14]*Ibid.*, p. 4

[15]*Ibid.*, pp. 4-5.

[16]Rush to Jeremy Belknap, June 21, 1792, *Rush Letters I*, p. 620.

[17]Rush to Rev. Elhanan Winchester, November 12, 1791, *ibid.*, p. 612.

[18]Rush to "Ministers of the Gospel of All Denominations: An Address upon Subjects Interesting to Morals", June 21, 1788, *ibid.*, p. 466-467.

[19]Rush to Elias Boudinot? "Observations on the Federal Procession in Philadelphia;, July 9, 1788, *ibid.*, p. 475.

[20]Rush to Rev. Elhanan Winchester, November 12, 1791, *ibid.*, p. 611.

[21]Rush to Elias Boudinot? See note 19.

[22]Rush to Rev. Elhanan Winchester, November 12, 1791, *ibid.*, pp. 611-612.

[23]Rush, *Three Lectures upon Animal Life*, in *Medical Inquiries and Observations* (5th ed., 2 vols., Philadelphia, 1818), I pp. 53-54.

[24]George W. Corner, ed., *The Autobiography of Benjamin Rush: His "Travels through Life" together with His Commonplace Book for 1789-1813* (Philadelphia: The American Philosophical Society 1948), p. 161.

[25]Rush to James Kidd, November 25, 1793, *Rush Letters II*, p. 746.

[26]*Essay on Man.*

[27]The theme is well developed in Mrs. Anne Carroll's Wanderer Forum Lectures.

[28]*Matt.*6:33 (emph. added); *cf.* John Card. Wright, *The Fact and Nature of the Nativity Revolution* in *L'Osservatore Romano* (Eng. ed.) Jan. 6, 1977, 5, 10.

[29]Rush to Granville Sharp, April 2, 1799, John A. Woods, ed., *Correspondence of Benjamin Rush and Granville Sharp 1773-1809* in *Journal of American Studies I* (April 1967), pp. 32-33.

[30]See, *e.g.*, the Holy Father's *Joy and the Cross in the Civilization of Love* in *L'Osservatore Romano* (English ed.), January 22, 1976, ·p. 1.

# 3.
# John Adams:
# Revolutionary as Manichaean

On October 9, 1774, a stranger entered St. Mary's Roman Catholic Church in Philadelphia, studiously avoided blessing himself with holy water, and sat down without genuflecting before the Blessed Sacrament. John Adams (1735-1826) of Massachusetts—the future President of the United States—was in town for the Continental Congress, which was meeting down the street at Carpenters Hall. "Wearied to Death" by it all, he had decided to relieve his ennui with a tour of the city's churches.[1] As a proud New Englander, moreover, he wished to confirm the superiority of his ways in the city of Brotherly Love where even Roman Catholics were allowed to worship in public.

In Massachusetts, Roman Catholics were "as scarce as a comet or an earthquake," Adams had noted.[2] And as far as he was concerned, that was a good thing. "The Church of Rome has made it an article of faith that no man can be saved out of their church," was the way Adams had put it, "and all other religious sects approach to this dreadful opinion in proportion to their ignorance, and the influence of ignorant or wicked priests."[3] Now, on this autumn day, he was sitting in a papist church surrounded by Catholics and listening to a Roman Priest deliver what he conceded was "a good short, moral essay" on parental duty.[4]

It would be edifying to say that John Adams, having come to scoff, remained to pray. Unfortunately, it would also be untrue. "This afternoon's entertainment was to me most awful and affecting," he explained to his wife, Abigail.

*36*

The poor wretches, fingering their beads, chanting Latin, not a word which they understood, their Pater Nosters and Ave Marias. Their Holy Water—their crossing themselves perpetually—their bowing to the name of Jesus, wherever they hear it—their bowings, and kneelings, and genuflections before the altar . . . . But how shall I describe the picture of our Saviour in a frame of marble over the altar at full length upon the Cross, in the agonies, and the blood dropping and streaming from his wounds.[5]

John Adams, good Puritan that he was, defiantly resisted the Tridentine Mass celebrated on the "very rich" altar with "little images and crucifixes about—wax candles lighted up," and sung to the accompaniment of organ music and Gregorian chants. "Here is everything which can lay hold of the eye, ear and imagination. Everything which can charm and bewitch the simple and ignorant. I wonder how Luther ever broke the spell."[6]

The Faith that charmed and bewitches "simple and ignorant" minds like those of St. Augustine and St. Thomas Aquinas was to remain inaccessible to Harvard-trained John Adams and, indeed, he was later to abandon even the Calvinism of his youth and early middle age for a paler Unitarianism by the time of his death in 1826. For, like many other New Englanders of his generation, Adams struggled unconsciously during his lifetime to free himself of "frigid" John Calvin's theology and discover again that abundance of life that Christ had promised in His true Church. These were the promptings of his restless heart, which we can perhaps glimpse ever so dimly in his letter to Abigail in visiting St. Mary's Church.

But, if on one hand Adams was groping for the pre-Reformation Faith of his fathers, if he was trying to work his way back to the Church of the Apostles, it was also true that, on the other, the anti-Catholic bias of his New England tradition proved too strong to overcome. And what seemed to have happened in the end was that Adams, largely if not solely because of his consuming hatred for the Roman Catholic Church—which in all justice can only be called monomaniacal—arrived by degrees at a final and inevitable position in Unitarianism which denied altogether Jesus's Messiahship.

John Adams was thirty-nine years old when he came to Philadelphia as a delegate to the Continental Congress. Already he was being called "honest John Adams," this proud son of Massachusetts yeoman farmers, and he delighted in affecting his New England accent and mannerisms in the plain, Quaker city. Even after he had renounced Calvinism in his late middle age, Adams liked to praise his Calvinist ancestors who had fled to America in 1636 to escape Anglican persecution and who had "multiplied like the sands on the seashore."[7] As a boy in Braintree, Adams suggested unwittingly a half century later, he had begun the long journey that would lead him farther and farther away from belief in the divine Sonship of Christ. "[I] became a reader of polemical writings of religion," Adams recalled, "as well as politics, and for more than seventy years I have indulged myself in that kind of reading, as far as the wandering, anxious, and perplexed kind of life, which Providence has compelled me to pursue, would admit. I have endeavored to obtain as much information as I could of all the religions which have ever existed in the world."[8] Adams's father, a deacon in Braintree, had wished him, in fact, to become a Congregational parson, and had sent him to Harvard in 1750 to prepare for the ministry.[9]

John's father no doubt had had some misgivings about sending his boy to Harvard. The college was under the presidency of Edward Holyoke at mid-century, and Holyoke was an Enlightenment liberal who was rumored to be using his office to subvert Calvinist orthodoxy at the leading New England seminary.[10] In any case, young Adams studied theology under President Holyoke for four years in a program that emphasized "logical analysis" of the Scriptures, and when he graduated came away skeptical of Calvinist doctrine, if not quite prepared to accept Holyoke's insistence that "every man therefore is to judge for himself in these things."[11] At the same time, John was drawn, through his father's position in the Braintree congregation, into a theological controversy involving the alleged Arminianism of the local minister. The "spirit of dogmatism and bigotry in clergy and laity" alike troubled him. "Very strong doubts arose in my mind, whether I was made for a pulpit in such times, and I began to think of other professions."[12]

In the village of Worcester, where Adams was appointed Latin schoolmaster, the recent graduate read Deist and other authors and debated theology and philosophy with the town freethinkers, while his deliberation about a profession edged him more and more towards law and politics. Finally, Adams decided to study law and took up lodgings with James Putnam, one of the leaders of the nonconformists circle. On March 7, 1756, he made clear in his diary that he had come round to agree with President Holyoke "that men ought (after they have examined with unbiased judgments every system of religion, and chosen one system, on their own authority, for themselves), to avow their opinions and defend them with boldness."[13] As we have seen, Adams always liked to think that he had conducted a rigorous inquiry into every "system of religion" in his lifetime—that he was the perfect Protestant—but we should note that from the first he omitted Roman Catholicism and other "high church" religions from his program of study.[14]

"Where do we find a precept in the Gospel requiring ecclesiastical synods? Convocations? Councils? Decrees? Creeds? Confessions? Oaths? Subscriptions? and whole cartloads of other trumpery that we find religion encumbered with in these days," he asked ingenuously.[15] Clearly, they were nowhere to be found in the Bible, according to Adams, literalist notions of exegesis, and therefore he concluded over the years that they were frauds perpetrated by that "monster," "Platonic, Pythagoric, Hindoo, and cabalistic Christianity, which is Catholic Christianity, and which has prevailed for fifteen years."[16]

From these beginnings, Adams elaborated over his long lifetime a world-view in which, sad to say, hatred for the Roman Catholic Church was central. Indeed, there is simply no understanding the mind of this founder of the American nation without entering into the scheme of his thought. And it would be false charity to deny this. Adams, honestly enough, was fond of saying that writers of history—and all men—should take the oath of Thuanus, the French historian who swore before God to tell the truth, the whole truth.[17] The irony is that Adams never besought himself to learn the truth about the Roman Catholic Church.

As Adams gradually turned away from the extreme predestination of Calvinism, the only norm for understanding Christianity he knew in his early years, he was attracted to avant-garde Deistic works like those of Thomas Morgan and Henry St. John, first Viscount of Bolingbroke. Morgan's *Moral Philosopher* (1737), which was the talk of Worcester's Deists when Adams arrived there, argued that an original pristine religion of nature had been corrupted by Moses, Aaron, and other wily and Judaizing priests, especially in the early Catholic hierarchy.[18] Adams was already familiar with Bolingbroke's historical and political writings while a student at Cambridge, but now Mr. Putnam, his legal mentor, lent him the Englishman's religious essays too, and Adams read them and Bolingbroke's entire works first in Worcester and then over and over again—five times in all—during his busy career. "I arose by the dawning of the day," he remembered years later, "and by sunrise had made my fire and read a number of pages in Bolingbroke."[19]

More than any other author, Bolingbroke—the teacher of Voltaire—seems to have influenced young Adams with many of his religious and political ideas, ideas that were nonconformist enough to suit an ambitious bourgeois lawyer determined to find his own way in a New England society fast losing its faith in the old Calvinist pieties. Bolingbroke, for example, denounced St. Paul's teaching on predestination and other traditional articles of Christianity as "often absurd, or profane, or trifling." He attacked the Old Testament as mere Jewish history, viewed Moses with "contempt" and "horror", and blamed the Fathers of the Church for introducing their "wild allegories" into natural religion. But his special hatred was for Plato who, like the schoolmen—those "pneumatical madmen" of the Middle Ages— had corrupted the simple theism of rational men with his "pompous jargon of mystery."[20] The study of metaphysics, wrote Lord Bolingbroke, was "delirium," and practitioners were "learned lunatics." The only philosophers worth reading were, of course, Englishmen: Francis Bacon and John Locke.[21] These were all opinions that Adams came to share, although to the end of his days he could not brook the Viscount's skeptical belief in the finality of death.[22]

Bolingbroke's historical method, crude and empirical as it was, led Adams to make his own dilettante researches not only into the origin of the "artificial theology" of Christianity but into the beginnings of politics and government. "History," said the popular author of *The Study and Use of History*, was "philosophy teaching by examples."[23] And the philosophy of history taught that events were caused by personal intrigue and a Hobbesian war of all against all for power. Hence, Bolingbroke concluded—and this became Adams's fundamental conception in political philosophy—that democracy and other simple forms of government tended to be governments of arbitrary will and that in a constitution like that of England "the safety of the whole depends on the balance of the parts, and the balance of parts on their mutual independency on each other."[24] Men must be restrained from their insane lust for power, their interests must be so balanced as to discourage "party spirit" and unite them in liberty under a constitutional monarch who, in truth, would be a "Patriot King."[25]

These ideas were in the background of Adams's thinking when he began practicing law before the Boston bar in November 1758. They formed in the mind of the doubting Puritan a kind of secularized Calvinism, whose leading principle was a deep suspicion of human nature and a radical distrust of any human claim to power and authority. His pride in the New England Independency of his ancestors, however, waxed more vigorous as he now read English history and law and was drawn, hopelessly as it turned out, into the naive anti-medievalism of the age. He got hold of William Robertson's *History of Charles V*, acclaimed by Voltaire, and found ample confirmation of his prejudices against medieval Catholic civilization. While in the sermons and pamphlets of the fiery Boston Unitarian preacher, Jonathan Mayhew, he was made starkly aware of what he, Mayhew, and their liberal coterie believed to be dangerous parallels between the tyranny of church and state in the Middle Ages and the new imperial policy of Great Britain.[26]

When he pored over Rousseau's recently published *Contrat social* in February 1765, a book his Boston study club was reviewing in connection with their study of feudal law, Adams lighted upon a passage condemning the feudal system as "the most iniquitous and absurd form of government by which human nature was so shamefully degraded."[27] This served to provide him with a unifying conception for the religious, historical, and political ideas that he had borrowed from many different sources. Adams's paper, *A Dissertation on the Canon and Feudal Law*, read before the club that spring and published anonymously in the *Boston Gazette*, synthesized his views on the subject in a typically crude anti-Catholic 18th century understanding of Western history; but one that, nevertheless, was to remain his "philosophy" of history.[28]

In the foreground of Adams's essay was the Stamp Act of 1765, which his older and admired colleague, James Otis—also a member of the Boston law club—denounced as "taxation without representation", as he had the Sugar Act before it. The *Dissertation on the Canon and Feudal Law* attacked the Stamp Act as a violation of individual rights and sought to demonstrate historically that the new British tyranny was another example of corporate authority's love of power and cruel oppression of the people. "If it is this principle that has always prompted the princes and nobles of the earth, by every species of fraud and violence to shake off all the limitations of their power," Adams, the proud dissenter and student of Bolingbroke, argued, "it is the same that has always stimulated the common people to aspire at independency, and to endeavor at confining the power of the great within the limits of equity and reason."[29] Corporate authority's mad love of power could best be seen in "the two greatest systems of tyranny", the canon and feudal law, "a wicked conspiracy" invented by spiritual and temporal "grandees" to deprive men of their God-given rights.[30]

"By the former of these," Adams continued to elaborate his peculiar New England manichaeanism,

> the most refined, sublime, extensive, and astonishing constitution of policy that ever was conceived by the mind of man was framed by the Romish clergy for the aggrandisement of their own order. All the epithets I have here given to the Romish policy are just, and will be allowed to be so when it is considered, that they even persuaded mankind to believe, faithfully and undoubtingly, that God Almighty had entrusted them with the keys of heaven, whose gates they might open and close at pleasure; with a power of dispensation over all the rules and obligations of morality; with authority to license all sorts of sins and crimes; with a power of deposing princes and absolving subjects from allegiance; with a power of procuring or withholding the rain of heaven and the beams of sun; with the management of earthquakes, pestilence, and famine; nay, with the mysterious, awful, incomprehensible power of creating out of bread and wine the flesh and blood of God himself.[31]

And characteristically for Adams, the evil one or Ahriman of this gnostic piece, and of his entire thought, was the pope, who had enslaved human nature "for ages in a cruel, shameful, and deplorable servitude to him, and his subordinate tyrants, who, it was foretold, would exalt himself above all that was called God, and that was worshipped."[32]

It was the Protestant Reformers of the 16th century, Adams believed, and especially the English Puritans, who had overthrown this "infernal confederacy" of ecclesiastical and civil tyranny personified by the Stuart kings and raised up in New England a truly Christian government free of Rome's jurisdiction.

> They saw clearly, that of all the nonsense and delusion which had ever passed through the mind of man, none had ever been more extravagant than the notions of absolutions, indelible characters, uninterrupted succesions, and the rest of those fantastical ideas, derived from the canon law, which had thrown such a glare of mystery, sanctity, reverence, and right reverend eminence and holiness, around the idea of a priest, as no mortal could deserve, and as always must, from the constitution of human nature, be dangerous in society.[33]

Free in America of the "sordid, stupid, and wretched herd" of priests, Adams went on, the original Puritan settlers built schools and colleges to educate their descendants against the evils of the feudal and canon systems. They knew, as did Adams himself, that only an enlightened public could restrain the lust for absolute power and domination that was in the hearts of men. They discerned from the beginning God's hand in their work, that their coming to America was "the opening of a grand scene and design in Providence for the illumination of the ignorant, and the emancipation of the slavish part of mankind all over the earth."[34]

But now in 1765, Adams warned his countrymen, there seemed "to be a direct and formal design on foot, to enslave all America."[35] The Stamp Act, an unprecedented direct tax on the colonists, was clearly unconstitutional and feudal in character, obviously part of a conspiracy to restore the absolute government of the Middle Ages. The Church of England, which every perceptive American saw as a tool of Rome, was likewise trying to destroy Independency by sending missionaries to the Colonies and scheming to re-introduce episcopacy and other features of the hateful canon law. "The canon and feudal systems, though greatly mutilated in England, are not yet destroyed. Like the temples and palaces in which the great contrivers of them once worshipped and inhabited, they exist in ruins; and much of the domineering spirit of them still remains."[36]

This, then, was the perspective in which John Adams viewed not only the events of the American Revolution but the course of history itself. Time had not been ransomed. The Incarnation, Adams in his skepticism maintained, had no historical consequences. Priests, nobles, and kings—ecclesiastical, political, and all "parties"—still conspired for power; and power once achieved always sought to justify itself. "When and where were ever found, or will be found, sincerity, honesty, or veracity, in any sect or party in religion, government or philosophy?[37] "Power always sincerely, conscientiously, *de tres bon* [*ne*] *foi*, believes itself right. Power always thinks it has a great soul, and vast views, beyond the comprehension of the weak; and that it is doing God service, when it is violating all his laws," Adams wrote as a Unitarian in 1816.

> Our passions, ambition, avarice, love, resentment, etc., possess so much metaphysical subtlety, and so much overpowering eloquence, that they insinuate themselves into the understanding and the conscience, and convert both to their party; and I may be deceived as much as any of them, when I say, that Power must never be trusted without a check.[38]

This historical nihilism, which is what it really was, owed much to Adams's early Calvinism and his reading in Bolingbroke, Machiavelli, Hobbes, and Locke. It was also the root-principle of his constitutional doctrine of checks and balances which was so influential on the authors of the Federal Constitution of the United States.

In this, Adams's historical scenario, the leading roles in villainy were played by Plato, SS. Athanasius and Ignatius of Loyola, and Pope Leo X.[39] Martin Luther and John Calvin were spared their company, but only barely. For "Luther, and his associates and followers, went less than half way in detecting the corruptions of Christianity" and "acquired reverence and authority among their followers almost as absolute as that of the Popes had been."[40] And Calvin, he now admitted, had broken away from Rome only to set himself up as the "Pope of Geneva."[41] But what saved the two Reformers from Adams's total condemnation was their great success in weakening the medieval papacy.

The anti-heroes of Adams's "philosophy" of history were all, like Athanasius, Ignatius of Loyola, and Pope Leo X, defenders of orthodoxy. As a Unitarian, a position he shared with Jefferson, Adams scorned the Council of Nicea and St. Athanasius, its fearless champion. The Trinity, the Incarnation, and the Holy Spirit were, Adams believed, so many fabrications of ideas derived from Pythagoreanism and Platonism.[42] "The truth is that nothing was canonical till the Council of Nicea. Then and not till then was settled the norm of canonicality. And by whom?''[43] Why, by the devils of John Adams's world-view: the sectarian corrupters of that original religion of nature, which the man Jesus of Nazareth had taught and which Adams had read about in the books of the leading "higher critics" and Deistic freethinkers of the 18th century. "Indeed, Mr. Jefferson," he wrote in a letter of December 3, 1813, "what could be invented to debase the ancient Christianism, which Greeks, Romans, Hebrews, and Christian factions, above all the Catholics, have not fraudulently imposed upon the public? Miracles after miracles have rolled down in torrents, wave succeeding wave in the Catholic church, from the Council of Nicea, and long before, to this day.''[44]

It was these vicious distortions of truth and reality, Adams held, mainly by his enemy of enemies, the Roman Catholic hierarchy, that produced in time the dreaded canon and feudal systems of the Middle Ages, laid low by the Protestant Reformers of the 16th century only to rise again, as we have seen, in Adams's own day.[45] And the symbol of Roman Catholic power for Adams was St. Peter's Basilica in Rome, personified in his demonology by Pope Leo X, "the political Christian".[46]

> That stupendous monument of human hypocrisy and fanaticism, the church of St. Peter at Rome, which was a century and a half in building, excited the ambition of Leo the Xth, who believed no more of the Christian religion than Diderot, to finish it; and finding St. Peter's pence insufficient, he deluged all Europe with indulgences for sale, and excited Luther to controvert his authority to grant them.[47]

Not that Leo X was, in Adams's manichaean view, the only priest to exploit man's need for salvation. "There is a germ of religion in human nature," his Calvinism kept on reasserting itself, "so strong that whenever an order of men can persuade the people by flattery or terror that they have salvation at their disposal, there can be no end to fraud, violence, or usurpation.''[48] These evil men, the reprobate of Adams's secularized Calvinism, were for him the devils of "Jesuitry", "Platonic Christianity, Pharisaical Judaism or Machiavellian politics.''[49]

Adams, at first, idealized the American Revolution as the long-promised victory of New World "saints" over the decadent religious and political medievalism of the Roman Catholic Church. But soon a concatenation of events, notably the rise of "party spirit" here among the American leaders and people, with all its allied phenomena of demogogic rule and "bedollared" materialism, and the French Revolution abroad, with its violent excesses in Ropespierre and Napoleon, forced him to disabuse himself of this precious illusion.

Francophile and opposition leader Thomas Jefferson, later to be his close friend (after the political battles were over), presently stood forth as a bitter "intriguer" against that republican unity that Adams had celebrated in his *Defence of the Constitutions of Government of the United States* (1787-1788) and other political writings. The even more villainous Alexander Hamilton, that "Creole adventurer", had "never acquired the feelings and principles of the American people", and so was as dissolute in his allegiance to the nation as he was in his private life.[50] Finally, Adams came to see in his twisted perspective that Washington— Hamilton's patron and "excellent hypocrite"—was himself not above accepting canonization and even worship in the manner of the Catholic "Dark Ages".[51] "The feasts and funerals in honor of Washington, Hamilton, and [Fisher] Ames," he wrote in 1809, "are mere hypocritical pageantry to keep in credit banks, funding systems, and other aristocratical speculation. It is as corrupt a system as that by which saints were canonized and cardinals, and popes, and whole hierarchical systems created."[52]

This Hamiltonian system of "speculations, banks, paper money, and mushroom fortunes," as Adams described it to Dr. Benjamin Rush, he had abhorred as President of the United States and "shall die abhorring."

> The profits of our banks to the advantage of the few, at the loss of the many, are such an enormous fraud and oppression as no other nation ever invented or endured. Who can compute the amount of the sums taken out of the pockets of the simple and hoarded in the purses of the cunning, in the course of every year?[53]

The Hamiltonian system was, in fact, a new kind of feudalism, as odious as that evil system which priests and politicians had used to exploit the common people in the Middle Ages. "An aristocracy is growing out of" the banks "that will be as fatal as the feudal barons, if unchecked, in time."[54]

Hamilton, "the sovereign Pontiff of Federalism", was a leader of reaction whose designs coincided with those of the priests in "reestablishing darkness and ignorance, superstition and despotism."[55] And the priests who were behind the grand conspiracy to destroy America were, of course, the Jesuits, now in 1814 reconstituted as a society by Rome expressly to crush Protestant freedom and bring back the tyranny of canon law. In the United States, Adams believed, they were "more numerous than every body knows . . . in many shapes and disguises . . . in the shape of printers, editors, writers, schoolmasters, etc."[56] He even suspected that the Jesuits and their secret agents—for example, Chateaubriand, the French apologist and restorationist—were acting under the orders of a new Council of Nicea, "an ecumenical council of Pope, cardinals, and bishops" to restore to the Catholic hierarchy the privileged position it had enjoyed in the *ancien regime.* "[57] No "congregation of men" was ever more deserving of "eternal perdition on earth and in hell' than the company of that "mere monk" St. Ignatius of Loyola—not even the French *philosophes* whom Adams detested.[58]

Indeed, Voltaire, Rousseau, Diderot, Helvetius, d'Alembert, Condorcet, Mably, and other "blind disciples of Franklin and Turgot" were for Adams grasping "priests and politicians" themselves, really no different from the Jesuits and feudal barons they attacked. True, they had undermined the hierarchy of the Catholic Church in a country where "the power of pardon and absolution in the priests" had left the people corrupted beyond hope; and Voltaire and Joseph Priestley—an Englishman but one of their company—"had done more to propagate religious liberty than Calvin, or Luther, or even Locke."[59]

> The philosophers of France were too rash and hasty. They were as artful as selfish and as hypocritical as the priests and politicians of Babylon, Persia, Egypt, India, Greece, Rome, Turkey, Germany, Wales, Scotland, Ireland, France, Spain, Italy or England. They understood not what they were about. They miscalculated their forces and resources: and were consequently overwhelmed in destruction with all their theories.[60]

At the very time the deep and civilizing effects of the Protestant Reformation were beginning to transform Europe, when the feudal and canon systems of the Catholic Middle Ages were about to disappear forever, the *philosophes* rushed headlong into their dangerous and reckless experiment, Adams believed. "The public mind was improving in

knowledge and the public heart in humanity, equity, and benevolence,''
he argued from his historical dualism.

> The fragments of feudality, the inquisition, the rack, the cruelty of
> punishments, Negro slavery were giving way, etc. but the philosophers
> must arrive at perfection *per saltum*. Ten times more furious than Jack
> in the Tale of a Tub, they rent and tore the whole garment to pieces
> and left not one whole thread in it. They have even been compelled
> to resort to Napoleon, and [Edward] Gibbon himself became an ad-
> vocate for the Inquisition. What an amiable and glorious Equality,
> Fraternity, and Liberty they have now established in Europe![61]

The *philosophes*, with their cant about equality, Adams concluded
had been responsible for the loss of millions of innocent lives and tens
of millions of dollars in property. And their folly had brought about the
positive evils of Napoleon and, then, the Congress of Vienna. "The question now," he grumbled, "is whether Popes, Jesuits, and inquisitions
shall rule the human race?"[62]

So the *philosophes*, whose exaggerated rationalism Adams himself
shared, were in the end unwitting agents of Catholic reaction. There was
something good to be said about them, however. Their anti-clericalism
was salutary, their rejection of Trinitarianism and other false doctrines
of canon law in favor of reason was enlightened in the best sense, and
their liberal social teachings were truly progressive. But in their political
and philosophic elitism they failed the test of Adams's New England
Independency, of the people's sovereignty in all things, whether religious
or political.[63] Voltaire and others preferred rule by "enlightened despot."
Adams, believing himself true to Protestant principle, demanded
representative government, as in the Massachusetts Constitution of 1780
(which he helped write) and the United States Constitution. Rousseau,
it was true, came closest of all to Adams's position, but his doctrine
of the "general will" was too simple and democratic in the extreme to
be acceptable. Montesquieu's *Spirit of the Laws* he treated with respect,
and copied whole passages from it into his *Defence of the Constitutions*,
but the Frenchman's principle of the balance and separation of powers
he knew to be derived from John Locke.[64]

Once again, this time in his eightieth year, Adams posed the major
question which, prescinding from his characteristic sarcasm, reveals at
times an honest if not noble mind trying to make sense of reality.

The question before mankind is, how shall I state it? It is, whether authority is from nature and reason, or from miraculous revelation; from the revelation from God, by the human understanding, or from the revelation to Moses and to Constantine, and the Council of Nicea. Whether it resides in men or in offices. Whether offices, spiritual and temporal, are instituted by men, or whether they are self-created and instituted themselves. Whether they were or were not brought down from Heaven in a phial of holy oil, sent by the Holy Ghost, by an angel incarnated in a dove, to anoint the head of Clovis, a more cruel tyrant than Frederic the Great or Napoleon. Are the original principles of authority in human nature, or in stars, garters, crosses, golden fleeces, crowns, sceptres, and thrones?

This was the question (he went on to obscure his point with the old hatreds) that had "been agitated and discussed, before that vast democratical congregation, mankind, for more than five hundred years."

How many crusades, how many Hussite wars, how many powder plots, St. Bartholomew's days, Irish massacres, Albigensian massacres, and battles of Marengo have intervened? *Sub judice lis est.* Will Zinzendorf, Swedenborg, Whitefield, or Wesley prevail? Or will St. Ignatius Loyola inquisitionize and jesuitize them all? Alas, poor human nature! Thou are responsible to thy Maker and to thyself for an impartial verdict and judgment.[65]

In his old age, then, John Adams was still, like the *philosophes*, absolutizing reason and nature. Where his Calvinist ancestors had overemphasized grace, faith, and necessity to the detriment of "freedom" in their exaggerated Augustinianism, he as a dissenter from Calvinism absolutized reason and "freedom". Adams, paradoxically, saw man's nature as corrupted and yet denied the need for grace, that "celestial virtue, more than human."

Virtue, the basis of all happiness, he went so far as to argue, could be produced in men by a "well ordered constitution."[66] Indeed, Adams, who believed man to be the most "savage beast of the forest" without government, made an absolute of his constitutionalism, of "checks and balances", not just in politics but in religion and in all areas of human life. "Checks and balances," he applied this principle to religion in a letter to Jefferson in 1813, are our only Security, for the progress of the mind, as well as the security of body. Every species of these Christians would persecute Deists, as soon as either Sect would persecute another, if it had unchecked and unbalanced power. Nay, the Deists would persecute Christians, and Atheists would persecute Deists, with as unrelenting cruelty, as any Christians would persecute them or one another. Know thyself, human Nature![67]

"The passions" of men "will never be prevented," he echoes his youthful Calvinism, "they can only be balanced."[68]

Adams failed to see that politics and all things must be baptized—transfigured in Christ—not that Christianity should be politicized.[69] His Calvinist background, moreover, so biased his outlook on history that he never understood that the Middle Ages he loathed had produced, in its life and thought, especially that of St. Thomas Aquinas, the criteria for limiting political power and serving the common good that he extolled. The very natural rights philosophy to which he and others subscribed in the Declaration of Independence, Adams apparently never realized, had been elaborated by medieval Catholic thnkers, as was the idea of representative government itself. And little did he realize, evidently, that Catholic theorists like St. Thomas, Cardinal Bellarmine, and Francisco Suarez had led the attack on the divine right theory of monarchy. Had his caricature of the Middle Ages been revealed for what it was—mere anti-Catholicism—Adams would have seen that feudalism contained within itself that great respect for law, representation, legislative power of taxation, and the other constitutional ideas that he wished to embody in a model government.[70] In short, the absolutism that Adams was really opposing in his constitutionalism was not Catholic but Calvinist, modern not medieval, but he never seemed to grasp the difference.[71]

John Adams was a lawyer and revolutionary polemicist, with a temperament to fit those professions. He read much—perhaps more than any other Founding Father—and wrote in a style unique among them for its color and verve. But like Jefferson he was no deep thinker. And also like the Virginian he too often mistook his own narrow understanding for the measure of things.

The point, though, is that Adams was a *philosophe*, an Enlightenment rationalist to whom only the natural, tangible, and secular were real. And these were ultimately what John Adams said they were: he, not the Logos—which he ridiculed—not Christ was the measure of all things.[72] It was not for him to believe—"this awful blasphemy", he wrote in his ninetieth year—that the "great Principle which has produced this boundless universe, Newton's universe and Herschel's universe, came down to this little ball, to be spit upon by Jews."[73] God exists, and He has commanded us in our reason and in the Bible—"The best book in the world"—to do good to our fellow man.[74] "Let us be content therefore," Adams concluded with the positivists of his age, "to believe Him to be a Spirit, that is, an Essence that we know nothing of, in which originally and necessarily reside all energy, all power, all capacity, all activity, all wisdom, all goodness."[75]

It was, apparently, this religious philosophy that sustained John Adams in his final days. On January 14, 1826, in his last letter to Jefferson, Adams sensed the approach of his death and, characteristically, prepared for it with classical arguments.

> I am far from trifling with the idea of Death which is a great and solemn event. But I contemplate it without terror or dismay, "aut transit, aut finit [Either it is a transformation, or it is the end .]'", if finit, which I cannot believe, and do not believe, there is then an end of all but I shall never know it, and why should I dread it, which I do not; if transit I shall ever be under the same *constitution* and administration of Government in the Universe, and I am not afraid to trust and confide in it.[76] (emphasis added)

Reason, as he understood it, was Adams's guide to the end.

There is a final note, an ironic postscript that must be written to any biography of John Adams. And it is this. The 18th century *philosophe* who absolutized reason and condemned as medieval superstition "the poor wretches fingering their beads" in St. Mary's Church in 1774 turned out to be the great grandfather of America's most famous student of the Catholic Middle Ages. Henry Adams (1838-1918), the author of *Mont Saint-Michel and Chartres*, took another view of that medieval Catholic civilization his progenitor considered the source of all that was wrong with the West. The Virgin of Chartres—and necessarily the canon law that promoted her cult—Henry Adams idealized as the symbol of Western man's unity of thought, will, and sensibility, attained in the 13th century, but lost in the multiplicity of the modern world as symbolized by the dynamo.[77] Our Lady of the Rosary was "the ideal of human pefection" and her universal cult in the Middle Ages, Henry Adams believed, was recognition by men that simple faith, intuition, art, and love united them *vis-á-vis* the universe in a way that reason and science can never do.

After his death in 1918, Henry Adams's niece, Mabel Hooper La Farge—a convert to Catholicism—found among his papers a "Prayer to the Virgin of Chartres" in which her uncle declared himself a supplicant of Mary.[78]

## NOTES

[1]John Adams to Abigail Adams, October 9, 1774, Lyman H. Butterfield, ed., *Adams Family Correspondence* (2 vols.; Cambridge, Mass., Belknap Press, 1963) 1: p. 166; John Tracy Ellis, ed., *Documents of American Catholic History* (2 vols.; Chicago, Ill., Henry Regnery Co., 1967) 1: pp. 132-133.

[2]*A Dissertation on the Canon and Feudal Law* in Charles F. Adams, *The Works of John Adams* (10 vols.; Boston, 1856) 3: p. 456; Newman C. Eberhardt, *A Survey of American Church History* (St. Louis, B. Herder., 1964), p. 17.

[3]Diary, February 16, 1756, Norman Cousins, *In God We Trust; the Religious Beliefs and Ideas of the American Founding Fathers* (New York: Harper & Bros., 1958), p. 80. A useful anthology of writings with very little critical analysis.

[4]Butterfield, p. 167.

[5]*Ibid.*

[6]*Ibid.*

[7]Adams to Samuel Miller, July 8, 1820, Cousins, p. 111; to Dr. Benjamin Rush, July 19, 1812, John A. Schutz and Douglass Adair, ed., *The Spur of Fame: Dialogues of John Adams and Benjamin Rush, 1805-1813* (San Marino, Calif., 1966), p. 238.

[8]Adams to Samuel Miller, July 8, 1820, Cousins, pp. 111-112.

[9]*Autobiography, ibid.*, p. 77; Page Smith, *John Adams* (2 vols.; Garden City, N.Y.: Doubleday & Co., 1962) 1: p. 28.

[10]*Ibid.*, p. 15.

[11]*Ibid.*, p. 15, 18.

[12]*Autobiography*, Cousins, p. 77.

[13]Diary, *ibid.*, p. 81; *ibid., Autobiography*, pp. 78-79.

[14]Adams to John Taylor, no date, 1814, Cousins, p. 108.

[15]Diary, February 18, 1756, *ibid*, p. 80.

[16]Adams to Jefferson, July 16, 1814, Lester J. Cappon, ed., *The Adams-Jefferson Letters: the Complete Correspondence Between Thomas Jefferson and Abigail and John Adams* (2 v.: Chapel Hill: U. of N. Pr., 1959) 2: p. 435.

[17]Adams to Rush, July 23, 1806, Schutz, pp. 59-60. Jacques Aguste de Thou or Thuanus (1553-1617).

[18]*Autobiography*, Cousins, p. 78. Leslie Stephen, *History of English Thought in the Eighteenth Century*, with a Preface by Crane Brinton (2 vols.; New York:

Harcourt, Brace & World, Inc., 1962) 111:71-72.

[19]Quoted in Zoltan Haraszti, *John Adams and the Prophets of Progress: A Study in the Intellectual and Political History of the Eighteenth Century* (New York: Grosset&Dunlap, 1964), p. 49; *Autobiography*, Cousins, p. 79.

[20]Haraszti, p. 51; Stephen, III, 82-83.

[21]Haraszti, p. 80; Adams to Jefferson, Feb. 3, 1812, Cappon, II, p. 294.

[22]Haraszti, pp. 74-75.

[23]Stephen, X, p. 49.

[24]Quoted in *Ibid.*, X, p. 48; Haraszti, pp. 54, 253.

[25]Stephen, X, p. 52.

[26]*A Diss. on the Canon and Feudal Law*, C.F. Adams, pp. 464, 449n; Fulmer Mood, *Jonathan Mayhew [1720-1766]* in *Dict. of Am. Biog.* VI, pp. 454f. On "The Founding Fathers and the Middle Ages", see H. Wayne Morgan, *Mid-America: An Historical Quarterly*, XLII (1960), pp. 30-43.

[27]Quoted in *Dissertation*, C. F. Adams, pp. 454-455, Haraszti, p. 80.

[28]C.F. Adams's introduction to the *Dissertation*, pp. 447-448, provides details on the writing and publication of the essay.

[29]*Ibid.*, p. 448; Samuel E. Morison, *James Otis [1725-1783]* in *Dictionary of American Biography* VII. pp. 101-105.

[30]*Dissertation*, C.F. Adams, pp. 449-450.

[31]*Ibid.*, pp. 449-450.

[32]*Ibid.*, p. 450.

[33]*Ibid.*, pp. 453, 451, See Warren H. Carroll, *John Adams: Puritan Revolutionist*, unpublished ms; Richard B. Morris, *Seven Who Shaped our Destiny; The Founding Fathers as Revolutionists* (NY: Harper & Row, 1973), pp. 72-114.

[34]*Ibid.*, pp 452n, 453.

[35]*Ibid.*, p. 464.

[36]*Ibid.*, pp. 464, 453.

[37]Adams to Thomas Jefferson, June 20, 1815, Cappon, II, p. 445.

[38]*Ibid.*, February 2, 1816, Cousins, p. 268.

[39]Haraszti, p. 81; Adams to Jefferson, Dec. 25, 1813, Cappon II, p. 410.

[40]*Ibid.*, February 2, 1816, II, 461.

[41]Haraszti, p. 108.

[42]Adams to Thomas Jefferson, December 25, 1813, Cappon , II, p. 411.

[43]Haraszti, p. 296.

[44]Cappon, II, p. 404. Haraszti notes that "there undoubtedly was a deep neurotic strain in Adams," p. 4.

[45]Adams to Thomas Jefferson, December 3, 1813, Cappon, II, . p. 405.

[46]*Ibid.*, December 25, 1813, p. 410.

[47]*Ibid.*, February 2, 1816, p. 461.

[48]Adams to Benjamin Rush, June 12, 1812, Schutz, p. 224.

[49]Adams to Thomas Jefferson, November 14, 1813, Cappon, II, p. 394.

[50]Quoted in Haraszti, p. 7; Adams to Rush, Sept. 1807, Schutz, pp. 93f.

[51]*Ibid.*, March 14, 1809, p. 135; to Jefferson, Feb. 3, 1821, Cappon, II, p. 571.

[52]Adams to Benjamin Rush, March 14, 1809, Schutz, p. 135. Fisher Ames

(1758-1808) "by placing all his hopes on Hamilton, lost the confidence of the soundest portion of the other party and is now dying," Adams wrote to Rush, "under the gloomy feelings of his disappointments," Sept. 1807, Schutz, p. 94.

⁵³*Ibid.*, July 3, 1812, p. 228; July 25, 1808, p. 113.

⁵⁴Quoted in Haraszti, p. 6; to Jefferson, Feb. 2, 1816, II, pp. 461-462.

⁵⁵*Ibid.*, p. 462; Haraszti, p. 6.

⁵⁶Adams to Jefferson, May 6, 1816. Cappon, II, p. 474. See *e.g.*, Bernard Bailyn, "The Logic of Rebellion," in Jack P. Greene, ed., *The Reinterpretation of the American Revolution 1763-1789*, (New York: Harper & Row, 1968), note to p. 211.

⁵⁷Adams to Jefferson, December 3, 1813, Cappon, II, p. 405.

⁵⁸*Ibid.*, May 6, 1816 and November 4, 1816, pp. 474, 494; Haraszti, p. 254.

⁵⁹A. to Jefferson, Dec. 25, 1813, Cousins, 253; Haraszti, 19,21,204,206.

⁶⁰*Ibid.*, p. 257.

⁶¹*Ibid.*Adams here alludes to Edward Gibbon's "conversion" to Roman Catholicism while at Oxford.

⁶²*Ibid.*, p. 258.

⁶³*Ibid.*, p. 330, n 33.

⁶⁴*Ibid.*, p. 157.

⁶⁵Adams to F.A. Van der Kemp, July 13, 1815, Cousins, p. 103.

⁶⁶Adams, *Defence of the Constitutions of Gov't U. S. of A.*, Cousins, p. 97.

⁶⁷June 25, 1813, Cappon, II, p. 334, Haraszti, p, 257.

⁶⁸*Ibid.*, p. 229.

⁶⁹Cf. George H. Sabine, *A History of Political Theory* (3rd ed.; New York: Holt, Rinehart and Winston, 1966), pp. 364-365.

⁷⁰*Ibid.*, p. 222.

⁷¹For a discussion of Calvinist political theory, see *ibid.*, pp. 362-370.

⁷²Haraszti, pp. 293-294; A. to Jefferson, Feb. 24, 1819, Cappon, II, pp. 534f.

⁷³*Ibid.*, January 22, 1825, p. 607.

⁷⁴*Ibid.*, December 25, 1813, p. 412.

⁷⁵*Ibid.*, January 20, 1820, p. 560.

⁷⁶*Ibid.*, p. 613.

⁷⁷Henry Adams, *Mont-Saint-Michel & Chartres* (originally published in 1913; Garden City, New York: Doubleday Anchor Books ed., 1959), *et passim; idem, The Education of Henry Adams: An Autobiography* (New York: Random House, The Modern Library, 1931), *et passim*; Robert Mane, *Henry Adams on the Road to Chartres* (Cambridge, Mass., Harvard University Press, 1971), p. 224; M. Whitcomb Hess, *The Atomic Age and Henry Adams* in *The Catholic World* (Jan. 1951), pp. 256-263. Essential are Fr. John P. McIntyre, S.J., "Henry Adams and the Unity of Chartres" in *Twentieth Century Literature* VII (January, 1962), esp p. 167, and the same author's reply to Adam's biographer, Ernest Samuels, in *In Interpreting Henry Adams, An Answer to 20th Century Virgin* in *The Christian Century* (January 4, 1961), pp. 18-19.

⁷⁸See. e.g. Mabel Hooper La Farge, *A Niece's Memories*, in *Yale Review* IX (January, 1920), pp. 271-285, esp. 284-285.

# 4.
# Charles Carroll of Carrollton: Catholic Revolutionary

I have lived to my ninety-sixth year; I have enjoyed continued health, I have been blessed with great wealth, prosperity, and most of the good things which the world can bestow—public approbation, esteem, applause; but what I now look back on with the greatest satisfaction to myself is, that I have practiced the duties of my religion.[1]

So wrote Charles Carroll of Carrollton, the last surviving Signer of the Declaration of Independence, of his Roman Catholic faith just before his death in November 1832. These last words, recorded by Carroll's friend and confessor, Father Constantine Pise of Georgetown, were not the pious hyperbole of an old man. For the last Founding Father, who, next to his Bible, cherished Thomas á Kempis's *Imitation of Christ* as the greatest of books, was a courageous witness to the Roman Catholic Church throughout his life and strove, like Thomas, to find union with God in humility and self-denial, and especially in frequent reception of the Blessed Sacrament.

Carroll's witness to the Faith began from the moment of his birth in Annapolis, Maryland on September 19, 1737. He was born into a province to which his grandfather, Charles Carroll, had come in 1688 after Charles Calvert, the Third Lord Baltimore, had appointed him Attorney General of Maryland. The founder of the Carroll line in America had himself been born into a wealthy family in Ireland and had received an excellent education including legal training in law at the famed Inner Temple in London. On arriving in Maryland, however, the new attorney general found many of Maryland's Protestants in rebellion against the legitimate proprietary government and all its officials. This was the New World version of the so-called "Glorious Revolution" in England which toppled Catholic King James II from his rightful place as sovereign, and usurped power over his subjects in the name of a Protestant legislature. In Catholic Maryland a renegade priest, the mysterious John Coode from St. Mary's County, led an army of some seven hundred men, known as the "Protestant Association", against the legitimate government of Lord Baltimore, forcing an end to Catholic proprietorship and a regime distinguished for its religious freedom for Catholic and Protestant alike. Calvert's enlightened Charter of 1632 was revoked in 1692, and the Maryland Toleration Act of 1649, guaranteeing religious freedom to all persons believing in Jesus Christ, soon became a dead letter as Maryland Catholics were denied religious and civil rights and priests were banished from the colony. What the fair-minded American historian George Bancroft acknowledged as the first government in history "to make religious freedom the basis of the State" now fell before the onslaught of bigoted men on both sides of the Atlantic. And without trial by jury and without any charge being brought against him, Catholic Lord Baltimore was, for all intents and purposes, stripped of his proprietary rule.

In 1692, the so-called royal government of Maryland passed an "Act of Religion" which imposed upon Maryland Catholics the same penal laws that were in force in England. The Church of England was established as the religion of all Marylanders, the majority of whom were not Anglican, and, in 1702, a tax for the support of the Establishment clergy was enacted into law. Quakers and Puritans subsequently were exempted from the penal laws, leaving the full burden on Maryland's Catholics who would be persecuted systematically right down to the American Revolution. Catholic lawyers were barred from the colony's courts. Priests were forbidden to celebrate Mass, or to teach the Faith. Parents were threatened with criminal action simply for teaching their children the doctrines of the Church in the privacy of their homes. Indeed, children were encouraged to disobey their Catholic parents and abandon the Catholic Faith; a law of 1715 required that Catholic children should be taken from their parents whenever possible and educated in the Protestant religion. Justices of the county courts were empowered to settle these children wherever they thought fit. And an inducement was held out to Catholic children who apostatized: they could inherit by law all family property rights.

Maryland Catholics were declared unqualified to vote in 1718, and barred from holding any office in the colony. But it was the French and Indian War that emboldened the illegitimate, anti-Catholic ruling party to reveal its deep, satanic plan for the total destruction of the Catholic Church in the land of St. Mary. And although the lands of the Jesuits were indeed to be confiscated in Maryland and elsewhere, and their very order suppressed, although Maryland Catholics were to be double-taxed and subjected to other penalties and indignities, a true son of St. Ignatius—and member of the Blessed Virgin Mary Sodality—Charles Carroll of Carrollton was to thwart the plan and help restore Maryland to Christ.

Charles Carroll's grandfather and father, after whom he was named, survived the harsh penal laws of Maryland in this period because of their deep and uncompromising faith in the true Church of Christ. The prominent Catholic families, of whom the Carrolls were one, seemed to have attained a remarkable degree of unity in their passive and sometimes active resistance to the anti-papist governments after 1688. As a boy, Charles was taught by his father the real character of the Revolution of 1688 as a Protestant rebellion against the Catholic governments of England and Maryland. In this historical perspective, the much-vaunted "Glorious Revolution" was revealed as little more than another rebellion against Catholic authority and civilization. Other Catholic boys and girls were secretly taught the facts of history by their parents, and some of the boys were fortunate enough to attend clandestine grammar schools like that at Bohemia Manor run by the Jesuit fathers. Even more fortunate were the sons of the few wealthy Catholic families who could afford to send their children to France for an outstanding classical education. But for most of Maryland's Catholic people there was no hope of escape from a cruelly oppressive Establishment.

Humanly speaking, the key to Catholic survival in Maryland in these pre-Revolutionary years was the existence of a superiorly educated and wealthy Catholic elite who could plan and lead the resistance against the state. This was achieved in what the Jesuit historian Father Thomas O'Brien Hanley has called a "Catholic counter-revolutionary society," which included the Carrolls and several other influential families. They intermarried, lent money to one another, educated their children in common, opened and maintained lines of communications with their brethren in England, and even occasionally deemed it necessary openly to violate the pseudo-laws of Maryland and go to prison in order to bear witness to their Catholic Faith. Charles's grandfather and father, despite their high station in Maryland society, were often imprisoned for breaking the penal laws against Catholics. Sometimes the weak and opportunistic fell away, like the apostate Daniel Dulany the Elder, who came as an indentured servant to Maryland, and whose more famous son by the same name was to act as the foil to Charles Carroll's greatness in the American Revolution—or Catholic Counter-Revolution. For, as we shall see, Charles Carroll's signing of the Declaration of Independence in 1776 meant to him and to practically every other Catholic in Maryland and elsewhere a counter-revolutionary victory over English totalitarianism, early modern style, as brazenly announced to the world in the Revolution of 1688 and seen in Parliament's policy of systematic rejection and erosion of the divinely-given rights of Englishmen and all men created in the image of God.

The Catholic counter-revolutionary society of Maryland, in which young Carroll was formed, emphasized the teaching of history, especially Irish and English, the classics, and law within the Western, Catholic tradition. The ideal of manhood was that of the Catholic knight of the Middle Ages. Charles Carroll was taught chivalry and that respect for woman which was already being eroded by the crudities of the post-medieval world. A true education, his father insisted, must be one of virtue. This counter-revolutionary education, forbidden by the anti-Catholic government of Maryland, was continued for young Charles Carroll, his cousins John and Daniel Carroll, and other boys at the Jesuit-run school at Bohemia Manor. Indeed, the Jesuits' influence on the formation of these boys—later to be prime movers in the American Revolution—cannot be exaggerated. At Bohemia Manor and, after 1748, at the Jesuit College of St. Omer in French Flanders, Charles Carroll and his cousins and friends were taught the Jesuit philosophy of limited civil government, especially as developed from the writings of St. Thomas Aquinas, Francisco Suarez, and Juan de Mariana. This exact understanding of government rested upon the classical and medieval conception of natural law as the ultimate humanly accessible criterion of right social and political order.

At St. Omer, where Maryland's and other Catholics were brought together, forming cells of opposition to English totalitarianism, young

Carroll spent six years reading the great books of Christendom. In St. Thomas's *Summa Theologica* he read these words, fully relevant today as they were to the government of Maryland and England then:

> St. Augustine says: "there is no law unless it be just." So the validity of law depends on its justice. But in human affairs a thing is said to be just when it accords aright with the rule of reason: and, as we have already seen, the first rule of reason is the Natural law. Thus all human-ly enacted laws are in accord with reason to the exent that they derive from the Natural law. And if a human law is at variance in any par-ticular with the Natural law, it is no longer legal, but rather a corrup-tion of law.[2]

Conscience rejected, and must reject, such pseudo-laws. St. Thomas con-cluded: "Man is bound to obey secular rulers to the extent that the order of justice requires. For this reason if such rulers have no just title to power, but have usurped it, or if they command things to be done which are unjust, their subjects are not obliged to obey them, except perhaps in certain special cases, when it is a matter of avoiding scandal or some particular danger."[3] Clearly then, as young Carroll had been taught by his father from the start, it was his duty to oppose, subvert, and finally destroy the illegal pseudo-governments of England and Maryland which, since 1688, had violated and perverted the true constitutions of Englishmen and Marylanders, indeed have violated and perverted the natural, God-given constitution of all men. And at an even deeper level of reality, the mature Charles Carroll was to come to see that, far beyond the natural law and reason of Thomistic philosophy, was the absolute, living norm of Christ Himself: "Because the Lord had said—*I am the Truth, not I am Custom or Constitution.*"[4]

At the time of the American Revolution and even afterwards, the object of Charles Carroll's life was, in his own words, "to be justified before God & man." And this meant unswerving fidelity to the Church, the mystical body of Christ. It is essential to understand this point, that Carroll as a Signer of the Declaration of Independence was fully and completely within this medieval, Thomistic tradition of the Roman Catholic Church, a tradition whose metaphysics presumed, as St. Thomas himself said, "the world to be governed by divine Providence." If this is forgotten, then Charles Carroll of Carrollton becomes just another natural-rights thinker like Jefferson and Franklin, prodigal and alienated sons of the Church, lost in the shadows of the modern world.

What Charles Carroll learned among the Jesuits at St. Omer and later at Reims and the College Louis le Grand in Paris during his nine years in France, was the true place of natural law in Catholic philosophy and the function of human or positive law as being that of working out the conclusions of natural law and, in St. Thomas' words, of restraining "evil men from wrongdoing by force and by fear." He learned that, according to Thomist legal philosophy, natural law, or what is basically the same thing, human reason, is not self-sufficient but must be perfected by grace. And this lesson, taken to heart, prevented Carroll from falling victim to the Enlightenment rationalism of Jefferson, John Adams, Franklin, and other American *philosophes*, while protecting him from the mock-Augustinianism of the New England Calvinists and other schismatics. He could subscribe to the natural-rights theory of the Declaration of Independence only in terms of the Church's teaching, after St. Thomas, that "the rights of the human person" have no abstract existence, but that the so-called "rights of man" have value only in the light of objective natural law and, ultimately, God's redemptive plan for man. The individual person, Jefferson not withstanding, was not and could not be the source of laws and standards. Such egoistic individualism violated natural law and order in its rejection of the "common good" and was unthinkable to the Jesuit-trained Carroll. One had to be demented like Thomas Hobbes or Rousseau, Charles Carroll believed, to accept this Protagorean relativism twenty centuries after Socrates had refuted it.

The Marylander's teachers in the College of St. Omer instructed him in the fatal weaknesses of Cartesianism. The Jesuits pointed out Descarte's angelism, the excessive rationalism of his dualistic philosophy which made man over into a kind of angel, who arrived at "self-evident truths" directly by intuition. Charles Carroll as a result was too well educated in Thomistic philosophy to adopt the naive realism—or, ultimately, the subjectivism—of Jefferson and other American *philosophes*. Interestingly enough, he read Voltaire's satires and admired in some degree his tolerance, but wrote that he abhorred Voltaire and others of his sort "who laugh at all devotion, look upon our religion as a fiction, & see its holy misteries as the greatest absurdities."[5] The same penetrating intellect, rigorously exercised in the best traditions of medieval scholasticism at St. Omer, made short work of other Enlightenment claims to naturalistic and rationalistic philosophy. And when the time came, in the 1760's and 70's, Charles Carroll was ready to bring to bear all of his critical powers, knowledge, and deep Catholic Faith on the issue of British tyranny.

Among the profoundly influential books he studied in France was Montesquieu's *Spirit of the Laws*. Published in 1748, the year young Carroll arrived in Europe, Montesquieu's book was to provide Carroll over the next ten years with ideas that confirmed, refined, and advanced his thinking as a Catholic counter-revolutionary. Montesquieu, like the Englishmen Richard Hooker and John Locke, helped revive the natural law tradition which had been slipping out of Western consciousness ever since the breakup of the Middle Ages, a Catholic tradition in which young Carroll was being educated by the French Jesuits. The author of the *Spirit of the Laws*, moreover, convinced the Maryland counter-revolutionary that the virtuous Roman Republic was not a thing of the past, lost forever, but an ideal form of government which could be attained again by his fellow-Catholics and other men of good will who loved their country and wished to restore the chartered civil and religious liberties taken away by the Revolution of 1688. The tyrannical Parliament which had usurped the government of England and Maryland in 1688 was the very same institution responsible for the unnatural and unconstitutional acts by which Maryland Catholics had been stripped of their religious and civil rights. As Montesquieu made clear, at least by implication to Carroll, this claim to, and seizure of, total power by Parliament violated the necessary division, separation, and balance of powers in a true constitution, the "mixed constitution" of St. Thomas. The judicial authority—ultimately based upon natural law, as St. Thomas taught—had been virtually destroyed in the English Constitution, explaining why Maryland Catholics and others were being increasingly deprived of their natural rights. Like the executive branch of government, the English judiciary could no longer check Parliament in its shameless bid for total control over the life of Englishmen.

Montesquieu's thesis of the separation and balance of powers was made even more convincing to the Maryland counter-revolutionary by the author's appeal to history for examples. Carroll knew the history of the oppression of his Catholic people intimately enough to see that this thesis described the pathology of English tyranny in Maryland. It led him to the conclusion, by the mid-1760's, that the only way to recover Catholic religious and civil rights—natural rights—was by restoring the Maryland Constitution, and that could only be done by gaining the independence from Britain. He was later to write in his classic *First Citizen* letters that "not a single instance can be selected from our history of a law favorable to liberty obtained from government, but by the unanimous, steady, and spirited conduct of the people. The Great charter, the several confirmations of it, the Petition of Right, the Bill of Rights, were all the happy effects of *force* and *necessity*."[6]

Ultimately, Carroll believed, it was the people—never the mob—who must depose a tyrant, whether legislative, executive, or judicial. He knew that the Jesuit philosophers, Mariana (1599) and Suarez (1613), had even justified tyrannicide in extreme cases. But before resorting to revolution and tyrannicide, Carroll held, appeal should be made to the judiciary as the institutionalized defender of natural law and natural rights. This "checks and balances system", operative among the three branches of government, was what Montesquieu taught in the *Spirit of the Laws* and what the Founding Fathers later adopted in the United States Constitution.

Even before he returned to America in 1765, Carroll believed that "the period of the English Constitution is hastening to a final period of dissolution." And, back home in Maryland, he wrote to a friend in England urging him to sell his property there "and purchase land in this province for liberty will maintain her empire . . ."[7] The Stamp Act, passed that very year, Carroll saw as tantamount to "political death" for Marylanders and all colonists; in his realistic appraisal, which was entirely too sophisticated for most Americans to appreciate, Parliament herself in this brazen, unconstitutional act was revealing to the world her contempt for natural law, English law, and the rights of man. Just as the corrupt and illegitimate parliament of 1688 had violated the civil and religious rights of English Catholics, so now the parliament of 1765, driven by an even greater passion for absolute power, was trying to reduce *all* men to slavery. True, it was easier for Carroll to see this, since the Revolution of 1688 and its Parliament had always been a symbol of tyranny for him and other members of the Catholic counter-revolutionary society. He did not, like Jefferson and Dr. Benjamin Rush, for example, have to re-evaluate and re-define the "Glorious Revolution," which they, as Protestant boys, had always been taught to revere, if not worship. Long before other colonial spokesmen, acting on good Catholic principles which they were too invincibly ignorant to recognize, saw the conspiratorial design of the Sugar, Stamp, Quartering, Declaratory, and Townshend acts, Carroll was denying Parliament's constitutional right not only to tax internally and externally but to regulate commerce and trade. This he could do because of the ancient charter of Maryland which reserved these privileges for the proprietor and freemen of that colony alone. Besides, as he wrote just before coming home, the Jesuits were "men of republican principles" (that is, men who taught that government was limited by divine and natural law) and he had been inspired by them with "a love of liberty."[8]

The Maryland Catholic counter-revolutionary society, of which Carroll was now a leader, enjoyed the support, to some extent, of anti-establishment and anti-clerical Whigs like William Paca and Samuel Chase and other Protestants who resented the opportunistic and doubtfully constitutional policies of the Maryland government. These dissenters were much less fearful of the Catholic minority than they were of the self-aggrandizing rulers of Maryland who, in league with the Church of England, were making a mockery of the lower house as representative of the people. Chase and Paca were Catholics in spite of themselves in appealing to natural law against the tyrannical government. They agreed with Carroll's argument from Catholic social doctrine that, "no stretch of the Prerogative of the general good will ever endanger our constitutions."[9] And they sympathized with the plight of Maryland Catholics who, since 1755, had suffered cruelly under the double-tax.

In 1765, at the very time the Stamp Act's repeal was being prepared in England, the governor and upper house in Maryland proclaimed new taxes in open disregard of the assembly's right to make tax policy. The principle of "no taxation without representation," urged against the Stamp Act by James Otis, Patrick Henry, Daniel Dulany of Maryland, and other patriots, was now being violated by a governor and his minister as they imposed new taxes by proclamation. What Britain's Parliament could not do, as the repeal of the Stamp Act in 1766 seemed to make clear, Maryland's government went ahead and did; and when the lower house protested the governor's usurpation of power over the purse, Governor Robert Eden prorogued the assembly. This tyrannical act by the governor outraged Carroll and the other members of the Catholic counter-revolutionary society, who were already smarting under anti-Catholic taxes. It also infuriated Whigs like Chase and Paca and the growing number of their followers among the non-Catholic inhabitants of the province. Daniel Dulany, the scion of a once-Catholic family which had weakened under years of persecution, had won fame throughout the Colonies and England for his eloquent opposition to the Stamp Act, but now the Cambridge-educated lawyer shamelessly abandoned his own principles and became the government's chief apologist for the new policy of taxation by executive proclamation. What was at stake in Maryland was nothing less than the constitutional right of the people to tax themselves, a question that Carroll quickly saw as transcending time and place and, indeed, offering a grand opportunity for a defense of natural law as he had learned it in his Thomistic and other studies. Against, "placemen" like Daniel Dulany, Charles Carroll of Carrollton now assumed the burden of Truth. This "Catholic burden" was to be carried by Charles Carroll right down to his death in 1832 when, as the last surviving Signer of the Declaration of Independence and the only living Founder of the American nation, he solemnly rededicated and reconsecrated the American Revolution to Christ in the Holy Eucharist.

The opportunity for Carroll to take a public stand on the new Maryland tax policy and indirectly to attack the double-tax policy against Catholics, came in early 1773. It was then, and only then, that Carroll, as a leader of the Catholic counter-revolutionary society, dared to test public opinion in Maryland on whether he as a member of the Catholic minority was entitled to freedom of speech. Public opinion in Maryland, Carroll knew from the signs of the times, was mounting against the proprietary government in the fee proclamation controversy. In January of 1773, the government's spokesman, Daniel Dulany, showed that he too was aware of this disaffection among all classes in the province. Dulany sought publicly to defend the new tax policy in the pages of the *Maryland Gazette* by means of a dialogue between two citizens, himself taking the part of the "second citizen" and arguing the constitutionality of the proclamation fees against the weak literary protests of the "first citizen." In truth, Dulany was employing the device of the "Second Citizen" to defend not only the governor and the upper house but himself as the minister responsible for the new tax policy. Now Carroll saw his chance.

He would use the device of the "First Citizen"—Dulany's straw man—to demonstrate that the Maryland governor and upper house were violating the English and provincial constitutions by denying the assembly's time-honored right to tax its people. The February 4th issue of the *Maryland Gazette*, accordingly, printed Carroll's argument against the new tax policy under the rubric of the "First Citizen," turning the tables on Dulany who now had to fight for his political life.

The Maryland Catholic counter-revolutionary society had entered the contest on the side of the Independent Whigs, as they were called; and it was this alliance that was to lead to the downfall of Dulany and of the tyrannical, anti-Catholic faction which had ruled since the Revolution of 1688. Dulany knew from the start who the "First Citizen" was— no one but Charles Carroll of Carrollton would dare to stand up to the famous and powerful author of the *Considerations on the Propriety of Imposing Taxes* (1765), a book which had established Dulany as an authority on constitutional taxation. But Dulany also knew that his only hope in the controversy was to discredit Carroll religiously and personally, since there was no way of refuting the Catholic's arguments that taxing power belonged in the lower house where the people were physically represented. He knew too that Carroll had behind him not only the force of his own powerful logic but the recognized authorities of constitutionalism: Bracton, Coke, Hooker, Grotius, Locke, and Montesquieu, who upheld the natural right to property and, emphatically so in the case of Montesquieu, insisted upon the separation and balance of the executive, legislative, and judicial departments of government. Taxation by proclamation, Carroll argued, clearly upset this balance and was a return to the unconstitutional practices of the Stuart kings.

Dulany tried every way he could to free himself from the net of Carroll's argument. The "First Citizen" was a Jacobin, a conspirator for the Pretender. As a "son of Saint Omer" Carroll was a Jesuit out to destroy the Church of England in Maryland, just as his father had tried to do years ago. Carroll, Dulany charged, was acting the role of "chaplain" to Pace, Chase, and the Independent Whigs. Finally, about to succumb, as he must, Dulany challenged Carroll's right as a Catholic to speak on public questions. This was exactly what Carroll had hoped Dulany would do, for, instead of impugning Carroll's motive, it had the opposite effect of discrediting the very anti-Catholic penal laws which indeed, as Dulany charged, should have prevented Carroll from exposing the government's conspiracy to take away the constitutional rights of Marylanders. The Independent Whigs and the majority of Maryland's people now, in 1773, came to see the true face of anti-Catholicism as it was unmasked by Carroll with the unwitting assistance of Daniel Dulany. "I have not," wrote Carroll, the First Citizen, "the least dislike to the church of England, though I am not within her pale, not indeed to any other church; knaves and bigots of all sects and denominations I hate, and I despise."[10] Penalties against Catholics were to be swept away three years later, thanks, in large part, to Carroll's brilliant intervention in the First Citizen controversy.

Indeed, after 1773, Charles Carroll was known in Maryland and the surrounding area as the "First Citizen"; and his support by both the Catholic counter-revolutionary society and the patriot party, the Independent Whigs, made him a leader in the struggle against unconstitutional government at home and abroad. He soon was rewarded with membership on the Annapolis Committee of Corrrespondence, the Maryland Convention, and the provincial Committee of Safety. In February of 1776 he was asked by the Continental Congress, meeting in Philadelphia, to join fellow-Marylander Samuel Chase, Benjamin Franklin, and his cousin, Father John Carroll, in a commission to Canada, whose purpose was "to promote or form a union" between the Thirteen Colonies and the estimated 150,000 Catholics who, as against less than 400 Protestants, constituted the population of the former French possession. Carroll accepted the charge and went to Canada; but largely because of the anti-Catholic policies of the Continental Congress, in its outrage over the Quebec Act, the commission failed and the American army retreated. Returning to serve in the Maryland Convention of 1776, Carroll helped significantly to commit Maryland to independence; and in July of that same year he was elected to the Continental Congress where he voted for independence on July 19 (the engrossed copy) and signed the Declaration of Independence on August 2.

One story has it that Carroll added the phrase "of Carrollton" after his name when someone observed that there were so many other Carrolls in Maryland that King George would not know whom to hang. More reliable is the anecdote about John Hancock's asking Carroll if he cared to sign it. " ' Most willingly,' was the prompt reply, and as he made his signature, a member standing near observed, 'There go a few millions,' and all admitted that few risked as much in a material sense, as the wealthy Marylander.''[11] Indeed, Charles Carroll was at the time the wealthiest person in the Colonies, the equivalent of a modern millionaire, for his grandfather and father had left him a great fortune which he was now committing wholly to the cause of the Catholic counter-revolutionary movement in America.

Fifty years later, to the very day on which he had signed the Declaration, Charles Carroll of Carrollton, the last surviving Signer (Adams and Jefferson had died the month before) wrote these stirring words rededicating the American Revolution to Christ:

> Grateful to Almighty God for the blessing which, through Jesus Christ our Lord, he has conferred upon my beloved country, in her emancipation, and upon myself, in permitting me, under circumstances of mercy, to live to the age of 89 years and to survive the fiftieth year of American Independence, and certifying by my present signature my approbation of the Declaration of Independence adopted by Congress on the fourth day of July, in the year of our Lord, one thousand seven hundred and seventy-six, which I originally subscribed on the second day of August of the same year, and of which I am now the last surviving signer, I do hereby recommend to the present and future generations the principles of that important document as the best earthly inheritance their ancestors could bequeath to them, and pray that the civil and religious liberties they have secured to my country may be perpetuated to the remotest posterity and extended to the whole family of man.[12]

Carroll had ever been a Revolutionary in order to free the Faith. He personified that truly Catholic Republicanism which is so elusive in our own day. Recognizing that a return to Christendom under the Pope was unrealistic in his day, he opted for the next best thing. Thus, in 1827, Carroll wrote to Rev. John Stanford of New York that "To obtain religious, as well as civil liberty, I entered zealously into the Revolution, and observing the Christian religion divided into many sects, I founded the hope that no one would be so predominant as to become the religion of the State. That hope was thus early entertained, because all of them joined the same cause, with few exceptions of individuals. God grant that this religious liberty may be preserved in these States, to the end of time, and that all believing in the religion of Christ may practice the leading principle of charity, the basis of every virtue."[13] God, not man, had been from the first at the center of Carroll's program. "Who are deserving of immortality?" he reflected in a letter to a woman who had published a flattering poem in his honor as the Last Signer. "They who serve God in truth, and they who have rendered great, essential, and disinterested services and benefits to their country."[14]

"The principal object" of government, Carroll insisted as always "should be the preservation of morals . . ."[15] His own personal and family life indicates how totally committed he was to stressing the importance of this view. In several letters to his only son, who was in declining health and was to predecease him, the aged hero of American Independence testified once again to his deep Catholic Faith.

> In writing to you I deem it my duty to call your attention to the shortness of this life, and the certainty of death, and the dreadful judgment we must all undergo, and on the decision of which a happy or a miserable eternity depends. The impious has said in his heart, "There is no God." He would willingly believe there is no God; the passions, the corruptions of his heart would fain persuade him there is none. The stings of conscience betray the emptiness of the delusion; the heavens proclaim the existence of God, and unperverted reason teaches that He must love virtue and hate vice, and reward the one and punish the other.
>
> The wisest and the best of the ancients believed in the immortality of the soul, and the Gospel has established the great truth of a future state of rewards and punishments. My desire to induce you to reflect on futurity, and by a virtuous life to merit heaven, have suggested the above reflections and warnings. The approaching festival of Easter, and the merits and mercies of our Redeemer . . . have led me into this chain of meditation and reasoning, and have inspired me with the hope of finding mercy before my judge, and of being happy in the life to come, a happiness I wish you to participate with me by infusing into your heart a similar hope. Should this letter produce such a change, it will comfort me, and impart to you that peace of mind which the world cannot give, and which I am sure you have long ceased to enjoy.[16]

And:

> God bless and prepare you for a better world, for the present is but a passing meteor compared to eternity . . . At the hour of your death, Ah! my son, you will feel the emptiness of all sublunary things; and

that hour may be much nearer than you expect. Think well on it, I mean your eternal welfare.[17]

Charles Carroll's son died in April of 1825, seven years before his father. The event certainly caused him to meditate on his own judgment which he knew must come soon:

> On the 20th of this month I entered into my eighty-ninth year. This, in any country, would be deemed a long life, yet . . . if it has not been directed to the only end for which man was created, it is a mere nothing, an empty phantom, an indivisible point, compared with eternity. Too much of my time and attention have been misapplied on matters to which an impartial judge, penetrating the secrets of hearts, before whom I shall soon appear, will ascribe no merit deserving recompense. On the mercy of my Redeemer I rely for salvation, and on His Merits; not on the works I have done in obedience to His precepts, for even these, I fear, a mixture of alloy will render unavailing and cause to be rejected.[18]

And in another letter:

> As I am fast approaching to the last scene, which will put an end to all earthly cares and concerns, I am looking to that state from which all care, all solicitude and all passions which agitate mankind are excluded. Revelation instructs us that eternal happiness or eternal misery will be the destiny of man in the life to come; the most pious, the most exemplary have trembled at the thought of the dreadful alternative. Oh! What will be the fate of those who little think of it, or thinking square not their actions accordingly.[19]

Finally, during the last three years of his life, Carroll witnessed and participated in two great events which symbolize his contribution to America: the completion of St. Mary's Roman Catholic Church in Annapolis, the first in the city where as a boy Carroll had been forbidden by law to attend public Mass; and the laying of the corner-stone, performed by Carroll himself, of St. Charles's College on land donated by Carroll for a Catholic college. His only request, characteristically, was "that Mass be said once a month for myself and family"and "That this gift may be useful to religion and aid our Church in rearing those who will guide us in the way of truth . . ."[20]

On November 14, 1832, in his ninety-fifth year, Charles Carroll of

Carrollton, the Roman Catholic and last surviving Signer of the Declaration of Independence, prepared for death in Christ. "On each side of his chair," one of his attending doctors remembered, "knelt a daughter and grandchildren, with some friends, making a complete semicircle; and just in the rear, three or four old negro servants, all of the same faith, knelt in the most venerating manner. The whole assemblage made up a picture never to be forgotten. The ceremony proceeded. The old gentleman had been for a long time suffering from weak eyes, and could not endure the proximity of lights immediately before him. His eyes were therefore kept closed, but he was so familiar with the forms of this solemn ceremony that he responded and acted as if he saw everything passing around. At the moment of offering the Host he leaned forward without opening his eyes, yet responsive to the word of the administration of the holy offering. It was done with so much intelligence and grace, that no one could doubt for a moment how fully his soul was alive to the act."[21] The doctor tried to make him take some food. "Thank you, Doctor, not just now; this ceremony is so deeply interesting to the Christian that it supplies all the wants of nature. I feel no desire for food."[22] Thus with the Eucharist on his lips, Charles Carroll performed that action the willingness for which may be taken as the acid test for all leaders who would truly benefit their nations. He left his beloved country, and without altering his principles, went home.

## NOTES

[1] Quoted by Fr. Constantine Pise in Kate M. Rowland, *The Life and Correspondence of Charles Carroll of Carrollton* 1737-1832 (2v., New York: G.P. Putnam's Sons, 1898) II: p. 370. The standard biography of the only Catholic Signer of the Declaration of Independence, from which the following essay is largely derived, is Fr. Thomas O'Brien Hanley, *Charles Carroll of Carrollton: The Making of a Revolutionary Gentleman* (Washington, D.C.: The Catholic University of America Press, 1970).

[2] *Summa Theol.,* 1a 2ae, 95, 2. Quoted in A.P. d'Entreves, *Natural Law: An Introduction to Legal Philosophy* (London: Hutchinson University Library, 1951), pp, 42-43. *Cf.* Christopher Dawson, *The Gods of Revolution: An Analysis of the French Revolution,* edited by John J. Mulloy, with an Introduction by Arnold Toynbee (New York: Minerva Press Edition, 1975), esp. ch. ii. pp. 14-31.

[3] *Summa Theol.,* 2a 2ae, 104, 6.

[4] A commentator on Gratian, quoted in d'Entreves, p. 34.

[5] Quoted in Hanley, *Charles Carroll,* p. 65. See Maurice De Wulf's

Philosophy and Civilization in the Middle Ages (New York: Dover Publications, Inc., 1953).

⁶ Rowland, *Life and Correspondence*, I: p. 347. Also, see Peter S. Onuf, ed., *Maryland and the Empire, 1773: the Antilon-First Citizen Letters* (Baltimore: The Johns Hopkins University Press, 1974); Hanley, *Charles Carroll*, p. 62 *et passim.*

⁷ Quoted in *ibid.*, p. 212.

⁸ *Ibid.*, p. 133.

⁹ *Ibid.*, p. 214.

¹⁰ Rowland, *Life and Correspondence*, I: p. 358. On anti-Catholicism in America at this time, see Sister Mary Augustina Ray B.V.M., *American Opinion of Roman Catholicism in the Eighteenth Century* (New York: Columbia University Press, 1936). Standard also is Charles A. Barker, *Background of the Revolution in Maryland* (New Haven: Yale University Press, 1940).

¹¹ Rowland, *Life and Correspondence*, I: p. 181; John Tracy Ellis, *Catholics in Colonial America* (Baltimore: Helicon Press, 1965); Charles H. Metzger, S.J., *Catholics and the American Revolution. A Study in Religious Climate* (Chicago: Loyola University Press, 1962).

¹² Rowland, *Life and Correspondence*, II: title page. Carroll wrote this on a copy of the Declaration of Independence preserved in the New York City Public Library.

¹³ October 9, 1827, *ibid.*, p. 358.

¹⁴ September 14, 1826, ibid., p. 346.

¹⁵ June 25, 1827, *ibid.*, p. 354.

¹⁶ To Charles Carroll of Homewood, April 12, 1821, *ibid.* pp. 327-328; Ellen Hart Smith, *Charles Carroll of Carrollton* (Cambridge, Mass.: Harvard University Press, 1945), pp. 299ff.

¹⁷ To Charles Carroll of Homewood, 1809, 1815, Rowland, *Life and Correspondence*, II: p. 335.

¹⁸ September 1825, *ibid.*, p. 336.

¹⁹ To Charles H. Wharton, July 19, 1826, *ibid.*, p. 340.

²⁰ *Ibid.*, p. 362.

²¹ *Ibid.*, p. 369.

²² *Ibid.*

# 5.
# George Washington: The Founder as Stoic

The massive figure of George Washington, half-draped in Roman toga, with one hand raised in virtuous salute to heaven and the other offering the sheathed sword of reconciliation, is a familiar sight to the tourist visiting the Smithsonian Institute in the nation's capital. The twelve-ton marble statue, laboriously executed in 1843 by America's first professional sculptor, Harvard-educated Horatio Greenough, fails artistically but succeeds in depicting Washington, the "Father of his Country," and the times he lived in.[1]

Greenough, apparently, was a better classicist than a sculptor. Neither talent was, in any case, much prized in the Age of Jackson when Greenough's masterpiece became something of a laughing-stock.[2] Washington himself, ironically, knew little Latin and no Greek, and was poorly read in the classics. But what is important about the American's gigantic statue, what endows it with historical value, is its representation of Washington as a Roman, down to sandals and short sword, a representation which from the point of view of Washington and many of the Revolutionary patriots could not have been more flattering or true. Indeed, Greenough's work, the most celebrated of many "Roman" Washingtons, beginning with Houdon's sculpture during the President's lifetime, provides the best clue to the nature of the most enigmatic of the Founding Fathers.[3]

Washington, in Marcus Cunliffe's felicitous term, was both a man and a monument, rather more of the latter than the former.[4] And, so we shall argue, Greenough's mass of marble symbolizes well the character of the man and perhaps that of the nation he helped found as well.[5]

Washington was a soldier. Not just some of the time but all of the time—in his very nature as a man. Not only did he, perhaps imitating the regular British officers he served with in the French and Indian War, distrust militia soldiers. As a young Virginia officer, he tried in vain to win a regular commission from the British authorities, and later as Commander-in-Chief of the Continental Army desired nothing more than to lead well-trained regulars against the enemy in European-style combat.[6] "Order, Regularity and Discipline" was his motto, whether on the field of battle or in private life.[7] His discipline of himself and others was Roman, not lax like that of the sometime warriors who led the militia units. The citizen-soldiers, he wrote his brother, John Augustine Washington, in 1777, were "here today and gone tomorrow—whose way, like the ways of Providence are almost inscrutable."[8] He hanged Major André, admitting him to be "more unfortunate than criminal," to the outrage of many on both sides, and did not scruple to exact the same kind of justice against deserters in his command.[9] As Greenough knew, Washington could use the short sword like a Roman.

The Roman soldier Washington would have liked most to be compared to was Marcus Aurelius, the Stoic emperor whose virtues and qualities he admired as a young man. There is no evidence that he read the *Meditations*. But he did have a copy of *Seneca's Morals by Way of Abstract* (1746), a popular introduction to Stoical philosophy, which he appears to have studied with great application when a lad of seventeen.[10] The Stoical ideal in Marcus Aurelius and Seneca was the same, and like a true Roman Washington came away from reading Seneca with the belief that the theoretical should be subordinated to the practical—that ethics was the essence of philosophy. It was not so much classical influence in a formal sense as it was that Washington's own outlook was practical, and the highly popularized Stoicism of the times mirrored well the values of a young man ambitious to rise in the world.[11]

Washington was only eleven in 1743 when he lost his father, Augustine Washington, a man of modest wealth—he owned twenty slaves—and good standing among the Virginia gentry. Augustine had gone to school at Appleby, in northern England, and had managed to send George's half-brothers, Laurence and Augustine, back to the mother country for a gentleman's education. George, envious of their advantage, was awaiting his turn when tragedy struck his family. Never was he to go to Europe, and only once did he leave what is today the United States, when some years later he accompanied his consumptive friend and brother, Laurence, to Barbados in search of health.[12]

Laurence, his senior by fourteen years, was the man George now considered the head of the family, next to Mrs. Mary Ball Washington, a woman of complaining disposition whom her children seemed on the whole to have respected more than loved.[13] Even before his father's death, George had seen in his elder brother a model for all that he wished to be. Laurence was a soldier, a captain in the American regiment which had accompanied Admiral Edward Vernon's expedition against the Spanish Main port of Cartagena in 1740. George remembered how proud he had been of Laurence's serving with British regulars, one of only four Virginians chosen as officers in the command. He would recall in years to come how his half-brother had spoken angrily of the condescending attitude of the British officers toward the colonials. But for the Admiral himself, Laurence had only praise, as seen in his naming his Hunting Creek estate Mount Vernon and hanging a portrait of the naval hero there for all to see. After Washington inherited the property in 1761, Laurence's widow dying that year, he sought to purchase from England busts of the great military commanders to add to Mount Vernon's gallery of heroes.[14]

That young Washington should be attracted to the military tradition was not at all surprising. Outside those areas settled by the Quakers, whose pacifism Washington never understood or appreciated, the arts of war engaged the attention of nearly everybody. The very year Washington was born, February 1732, the colony of Georgia was chartered as a base for British military operations against Spanish Florida. Virginia and the other colonies were preparing too for another war against France and Spain—King George's War—which would break out by the end of the decade. And, if Britain's old enemies, with whom she had been at war since 1689, were quiescent for the moment, there were always the Indians to drive farther back into the trans-Appalachian wilderness.

Tall and husky for his age (perhaps six feet three when fully grown), and keenly intelligent in a practical way but by no means scholarly in temperament, Washington had the personal qualities that allowed him easily to conform to his bellicose times and roughhewn frontier environment. One speculates that a formal education beyond grammar school, like that which Laurence had received in England, or the regular army commission that he likewise wanted so ardently, would have spoiled him, made him into a proper English gentleman, and disqualified him for his role as leader of largely nondescript rebel forces in 1775. Brother Laurence's military ambitions were apparently satisfied with his appointment as adjutant general of the Virginia militia and his bourgeois social aspirations to higher rank fulfilled by marrying Anne Fairfax, the daughter of one of the great men of Virginia.[15] George Washington, before the Revolution, was to try but never win preferment from the leading families, although he did enjoy some of the benefits of Laurence's new status.

It was in the high society of the Fairfaxes, at their Potomac estate called Belvoir, that young George learned the ways of the First Families of Virginia, or the "better sort"as they were known in colonial parlance. Belvoir was not far from Mount Vernon, Laurence's seat, where the elder Washington had arranged for his brother to live. No doubt Laurence's kind purpose was to tear the boy from his mother's apronstrings and to include George in the more polished society that he had entered as a result of his marriage to Ann Fairfax.

George's handicaps were many and embarrassing. Except for Laurence, he seems not to have had any pride in his family. His father was dead and could help him no longer. His mother, a good but coarse woman, he and Laurence scarcely mentioned in polite company. As for social etiquette, observed with great care at Belvoir, he must rely on Francis Hawkin's *Youth's Behaviour,* a handbook of the rules of civility, which his schoolmaster had made him copy and memorize.[16] At sixteen, moreover, George Washington appears to have had no religious formation. He and his family belonged to the Church of England and, nominally at least, accepted its ritual, but George seems already to have begun that reduction of religion to morality which he would later hold with so many men of his age.[17]

There was one qualification, however, that George possessed, one so uncommon at the time as to make him invaluable to Lord Fairfax: the gangling country boy knew surveying. He may have been weak in every other subject, but in practical mathematics he was outstanding, and Lord Fairfax hired him to survey his extensive lands in the Shenan-doah Valley.[18] Not the College of William and Mary, which other young Virginia gentlemen attended, but the dark and bloody frontier now became his lecture hall, as he carried out surveys for the master of Belvoir. There was no better school for the future commander of the Continental Army.

It is hard to picture the life that George led in these years as friend and employee of Lord Fairfax, partly because of the striking contrasts between Tidewater elegance at Belvoir and Mount Vernon and the rigors of frontier survival which he now experienced. He learned quickly in the backwoods how to endure deprivations of every kind, and most im-portant of all, how to trust oneself in making life-or-death decisions, whether in avoiding an Indian war party or finding one's supper among the denizens of the forest. In the Fairfax circle, to which young Washington eagerly returned after the mappings were done, a slave-based economy offered a life of leisure and an aristocratic culture which boasted the latest Enlightenment ideas and attitudes. Among these was the classical ideal, of Stoicism in particular, which taught values like courage and self-sufficiency, values highly plausible to a wilderness surveyor who repeatedly braved the unknown.

The Fairfaxes of Belvoir, like so many other wealthy and educated families in the Old Dominion and at home in England, seemed to have lost their faith in Christ—if they ever had it— and looked instead to the pagan philosophy of Seneca and Marcus Aurelius for life's meaning in the post-Christian Age of the 18th century Enlightenment.[19] Lord Fair-fax, his eldest son, George William, his wife, Sarah Cary, and Laurence and Anne Fairfax Washington formed a Roman circle along the Potomac in which George listened to readings from Plutarch and wise sayings from Epictetus. Here he read Seneca's *Morals* for the first time, pro-bably on the recommendation of Lord Fairfax, and discovered in Stoicism a philosophy of life.[20] These Romans were soldiers, practical men like those of Washington's own ideal who knew how to cope with the vicissitudes of frontier life in their own day. In his encampment against the northern barbarians on the Danube, the Emperor Marcus Aurelius had written of the good life and true virtue as the means to achieve it. Wisdom, the good life, Aurelius agreed with Seneca, must be conquered by the will, which alone could purge man of the emotions which lead to vice and the loss of self-sufficiency. Pain, pleasure, fear, desire, all the emotions must be subjected to the higher reason of man who possesses in this divine spark the means by which to harmonize his will with that of God.[21]

Washington, largely untutored as he was, could sympathize with Seneca's attack on grammar and the liberal studies of his time as mere intellectualism without any practical consequence. What was important, the philosopher insisted, was liberating oneself from the thralldom of desire, seeing all things in the light of Eternal Reason, and conforming one's life to the order of nature which is another name for God. Such a purpose was not just for any man. In fact, Seneca went on, the commonalty of men are bad, and their depravity will continue until the great conflagration at the end of the world. Only the true philosopher strives to form his life in virtue, and thus to worship that divine Being who loves and cares for man in his Providence.[22] Seneca, the "physician of souls," in these ideas gleaned from Washington's own reading and the bourgeois classicism of the Fairfaxes provided the young Virginian with a philosophical religion which supported him to his final days.[23]

This philosophical religion of action in accordance with nature, rather than contemplation, suited Washington's practical temperament. But the ideal was action at a distance, participation in the Heraclitic world of flux without deep personal involvement—a secular, dechristianized version of living *in* but not *of* the world. Emotionlessness, or "apathy" as the Stoics called it, was already a predisposition, a latent native trait in the man, and over the years he perfected it into a distinguishing characteristic. Washington sought to model himself after the complete Stoical wise man of Seneca's description: free, beautiful, rich and happy; knowing how to govern as well as obey; indifferent to pain and unafraid of death, even preferring the latter to dishonor; jealous of his peace of mind and tranquility of soul; above any show of favoritism in the discharge of his sacred duty; tireless in working to build a cosmopolis of all men as a reflection of the rationally ordered physical world.[24] Washington, however, believed he could not hope to emulate the wise man as orator, poet, and prophet; his formal education was too sketchy for that.[25]

There were grave dangers in this philosophical religion, and they can be seen writ large in Washington's private character. Yet, in his public role his Stoicism, his pagan-style "Christianity," may have made some things easier for the military hero and idol of his country. Revolutions like that of 1776, whatever their ultimate meaning in history, are too morally complex to be the central aim of either great saints or more humble folk who aspire for nothing but to follow Christ.

Stoicism had developed in Hellenistic-Roman times as a philosophical compensation for the loss of the state religion. The new skepticism about a public and common religious faith turned men away from the larger, more fundamental Platonic and Aristotelian conceptions about God and His worship to an almost exclusive concern with the conduct of life and individual morality.[26] Less than fifteen centuries later, with the decline of medieval Christian faith, much the same profound doubts about man's objective, social relationship to God promoted a revival of Stoicism among Renaissance thinkers like Montaigne and George Chapman. The age in which Washington and his contemporaries—notably Jefferson—lived, the Enlightenment, was no different.

Like Jefferson, who was much more articulate about it, Washington neither understood nor accepted the Judeo-Christian claim to Revelation; and without the objective prescription of Revelation there could be no shared, corporate religious worship. Both men, in a decidedly modern way, summarily rejected what they called "dogmatism."[27] It was logical, then, that Washington, Jefferson, and others, ignorant as they were of medieval Christian culture's synthesis of faith and reason, and deficient in the great systems of Platonism and Aristotelianism, should reduce philosophy and religion to Stoical ethics or some variation of it. Washington and Jefferson seem never even to have glimpsed man's ontological relationship to God in the Catholic Church, whose sacraments make Christ the Redeemer ever present to His people.[28] "Right reason," not grace, "is the perfection of human nature," they believed with the pagan Seneca. Philosophy was the guide to life, wisdom "the perpetual tranquility of mind."[29]

Right reason, Washington knew beyond a doubt, made clear that God existed. And what is God? Washington answered with Seneca: "An immense and an almighty power; great, without limits; and he does whatsoever pleases him."[30] Washington was a Deist, like Jefferson, in the sense that Dr. Samuel Johnson defined the word in his celebrated *Dictionary*. A Deist was "a man who follows no particular religion but only acknowledges the existence of God, without any other article of faith.'' Washington, however, following Seneca and the Stoic philosophers more closely, repudiated the radically transcendentalistic Deist conception of the ''absentee God''—the Unconcerned It—which Jefferson, Benjamin Franklin, Thomas Paine, and other American *philosophes* accepted as proof against divine intervention. ''The will of Heaven,'' he wrote as a perfect Stoic, ''is not to be controverted or scrutinized by the children of this world. It therefore becometh the creatures of it to submit to the will of the Creator, whether it be to prolong or to shorten the number of our days, to bless them with health, or afflict them with pain.''[31] And near the end of his life, commiserating with his friend, General Henry Knox, who was mourning the death of two children, he elaborated on the ancient teaching further: ''It is not for man to scan the wisdom of Providence. The best we can do, is to submit to its decrees. Reason, religion, and philosophy teach us to do this; but 'tis time alone, that can ameliorate the pangs of humanity and soften its woes.''[32] Man's duty—and the word was an important one for the Roman stoics and Washington—was submission to the will of God, which Washington nevertheless believed could often be discerned by man.[33] Indeed, throughout the Revolutionary War it was almost an article of faith with him that Providence was shielding him from every danger in order to fulfill his and the American people's destiny.[34] And the theme of Washington's divine favor, like that of Marcus Aurelius centuries before him, was given wide currency in pulpit sermons and Fourth-of-July orations during and after his lifetime. Parson Weems's enterprising story of young Washington's not being able to tell a lie is only one transparently silly variation of this deeply held national myth.[35]

In his public addresses, Washington used the word Providence rather than God, and never anywhere seems to have referred to Christ.[36] Jefferson referred to Christ, but of course only as a man. Neither Founding Father, so far as the evidence reveals, was a Christian; yet, while Jefferson expressly renounced the divinity of Christ, Washington appears simply to have ignored the Nazarene's claim, preferring what might be called a more Roman, i.e. polytheistic, than modern approach to the question of the nature of the Godhead.[37] Perhaps one reason for this was Jefferson's more physical or ''scientific'' orientation to truth, as the word was understood in the Enlightenment. It was so to speak the disadvantage of his formal education in the works of Bacon, Locke, and Newton. Washington, as a practical surveyor, was innocent of Newtonian physics and its overweening confidence in mechanistic explanations of nature, even to the point of believing in miracles! Like Seneca and the other latter-day Roman Stoics, the dilettante philosopher of Mount Vernon was concerned almost exclusively with happiness, the ethics of his own perfection in virtue.[38] "Happiness," he declared in this tradition, "depends more upon the internal frame of a person's own mind, than on the externals in the world."[39]

But if Washington did not deny Christ, it would nevertheless be misleading to say that his Stoicism was compatible with Christianity. The Stoical idea of Providence, held by Washington, is by no means Christian. The word itself is only used twice in the New Testament and then in a different sense from that of the Stoics.[40] Even so, the richer, more inclusive Christian idea of Providence is integral to the New Testament. Whereas Seneca wrote that the gods "are supreme commanders in the universe, controlling all things by their power and acting as guardians of the human race, even though they are sometimes unmindful of the individual,"and Cicero that "The gods care for great things but neglect the little." Christ declared that not a hair of our head shall perish.[41] For God is our Father and the God-Man our brother, so that every detail of our lives is the object of His loving care and everything that happens, no matter how inscrutable to our finite intelligence, advances the divine plan of benevolence for mankind.

The Stoical idea of Providence, moreover, is contradicted by another teaching of the Stoa, that of Fate or Chance. "Surrender everything to the Deity, to Fortune," says Epictetus.[42] And there are echoes of the same resignation in Washington's writings. This arbitrariness at the center of things is antithetical to Christian hope, as witnessed by the Stoic's acceptance of suicide as a philosophical release from the terrors of life. Zeno of Citium, Seneca, and other members of the school ended their lives by their own hand, for without the *supernatural* virtue of Christian hope there can only be despair in the midst of sudden changes of fortune. If man is not immortal, not made in the image of a perfectly loving God who entered history at the Incarnation and restored divine sonship and eternal life to His wayward children, then there only remains a philosophy of suffering, which is what Stoicism was to the despairing cultured elite of Hellenistic times and their counterparts in the modern world.[43] Washington certainly was no Montaigne or, say George Chapman, but like them and other post-medieval and increasingly post-Christian men he found in Stoical philosophy a quasi-Christian view of life, an "enlightened" religion free of the supernatural, in which man could live in harmony with nature and man and possess his soul in peace.

This is not to say that Washington was a profound or even critical, systematic thinker. On the contrary, John Adams was perceptive as usual when he observed in the privacy of his correspondence with Rush that the Virginian was "but very superficially read in history" as well as in other subjects and was no intellectual.[44] But neither is Stoicism known in the history of philosophy for its comprehension and depth of insight into reality. On the nature of God for example, Washington was satisfied with a vague Stoical conception of immanent, absolute Being despite seventeen hundred years of Christian theology. Did he never read the Bible and wonder at the Judeo-Christian conception of God as the ultimate Person, of He who is? Apparently not. An isolated and unredeemed man for Washington, as for the Stoics, lacked freedom: it was not so much doing the will of God with him, it was resigning oneself to it. The future "is known only to the great ruler of events; and confiding in his wisdom and goodness, we may safely trust the issue to him, without perplexing ourselves to seek for that which is beyond human ken, only taking care to perform the parts assigned to us in a way that reason and our own consciences approve of."[45] Man's conscience did not tremble before good and evil, as in the Catholic tradition, but served the cosmic destiny, the Eternal Reason of Stoicism. This fatalism lurks in Washington's mature writings and evinces a heroic pessimism inconsistent with Christianity. John Adams was more insightful than he realized when he characterized Washington as an actor.[46] Unlike Hamilton, a much deeper man, Washington seems never to have had a religious conversion, to have been surprised by perfect joy. He never made the decisive passage from naturalistic Romanism to Christianity. Here, Greenough's statue of Washington in Roman dress and manner is again symbolic.

It is no exaggeration to say that Stoicism, pure or in its bourgeois 18th century variety, tended to change normal men into cold, marble-like figures. Monumentality, not humanity, became the criterion of perfection. Washington, said Ralph Waldo Emerson, seemed to absorb, "all the serenity of America, and left none for his restless, rickety, hysterical countrymen."[47] The emotions, in this ultimately Platonic way of thinking, are at war with calm reason and must be destroyed—not transformed and spiritualized, as Christianity teaches. It is not strange, then, that Washington was never seen to kneel at Anglican or other services, let alone as legend has it in prayer in the snow at Valley Forge.[48] Stoics and other proud men do not genuflect, only Christians do. Washington's stolidity and frigid reserve are well known. Gouverneur Morris, so the story goes, once put his hand on Washington's shoulder in a gesture of friendship, only to have the General remove it with an icy rebuff.[49] One is inclined to believe that Washington's lifetime ambition to perfect his character, after the teachings of the Stoics, left little room for true friendship.[50]

By trying to attain that practical wisdom, that "apathy" and independence which was the end of Stoicism, Washington recapitulated in his own life, as it were, the history of the school. For the Stoical ideal of the wise man, which he pursued in his own way, isolates and dehumanizes man—as it did George Washington—depriving him of that very brotherhood which the Stoics professed and which only Christianity can achieve in the radical conversion of hearts.

## NOTES

[1] Howard Mumford Jones, *O Strange New World: American Culture: The Formative Years* (New York: The Viking Press, 1968), p. 265; Adeline Adams, "Horatio Greenough," *DAB*.

[2] Jones, p. 265.

[3] *Ibid.*, pp. 264-265.

[4] Marcus Cunliffe, *George Washington, Man and Monument* (Boston: Little, Brown and Company, 1958).

[5] James M. Smith, ed., *George Washington: A Profile* (New York: Hill and Wang, 1969) is a helpful anthology of essays.

[6] *Ibid.*, pp. 3-4; Cunliffe, p. 125. The comparison between Washington and Lucius Quinctius Cincinnatus, the hero of the old Roman republic and paragon of virtue, is well known. Even Lord Byron called Washington "the Cincinnatus of the West." Both men, it is true, left their ploughs to save a nation. But it should not be overlooked that, while he professed great love for Mount Vernon—hardly a modest Roman farm—he was a military man through and through. His ambition was to be a professional soldier, and in his exaggerated respect for governmental authority there is an ominous note, epecially in view of 20th century developments. Washington's fondness for uniforms has often been observed.

At the Second Continental Congress, he was the only delegate in military dress, *ibid.*, pp. 16-17, 63-65. He never refused a war.

[7] *Ibid.*, p. 124-125.

[8] Quoted in *The Washington Papers: Basic Selections from the Public and Private Writings of George Washington*, edited and with Introduction by Saul K. Padover (New York: Harper & Brothers Pub., 1955), p. 404; Cunliffe, p. 125.

[9] *Ibid.*, pp. 54, 116. "André has met his *fate*, and with that fortitude, which was to be expected from an accomplished man and gallant officer . . ."(my italics), GW to Lt. Col. John Laurens, October 13, 1780, quoted in Padover, p. 367. In an earlier letter to Governor Robert Dinwiddie of Virginia GW, after informing his superior of his hanging two militiamen, asked to be excused for "hanging, instead of shooting them. It conveyed much terror to others and it was for example sake, we did it." (August 1757) quoted in Cunliffe, p. 54.

[10] James Thomas Flexner, *George Washington; The Forge of Experience (1732-1775)* (Boston: Little, Brown and Company, 1965): p. 241 *et passim;* Roger L'Estrange, *Seneca's Morals By Way of Abstract to which is added a Discourse under the title of an After-thought* (London 1746). An excellent general discussion of GW's Stoicism is Samuel Eliot Morison, "The Young Man Washington," in Smith, ed., pp. 38-58.

[11] Cunliffe, p. 55; Douglas Southall Freeman, *George Washington, A Biography* (7 vols.; New York: Charles Scribner's Sons, 1948): Vol. II, *Young Washington*, pp. 387-389.

[12] James Thomas Flexner, *Washington: The Indispensable Man* (Boston: Little, Brown and Company, 1974), pp. 4-5, 8; Cunliffe, pp. 29, 41. GW himself accumulated 62,000 acres and had 200 slaves, whose manumission he provided for after the death of Martha. Paul F. Boller, "Washington, the Quakers, and Slavery," in Smith, ed., p. 187. GW was reluctant to have his slaves punished by whipping and he was unwilling to sell them without their permission. Flexner, *Washington: The Indispensabe Man*, pp. 193-194.

[13] Flexner, *George Washington; The Forge of Experience*, pp. 19-20.

[14] *Ibid.*, 16-17; Cunliffe, pp. 35-36; Curtis P. Nettels, "Washington on the Eve of the Revolution," in Smith, ed., p. 67.

[15] James Thomas Flexner, *George Washington and the New Nation* (Boston: Little, Brown and Company, 1970), p. 21; Paul F. Boller, "George Washington and Religious Liberty," in Smith, ed., p. 178. As a secularist, GW believed that even conscience must be secondary to what he called "the protection and essential interests of the nation . . . ," quoted in Norman Cousins, ed., *In God We Trust: The Religious Beliefs and Ideas of the American Founding Fathers* (New York: Harper & Brothers, 1958), p. 60. This same reply to the Quaker's Address of 1789 makes clear GW's disapproval of their and all pacifism.

[16] Freeman, *Young Washington*, pp. 195-196; Cunliffe, p. 36; Flexner, *George Washington: The Forge of Experience*, pp. 26, 30.

[17] Freeman, *Young Washington*, pp. 387-388; Dixon Wecter, "President Washington and Parson Weems," in Smith, ed. p. 24. GW retained nominalistic

ties to the Church of England, but typically for a Stoic he seems never to have understood the depth of man's religious feelings and convictions. "Religion" for him appears as a technique for dealing with the mystery of life than a religion. Here his modernity is strikingly evident. Helpful but superficial is Paul F. Boller, Jr., *George Washington & Religion* (Dallas, Southern Methodist University Press, 1963).

[18] Morison, p. 43; Cunliffe, p. 39.

[19] Morison, pp. 45-46. GW always wanted to be an aristocrat. Once he rose above his early bourgeois station, he was careful to maintain his new social role. His ambivalent relationship with Tom Paine, that hater of aristocrats, is worth exploring with this in mind.

[20] Morison, p. 41. GW now read Joseph Addison's tragedy *Cato* (1713), immensely popular with the pre-Revolutionary generation of Americans, and found the Stoicism of its main character Marcus Porcius Cato, much to his liking. The play was GW's lifelong favorite, and he may have acted a part in an amateur production of it at Belvoir. When morale was low at Valley Forge, he ordered that the play be performed for the troops, *ibid.*, pp. 46-48.

[21] See, e.g., Samuel Dill, *Roman Society from Nero to Marcus Aurelius* (Cleveland: World Publishing Co., 1956), pp. 308-309, *et passim.*

[22] L'Estrange, *Seneca's Morals*, pp. 98-100, 362; Dill, pp. 299-308.

[23] GW's philosophical religion of Stoicism, with its exaltation of the role of the will in the perfection of character, explains in large part his notorious failure to respect political, religious, and other genuine differences among men in a pluralistic society. The unity of will that GW and the Stoics demanded of men and the state is based on too narrow a conception of nature. Hence, it is itself unnatural, i.e. artificial, and violative of the principle of subsidiarity. The result is elitism of a subtle kind. Hence, GW was an uncompromising supporter of the totalitarian Alien and Sedition laws. Marshall Smelser, "George Washington and the Alien and Sedition Acts," *American Historical Review* LIX, No. 2 (January, 1954), pp. 322-334.

[24] GW's attitude towards his own death seems to have been Stoical in the best tradition. It was, he told his secretary, a "debt which we must all pay." When he became convinced that his illness (probably a streptococcus infection of the throat) was fatal, he ordered his slave overseer to bleed him and, despite Martha's protestations, urged that more and more blood be taken. The attending physicians repeated the treatment and GW grew weaker. His only expression of fear was that he might be buried alive: "I am just going. Have me decently buried, and do not let my body be put into the vault in less than three days after I am dead. Do you understand me?" The secretary nodded. " 'Tis well." Thomas T. Flexner, *George Washington, Anguish and Farewell* (1793-1799) (Boston: Little, Brown and Company, 1969), pp. 456-462; Cousins, p. 48.

[25] Certainly, this awareness of his own poor education was a major reason for his support of a national university which he and others hoped to found in the District of Columbia. Cunliffe, p. 206.

[26] Wilhelm Windelband, *A History of Philosophy* (2 vols; New York: Harper & Brothers, Pub., 1958) I; pp. 155-158.

[27] Boller, "George Washington and Religious Liberty," p. 168. Once GW was challenged by Presbyterians as to why the Constitution did not explicitly acknowledge "the *only true God and Jesus Christ whom he hath sent.*" "I am persuaded," he replied in a formal statement, "that the path of true piety is so plain as to require but little political direction. To this consideration we ought to ascribe the absence of any regulation, respecting religion, from the Magna-Carta of our country." (*Ibid.*, 179, and Cousins, p. 60) Typically for his age, GW was willing to accept some kinds of authority, but not others, especially that of Revelation.

[28] Like Jefferson and others, GW uncritically identified religion and conscience. See, e.g., his reply to an address of the United Baptist Churches of Virginia, May, 1789, in Cousins, p. 58.

[29] Quoted in L'Estrange, *Seneca's Morals*, pp. 98-99.

[30] *Ibid.*, 361; Flexner, *George Washington in the American Revolution*, p. 404n.

[31] To George Augustine Washington, January 27, 1792, Padover, *The Washington Papers*, p. 395.

[32] March 2, 1797, *ibid.*, p. 409; Boller, *George Washington and Religion*, pp. 99-100. North Callahan, *Henry Knox; General Washington's General* (New York: Rinehart & Co., Inc., 1958), pp. 156, 198, *et passim*. GW's own stepchildren, Jacky (John Parke Custis) and Patsy (Martha Parke Custis) died at seventeen and twenty-five respectively, Smith, p. xxvi.

[33] Flexner, *George Washington in the American Revolution*, p. 549.

[34] Dixon Wector, p. 2.

[35] Cunliffe, p. 44; Dixon Wector, pp. 1-37. Perhaps the first minister to predict GW's future greatness in his country's history was Rev. Samuel Davies in his *Religion and Patriotism the Constituents of a Good Soldier* (1755), see Lyman H. Butterfield, ed., *The Letters of Benjamin Rush* (2 vols; Philadelphia: The American Philosophical Society, 1951) I: p. 1125n. "From the first ages of the world," declared Representative Benjamin C. Howard of Maryland in a speech before Congress (1832) "the records of all time furnished only two instances of birthdays being commemorated after the death of the individual: those two were the 22nd of February and the 25th of December." And Rev. J.N. Danforth of Virginia said in 1847 that "To 'Mary the Mother of Washington,' we owe all the mighty debt due from mankind to her immortal son." Daniel J. Boorstin, "The Mythologizing of George Washington," Smith, p. 281.

[36] Boller, "George Washington and Religious Liberty," p. 166. There is what must be characterized as a missionary reference to "the religion of Jesus Christ" in a speech to Delaware Indian chiefs, May 12, 1779, in Cousins, p. 55; Wecter, p. 24.

[37] Apparently, as a Stoic, a non-believer, GW was indifferent to this and other theological questions. He was, therefore, tolerant of Roman Catholics—

or better, indifferent to their claims. See, e.g., GW to Benedict Arnold, September 14, 1775, in Cousins, pp. 49-50, on the treatment of Roman Catholics, and his Farewell Address of 1796. In arranging for workmen at Mount Vernon, he wrote that he did not care whether they were Mohammedans, Jews, Christians, or atheists. Flexner, *George Washington; The Forge of Experience* p. 243n. Cf. Boller, *George Washington and Religion*, pp. 66-91.

[38] See GW's comments on arithmetic and mathematics in Padover, ed. *The Washington Papers,*, pp. 383, 402. We have already pointed out this elitism in GW's character. Again, he and Marcus Aurelius come into comparison, as more concerned with realizing the Stoic ideal of perfection in themselves than in any other duty.

[39] To Mrs. Mary Washington, February 15, 1787, in *ibid.*, 396; Dilly, p. 309

[40] Ralph Stob, "Stoicism and Christianity," *The Classical Journal* XXX, No. 3 (December 1934), p. 221.

[41] Luke xxi, 18. The quotations are in Stob, pp. 221-222.

[42] Quoted in *ibid.*, 222.

[43] Cf. W. G. De Burgh, *The Legacy of the Ancient World* (Baltimore: Penguin Books edition, 1965), p. 208n.

[44] September, 1807, in John A. Shutz and Douglass Adair, eds., *The Spur of Fame; Dialogues of John Adams and Benjamin Rush, 1805-1813* (San Marino, Calif.: The Huntington Library, 1966), p. 94.

[45] Quoted in Flexner, *George Washington; The Forge of Experience*, pp. 24-245; cf. Cunliffe, p. 24; Stob. p. 218.

[46] Adams to Rush, June 21, 1811, Schutz, p. 181.

[47] Quoted in Morison, p. 39.

[48] Quoted in Cunliffe, p. 65.There is strong evidence that GW never received Holy Communion. One Sunday in Philadelphia he was chided indirectly for not receiving the sacrament. He never returned to the church for services, Wecter, p. 24, Boorstin, p. 275. *Ibid.*, pp. 33-34. The episode at Valley Forge, typically enough, has been called Washington's "Gethsemane," cited in Paul F. Boller, Jr., *George Washington and Religion* (Dallas: Southern Methodist University Press, 1963), p. 10.

[49] *Ibid.*, 18

[50] Cf. Cunliffe, p. 189.

# 6.
# Alexander Hamilton: From Caesar to Christ

> Where now. O! vile worm, is all thy boasted fortitude and resolution? what is become of thy arrogance and self-sufficiency?—Why dost thou tremble and stand aghast? How humble—how helpless—how contemptible you now appear. . . . Oh, impotent presumptuous fool! How darest thou offend that omnipotence, whose nod alone were sufficient to quell the destruction that hovers over thee, or crush thee to atoms? . . . He who gave the winds to blow and the lightnings to rage—even him I have always loved and served—his commandments have I obeyed—and his perfection have I adored.—He will snatch me from ruin—He will exalt me to the fellowship of Angels and Seraphs, and to the fulness of never ending joys.[1]

Alexander Hamilton wrote this not in the final, tragic years of his life, after his disillusionment with politics and rebirth as a Christian, but in 1772, when as a boy of fifteen in St. Croix, West Indies, he described his reaction to a terrible hurricane that slammed into the islands and wrecked the Danish settlement on the night of August 31.[2] Even so, the labored, youthful account, modelled after the heroic compositions of Pope and his other favorite authors, was prophetic of the mature Hamilton's deep sense of contingency and trust in God after his political and other battles had been lost. For, as we shall see, when Hamilton lay mortally wounded after his duel with Aaron Burr he truly believed that Christ would "snatch me from ruin" and "exalt me to the fellowship of Angels and Seraphs, and to the fulness of never ending joys." And, on July 12, 1804, after having received Holy Communion from Episcopal Bishop Richard Moore, Hamilton's soul found its peace at last.

Hamilton died in New York City, surrounded by his wife and seven children and mourned by a nation. Half a century earlier, his coming into the world, on Nevis Island, British West Indies, had had none of this celebrity. Indeed, Hamilton's parentage, as John Adams and others sneered, was irregular.[3] He was the son of James Hamilton and Rachel (Fawcett) Levine, who, separated from her legal husband, was prevented from a licit union by her failure to obtain a divorce and who soon found herself deserted by the boy's ne'er-do-well father. At age eleven Alexander lost his mother too, when the poor, heart-broken woman could struggle no longer against her deepening misfortune.

Orphaned as he was, young Hamilton was thrown on the charity of the island gentry, and in 1769 he was placed in the trading house of Nicholas Cruger as an apprentice clerk. Cruger was one of the most prosperous merchants of St. Croix. His store in Christianstadt was the center of the Island's trade, and Hamilton soon learned to excel in record-keeping, buying and selling, and all the other activities of the bourgeois merchants. Perhaps, as one of his biographers, Nathan Schachner, has speculated, Hamilton's Calvinist inheritance on his mother's side may have fitted him for the economic life, as a model apprentice clerk in the early years and as the architect of American capitalism in the post-Revolutionary era. In any case, to a boy in his straits there was no alternative to success.[4]

Nor was the lad's education neglected. Dr. Hugh Knox, the Presbyterian minister who had been so helpful to his mother, saw after his education in Latin, mathematics, and French; and in 1772 Dr. Knox and others arranged for him to continue his studies on the mainland. Hamilton's first choice was Princeton, where Dr. Knox had graduated. However, the College would not accept his proposal for an accelerated program of study, so the West Indian decided on King's College in New York. There is no doubting that Hamilton was serious about college, yet he was ambitious and impatient to make his way in the world, and back home he had revealed to a close friend that he "would willingly risk my life, though not my character, to exalt my station."[5] All that he needed was an overpowering cause, a noble one that he could exploit to the fullest, and win that glory that he had read about in the pages of Caesar and Plutarch while an orphan boy in St. Croix.

The mainland colonies were astir those days with such a cause. In

May of 1773 Parliament enacted the Tea Act, threatening to give the British East India Company a monopoly on the colonial market. This was only one of a long train of laws, passed since 1763, which colonial spokesmen held to be unconstitutional. Hamilton agreed. Dr. Knox and other opponents of Parliament's new imperial policy in St. Croix had already explained to him how all Englishmen were being deprived of their historic rights by Lord North's arrogant stratagems. But is was the Boston Tea Party of December 1773 which led Hamilton as a student at King's to become personally involved in the crisis by writing his "Defence of the Destruction of the Tea" and publishing it in *Holt's Journal*, where it attracted the attention of many patriot New Yorkers over the next few months. He contributed still other articles, was emboldened to give public speeches on Parliamentary oppression, and determined to take an even more active role in the controversy with the mother country.[6]

It was this last resolution which caused Hamilton to defend the Continental Congress, meeting in Philadelphia, in another pamphlet, and to attack the liberal Quebec Bill of 1774, which recognized the Roman Catholic Church in Canada, as a ministerial conspiracy to destroy the Protestantism of the colonist by establishing popery among their neighbors to the north. Here, in his "Remarks on the Quebec Bill," which reflected the thinking of the Continental Congress itself, the eighteen-year-old Hamilton revealed not only the Whig sentiments of his West Indian tutor, Dr. Knox, but his prejudices as well. It is ironic that, in taking this line of argument—or, better, in making this emotional outburst—the man who would become the new nations's most vocal spokesman for centralized, Federal power helped in this instance to bring about the opposite effect, as the French Canadians, smarting at this kind of treatment, remained loyal to Britain and would have nothing to do with anti-papist bigotry.[7]

Hamilton had found his noble cause, liberty, and his pamphlets and speeches were serving it well, at least in keeping Parliamentary tyranny before the public eye. But there was still his dream of military glory, of Casear-like conquests that would rescue him from his obscure and shadowed beginnings. "I mean to prepare the way for futurity," he had confided to a friend in St. Croix. "I wish there was a war."[8] Now, in March of 1776, after the blood-letting at Lexington and Concord, there was one, and Hamilton used his connections among the New York Sons of Liberty to obtain the rank of captain of artillery in the local militia. Never, as it turned out, was a political appointment more fitting, since he had studied all about artillery and ballistics on his own, like the self-taught Henry Knox, and was to serve the Revolutionary cause with distinction. The opportunity to excel at arms soon presented itself.[9]

In the retreat across New Jersey later that year, Captain Hamilton was assigned to Washington's rear-guard on the banks of the Raritan River and handled his battery with such skill and gallantry as to allow the main body to withdraw safely to Princeton. General Washington himself was impressed, although in the end it was Hamilton's other talents—his gift for writing and keen intelligence—which led the commander-in-chief on March 1, 1777 to name the young captain his aide-de-camp with the rank of lieutenant-colonel. At twenty Hamilton's meteoric rise to power had begun. It appears so dramatic that perhaps one can understand the temptation of some writers to charge that Hamilton, who was born while Washington was in the Barbados, was none other than the General's natural son.[10]

As secretary and aide to Washington, the Virginian being for all intents and purposes secretary of war as well as commanding general of the army, Hamilton soon became privy to the inner workings of the Articles of Confederation government and the military system, both of which he now sought to purge of their defects by constructive reforms. Even at this early date, Hamilton called for a constitutional convention, apparently the first proposal of its kind, to centralize power in Congress; and urged the establishment of a national bank in a letter to Robert Morris, the new nation's superintendent of finance.[11] It was, of course, only as Washington's trusted adviser, his intimate rather than merely his aide-de-camp, that Colonel Hamilton could presume to write to the older leaders of the Revolutionary cause and indulge his pet theories. Or, more directly, Hamilton began now cleverly to manipulate Washington who, at forty-five, was more than twice his age and who seems to have developed from the start a fatherly attachment to the brilliant young officer. It is this manipulative ability, this capacity to use people—Washington and many others—as a means to what he conceived to be a higher end, that describes Hamilton best in his vigourous middle period. This higher end or purpose of Hamilton in the years from, say 1777 to 1801, was the construction of his own political utopia in America.

From his vantage point in Washington's military household, where for four years he was the General's alter ego, Hamilton could see the critical weaknesses of the Articles of Confederation government and the men who administered it. After the War, and a term in the Continental Congress (1782-83) where more internal problems became disturbingly apparent, the now fervid nationalist searched for ways to remedy the defects of the union by strengthening the central government at the expense of the states. In New York, where he had married Elizabeth, the daughter of the prominent, well-connected General Philip Schuyler, in 1780, Hamilton advanced his career further by taking advantage of the new test laws which, by disbarring older Tory lawyers, enabled him to win quick admission to the legal profession.[12] Not yet thirty years of age, Hamilton had skillfully maneuvered himself into a position from which he might aspire to a leading role in the formation of a new nation.

Like his father-in-law, General Schuyler, he pressed for a constitutional convention to deal with the revenue problem, the threat of mutiny at Newburgh, and other emergencies which the loose Confederation simply could not handle. In particular, Schuyler insisted upon Congress's having control over interstate and foreign commerce, one of many centralist views which he shared with Hamilton; and in 1786 he used his considerable influence in the New York Senate to appoint Hamilton one of six commissioners to the Annapolis Convention where regulation of commerce among the states was to be discussed. As is well known, the Convention failed, but Hamilton, seeing in this confirmation of his belief that political unity was indispensable to commercial harmony, inveigled and manipulated the other delegates into signing a report which called for another meeting in Philadelphia the following spring "to take into consideration the situation of the United States, to devise such further provisions as shall seem to them necessary to render the Constitution of the Federal Government adequate to the exigencies of the Union, and to report an act for that purpose to the United States and Congress assembled."[13] Just as he had done on several critical occasions earlier in his life, so he again orchestrated events his way. Hamilton was succeeding by one ingeniously calculated move after another in imposing his will on his newly adopted country, which must now be fitted to Hamilton's procrustean scheme for a highly centralized government.

The convention at Annapolis over, Hamilton returned to the New York assembly, where he held his seat with the powerful support of the business community. There he was the master strategist in committing the legislature, despite Governor George Clinton's anti-Federalist opposition, to participation in the Philadelphia meeting. True to form, Hamilton managed to get himself appointed to the New York delegation as the sole Federalist. Clearly, though, much more work needed to be done in breaking down the resistance of Clinton and the radical localists who feared a strong national government. If the state laws disfranchising Tories could be repealed over the opposition of the anti-Federalists, these conservative men of property could be expected to vote for a more vigorous constitution to protect them against the states-rights radicals. So Hamilton, acting on these and purer motives of justice, spoke passionately for repeal.[14]

In Philadelphia the other New York delegates soon bolted the Convention, furious over what they believed to be the excesses of the Convention in drafting a new Constitution rather than amending the Articles of Confederation. Hamilton, for his part, thought the debates had not gone far enough in saving the nation from anarchy. He took a whole day to propose his own system of government which, while not ideal from his point of view—since the people, he believed, were agog with republicanism and incapable of political realism—came closest to the limited monarchy he secretly preferred. The chief executive and senators should hold office for life, subject only to good behavior. The president must have a veto over all Federal and state laws, he held, in order to balance a democratic lower house against the propertied interest of the senate. And, finally, governors of the states—mere administrative units in Hamilton's conception—should be appointed by the president, whose only check would be from congress and a Federal judiciary empowered to declare laws unconstitutional.[15]

The expected then happened. The proposal was voted down overwhelmingly, but Hamilton once again had shown his managerial skill with men. "I revolutionized his mind," he said of one of them, Rufus King of Massachusetts, perhaps the most eloquent speaker in the assembly, who came over the Hamilton's position from the opposite side.[16] Hamilton always prided himself on having his way with people, as he had with Washington, Schuyler, King, and others. In boldly arguing this scheme of government before the convention he was likewise trying to manipulate other highly influential men, national opinion-makers, into a favorable attitude towards what he considered a more realistic theory of federalism by offering a plan of government which he knew to be too advanced for them to accept. As a result, later on September 17, 1787, when the final draft of the proposed Constitution was ready for signing, many ideas which hitherto had been unpalatable to the delegates were in it—thanks to Hamilton's stratagem. After urging all of them to sign, or else face the dangers of "anarchy and convulsion," Hamilton signed for New York, along with all but three of the 42 delegates. His own ideas were "more remote from the plan" than anyone else, he alleged, so imperfect was the Constitution, but in fact the new document incorporated many of Hamilton's ideas.

Hamilton had cajoled the Philadelphia assembly into drafting a new Constitution, but he must now turn to the more formidable problem of assuring its ratification in his own state. Robert Yates and John Lansing, anti-Federalists and Gov. Clinton's men in the Constitutional Convention, had already returned to New York to prepare for the coming battle. Hamilton knew that the anti-Constitutionalists there were powerful and well-organized. He also realized that without New York, which by its strategic location held the country together, there was no hope for the United States as a great nation. The battle over New York loomed in Hamilton's mind as critical for world history. Was the United States of America, which promised so much, a true nation or only a congeries of states? At a deeper level, the struggle for ratification was critical for Hamilton's psychological and moral development. For at issue was his very manhood, his utopian attempt to organize reality as it ought to be, his transcending wayward nature—in this case the unpredictable and quarrelling state—by imposing authority and order.

It was therefore no accident that his first articles defending the Constitution should appear in the New York *Daily Advertiser* under the name of "Caesar." These polemical letters against Gov. George Clinton, the "Cato" of the piece, rehearsed the old problem of the republic vs. the consolidated state. Hamilton, however, seeing that his high-toned writing was not having its desired effect, soon wisely exchanged polemics for argument and began contributing more moderate articles under the vaguer name of "Publius." These *Federalist Papers* (1788), some 77 essays in support of the proposed national government, authored by Hamilton with the help of James Madison and John Jay, proved much more effective not only with New Yorkers but with other Americans. Washington wrote that they had convinced him of the merits of the new charter, and even Hamilton's enemies grudgingly admitted the arguments were hard to refute.[17]

At the Poughkeepsie convention, held late that year to decide whether New York should ratify the Federal Constitution, Hamilton employed the same arguments, down to their very phraseology, and capitalized on the more favorable public opinion on the Constitution that his writings had helped bring about. His manipulative skills were perhaps never better, and once again fortune herself seemed to conspire with his plans, for news of ratification of the Constitution by New Hampshire and Virginia in late June left New York no real alternative. Either she must come into the New Union, join Virginia, Massachusetts, Pennsylvania, and the other large states, or perish.

Alexander Hamilton had helped make a nation and now was bending it more and more to his will by defeating the strong, resisting forces of localism and tradition, as the victory in his home state demonstrated. Hamilton was Caesar, and the empire of his vision was the modern, totalitarian state. In these years Hamilton, not yet a Christian, saw no real choice between Caesar and Christ, nor could he as his only reality at this time seems to have been the political, the economic, the tangible. Men were not angels, he agreed with Madison, but his pessimism went much deeper, perhaps because of his Calvinist background. The effects of what he called "the ordinary *depravity* of human nature" were everywhere, of "uncontrollable impulses of rage, . . . jealousy, . . . and other irregular and violent propensities."[18] There was yet no Christ in his thinking to redeem man, no supernatural virtue of love to overcome the war raging between man and man. Like Hobbes, whose view of human nature he shared, Hamilton saw the only hope for passion-driven man in the absolute security of the Leviathan state. Talk about the virtue of republics, with Montesquieu, Locke, and Jefferson, he believed, was not only idle and utopian but dangerous. There was no "exemption from the imperfections, the weaknesses, and the evils incident to society in every shape."[19] Not the protection of their natural rights to life, liberty, and property, but the lust for power, was the motive of men in political associations. Hamilton neither signed nor approved of the Declaration of Independence.

This pessimism about man left to himself, this fear of man's arbitrariness, was what motivated Hamilton to seek more and more centralization of government so as to save men from themselves. In true Hobbesian fashion, he was prepared to choose security as against liberty if the choice must be made. But in Hamilton's mind, it was not really security but the "general good" that must be served. Interspersed among his writings, as Clinton Rossiter has shown, is this phrase and many other terms like "the public safety," "the public interest," and even "the general will," all vaguely describing what he viewed as that transcending, ultimate end to which politics was only a means.[20] The very concept, Rousseauian in its nebulosity, shares with the ideas of the Frenchman and Hobbes too that utopian imprecision and casualness of language—that sloganeering character which modern advertising and mind-control technology knows so well how to exploit. "The first thing in all great operations of such a government as ours is to secure the opinion of the people," Hamilton wrote during the controversy over the Alien and Sedition Acts.[21] Public opinion was "the governing principle of human affairs," and he had no doubt that it could be conditioned to accept the totalitarian state that alone could prevent the abuse of human liberty.[22]

For it was, in truth, man's liberty that made Hamilton, as a secular utopian, skeptical of the Articles of Confederation government and any other loose union. Decentralization allowed man too much scope for his native unruliness. If, as Hamilton believed, it is "a maxim, that, in contriving any system of government, and fixing the several checks and controls of the constitution, *every man* ought to be supposed a *knave*," it followed that "it is therefore a just *political* maxim, that *every man must be supposed a knave*."[23] How could men like Hamilton, men of "stern virtue," the political elect "who could neither be distressed nor won into a sacrifice of their duty"—how could they save other men from their own destructive, selfish passions except by rendering them impotent as moral agents before the ethical state, which, as Rousseau and later Hegel asserted, was freedom *per se*. "Take mankind in general," he is reported to have said to the delegates at the Constitutional Convention.

> They are vicious, their passions may be operated upon. . . . Take mankind as they are, and what are they governed by? Their passions. There may be in every government a few choice spirits, who may act from more worthy motives. One great error is that we suppose mankind more honest than they are. Our prevailing passions are ambition and interest; and *it will ever be the duty of a wise government to avail itself of the passions, in order to make them subservient to the public good; for these ever induce us to action.*[24]

And, he subsequently noted in the *Federalist*, men's passions could be exploited for the public good by taking advantage of the fact that they generally did what they thought to be for their immediate benefit. Hence, the logic of Hamilton's fiscal program as Secretary of the Treasury when, in a series of reports on domestic and foreign debt, an excise tax, and a national bank he designed to align the selfish interest of the moneyed class with the new government. While he calculated, admittedly with little effort, to win over the masses of the people by advocating road-building and agricultural improvements. All this was consistent with this essentially Hobbesian belief that men are "rather reasoning than reasonable animals" and motivated by the pleasure principle.

Hamilton's assumption plan, by which the Federal government assumed the state's unpaid debts, catered to the upper classes solely in order to transfer their loyalty from the state to the new central government. The means of doing this, as Madison, Rush, and others protested, was immoral, since the original owners of the securities had had to sell them at a great loss to speculators, who now stood to gain unconscionably.[25] But Hamilton was here, and in his other state papers, only concerned with the overriding principle of establishing the public credit of the new nation so that the central government would be strengthened, American natural resources developed, and a capitalist economy settled upon the land. His critics, he believed, had no theory, no general principles. "Can that man be a systematic or able statesman who has none," he asked "I believe not. *No general principles* will hardly work much better than erroneous ones."[26] Apparently, it meant little to Hamilton that Revolutionary War veterans, their widows and children, and other poor people would suffer from this political manipulation. But, then, Hamilton in his utopian scheme for a great Federal power was prepared to use immoral means, and, as pointed out above, he had never subscribed to the Declaration of Independence with its doctrine of the natural rights of the person.

Hamilton, unlike Jefferson, never seems to have understood the Western concept of the person and his inalienable rights. His reading, evidently, was confined to highly selective ancient and modern authors like Demosthenes, Cicero, Plutarch, Bacon, Montaigne, Machiavelli, and Rousseau.[27] In the company of the great majority of his American contemporaries, he knew next to nothing about the Middle Ages and its Christian teaching of the primacy of the person made in the image of God. He was acquainted with natural law, for it was of course an integral part of the 18th century world-view, but from Locke's *Treatise of Government* Hamilton seems to have drawn implications that led more to the corporate idealism and collectivism of Rousseau than to the individualism of Jefferson. In any case, the Frenchman's concept of the "general will" rather than Locke's majority will was the fundamental tenet of Hamilton's political philosophy, at least before 1800. Accordingly, there was no place for minority rights, natural rights to life, liberty, and property in his ideal state which he tried to construct as Secretary of the Treasury and adviser to Washington.[28]

Like Rousseau and all utopians, secular and religious, Hamilton justified coercion of the individual—forcing him to be free, Rousseau called it—in order to achieve the perfect society of his dream. Freedom was a great treasure, Hamilton agreed with the ideologues, propagandists, social engineers, and manipulators of all ages, but it must be organized against abuse. Unrestrained man's freedom degenerated into license and anarchy. "Shall the general will prevail, or the will of a faction? Shall there be government or no government," was the way Hamilton put it in his "Tully" essays of 1794, written to prepare the people for the Federal government's military action against the Whiskey Rebels—Pennsylvania frontiersmen who opposed his excise tax—which he was already planning.[29] And Hamilton himself in September of that year, fantasizing about military glory, rode out with a militia army of 12,000 men to force the Whiskey insurgents to be free!

Just as he morally never appreciated the person's infinite worth, viewing man with Calvin and Hobbes rather than Locke, so Hamilton could never advance in his social and political thinking to the concept of localism, better, of subsidiarity, as normative in man's relationship to other men. His twisted conception of human nature prevented him from seeing that "Every agent is perfected by its own activity," which is the principle of subsidiarity. Society, he failed to see, exists only *in* and *for* its members. It has no higher unity under which the individual is subsumed, no ethical priority over its members. The common good, which Hamilton as a utopian confused with the totalitarian "general will" of Rousseau, and which he used force to impose on the backwoodsmen of western Pennsylvania, required that he place the good of the Whiskey insurgents before the collectivity of his ideal state. The common good also required that, as Madison proposed, the Federal government in its funding program discriminate between the original holders of certificates and speculators, but Hamilton himself would brook none of that. Like today's Marxists and other totalitarians, Hamilton did not realize that society, the state, or any organization exists for the good of the individual and not vice versa, that the community's *raison d'état* is to help man actualize the powers that God has given him.

Man, the principle of subsidiarity teaches, must be free to use his faculties, to act on his own initiative, employing his own means towards the end that he has chosen, without the regimentation of the state. This principle Hamilton rejected. He also violated the norm easily discoverable by reason, that the lower social unit, whether person, family, group, institution, or government has the right to exist and work out its rightful activities without the next superior unit interfering. As a social engineer who found man depraved and unpredictable, Hamilton committed the typical utopian error of "liberating" man from himself by trying to force him into static political and financial classes and structures which could then be absorbed by the total state into a transcendent unanimity. Not man, but his social relations preoccupied Hamilton: his thought was really more sociological than anthropological. Factionalism must be prevented, even if it meant the sacrifice of personal liberty. Ideological consensus in the perfected, universal state of Hamilton's conceit would make factionalism unnecessary, since—if Marxist terms be permitted—factionalism was a kind of alienation which must disappear once men came to realize where their real interest lay and praxis was at last achieved.[30]

The Declaration of Independence, in its concern for the person and his natural rights, is of course antagonistic to these Hamiltonian ideas and draws from that Western tradition which Hamilton himself seems never to have understood nor, at any rate, thought worthy of preserving in the New World. The idea that man's soul is ultimately the only real value in humanity, an Augustinian insight which had deeply influenced Calvin and Hamilton's other spiritual forefathers, lies at the center of the Judeo-Christian tradition, but along with it and qualifying it is Aristotle's and St. Thomas's insistence that man is a social animal by nature. Jefferson in the Declaration clearly had exaggerated the one aspect of that tradition while slighting the other, that of the common good, and the fault runs through his thought in general. His extreme individualism, as we have seen in Chapter one, soon evolves into relativism and subjectivism, which are destructive of the common good. Jefferson's atomistic conception of society, moreover, can be traced directly to this reliance on Locke, Algernon Sidney, and other "social contract" thinkers. Hamilton, on the contrary, looked to the tradition of Hobbes and David Hume, both of whom held in the words of the latter that "reason is and ought only to be the slave of the passions and can never pretend to any other office than to serve and obey them."[31] Neither reason nor natural law—mere hypotheses Hume called them—were present to guide man, according to this tradition. Government, the Declaration notwithstanding, is not based upon some fabled consent in the past, but upon accepted conventions. Its validity is not to be found in natural law and its self-evident truths of reason but in utility. There are, hence, no rationally discoverable absolute truths and values, according to Hume, to limit the modern state in its self-aggrandizement, and the way is opened to the absolutizing of the common good with Rousseau ("the general will"), Hegel's deification of the state, and Hamilton's totalitarianism.

That Hamilton in his politically active years saw the only hope for man in the perfectly organized modern state, in Caesar rather than Christ, can also be seen in his doctrine of implied powers and his support of the Alien and Sedition laws of 1798. Both illustrate too his consistent adherence to the principles of Hobbes and Hume, which rejected the medieval, Judeo-Christian and classical view of man's inherent rationality and dignity.

The preamble of the Federal Constitution, lodging all power and initiative in the people, was enough to mar the charter in Hamilton's estimation; for how could the impure, the non-elect organize a true common-

wealth. Hamilton's basic premise, we have noted, was that of all utopians, religious and secular: man's corrupted nature, issuing in license
rather than freedom, must be restrained by government, which can only
be organized by the elect. Only in this way could man be made to overcome his selfishness and live in the ideal society where his own good
was transcended by the public good. To this end, the realization of the
secular, where public virtue would replace private greed, the Federal
government must have much more power than the Constitution provided. This meant, Hamilton knew, attacking the principle of subsidiarity
wherever it could be found, but especially in the Constitution where the
rights of persons and states were protected against the encroachment of
the central government.

   Exploiting, again, his special relationship to Washington, which
allowed him to act the role of *de facto* premier in the national administration, Hamilton succeeded in 1792 in chartering a bank of the United States
over Jefferson's objection that Congress was not authorized to do so.
Jefferson and Madison also feared what they called the ''money
despotism,'' the influence of that wealthy class whom Hamilton was cour-
ting in his fiscal program, and who posed a threat to the local sovereignty
of the people. While Hamilton in his doctrine of implied powers argued
that Congress's power to establish the bank was implied in the Constitution as a necessary means to the collection of taxes and regulation of
trade, Jefferson and Madison defended the principle of subsidiarity here
by pointing out that Hamilton's loose constructionist view of the Constitution could be reduced to the absurdity of saying that Congress had
the total power to do whatever it thought good for the people of the United
States.[32] Here, again, Jefferson and Madison spoke, albeit unwittingly,
for Western, medieval Catholic tradition in citing the dangerous lack
of intermediate structures between the people and the central government in Hamilton's program. But the ultranationalist prevailed, for
Hamilton as a post-Reformation thinker knew next to nothing about the
organic society of the Middle Ages—which Edmund Burke at the time
was trying desperately to recover—and the spirited Virginians were, in
reality, powerless before the onslaught of the modern world.

   Much more aware of the subtle, hierarchical, organic nature of true
society, Jefferson and Madison were more likely to object to usury than
Hamilton; and of course there are overtones of such an objection in their
stand against Hamilton's plans for funding and establishing a national

bank. They seem to have understood, as Aristotle and the Church fathers did before them, that usury exploits man's misfortune; that, from the point of view of the state—Aristotle insists—usury leads to excessive wealth and materialism which prevent the citizen from engaging in the higher, fuller life of the intellect and spirit which is man's true end in the commonwealth.[33] Hence, Jefferson's well-known substitution in the Declaration of Independence of the phrase "pursuit of happiness" for "property" in the Lockean "Life, Liberty, and Property," and his harking back to agrarianism *vis-à-vis* the modern capitalistic, industrial state of Hamilton. And, hence the efforts of the two libertarians to protect the natural and other rights of man against the national government in the Bill of Rights and in the Virginia and Kentucky Resolutions (1798), consistent with the principle of subsidiarity, which they wrote to protest the unconstitutionality of the Alien and Sedition Acts—laws that did not go far enough, according to Hamilton, in curbing internal criticism of the Federal Administration.[34]

Hamilton's dependence upon legislation, so typical of the 18th century mentality, in the building of his nationalistic utopia appears, at first glance, to accord with the belief of the Founding Fathers in general that the best government is one of laws rather than men. But on closer study, what distinguishes Hamilton's legalism and rigid constitutionalism from the social and political thought of men like Jefferson, Madison, and especially Benjamin Rush and Charles Carroll of Carrollton, is the latter's recognition in varying degrees that justice, and ultimately charity, alone binds the good society together. Hamilton's philosophy of man and society is mechanistic and cold, legalistic in the extreme. Man is considered as important in this perspective, but always as the fictitious man or political man of classical liberalism, never as man *qua* man. Otherwise, Hamilton would have appreciated the rise of society in man's nature, his family, and the extended family, the village; and he would have realized that the true state is one in which men cooperate in reason, and in its perfection, love—not one in which they are forced to perform services for one another by a coercive, if well-meaning, government. Rule by law, in short, can be as tyrannous as government by men, if social charity does not prevail. Next best to love as the motive of society and the state, and included in it, is rational cooperation, which Plato and Aristotle as pre-Christian thinkers understood very well. Hamilton seems not to have perceived this. A striking contradiction in his basic premise is that of denying rationality and virtue to man—"men are reasoning rather than reasonable animals"—while attributing them to the ruling political and economic elites who in his ideal commonwealth prescribe the laws, economy, and mores of the state and *are* the state. This contradiction is of course glaring in socialism, capitalism, fascism, and all utopian systems which require "pure" elites for their operation. Politics and economics, despite Hamilton and so-called modern "scientific" thinkers, are moral sciences, since their ultimate concern is man, man who has a supernatural as well as a natural end.[35] States—even his beloved United States—laws, governments, economies, and banks exist for man, not conversely. The Declaration of Independence is a testament to this truth. Hamilton, like so many of us, confused his means and ends.

Finally, in this analysis of Hamilton's thought, we should observe a paradoxical outcome of his labors as America's apostle of ultranationalism and the corporate system. His motivation for the new nation's economy was not moral but political, reminiscent of the old mercantilists and foreshadowing at the same time capitalistic and socialistic appropriation of government for their own economic purposes. It was false motivation, in principle, treating man as a means rather than an end; and while this politicized economy at first served Hamilton's centralistic purpose by wedding the money interest to the national state, it has led in our own day, of mass production and larger and larger corporations, to cartels and other international combinations which dominate states rather than serve them. The corporate system which Hamilton conceived as the handmaid of nationalism turned out to be, instead, the mistress of states. Corporate systems, with incomes greater than some modern states, are creating a new kind of internationalism. That is the paradox. Only the small entrepreneur and the small holder of property, marginal in Hamilton's theory of the state, remain in the low condition to which he relegated them and continue to decrease in number as huge, international corporations multiply. Special interests, not the "common good," prevail and tyrannize over nations and their people.

Hamilton, weary and hard-pressed—he was only making $3500 a year—resigned from Washington's cabinet in 1795, his fiscal program for the new nation established but still under attack from Jefferson—that man "of profound ambition and violent passions"—and his followers.[36] Behind the scenes, however, he remained influential, advising the President on domestic and foreign affairs and even writing sections of Washington's Farewell Address which committed the United States to Hamiltonian power politics abroad.[37] He was never to return to civil office, his aspiration to the presidency blocked by the South's antagonism to his centralizing policies. Undoubtedly, in his own mind Hamilton rationalized this as a patriotic sacrifice of his greatest ambition for the good of the new Federal Union which Jefferson and the other Southern States-rights radicals were trying to destroy. Like other immigrants, then and now, he must prove his loyalty to the state at any price—even of his life, as we shall see later. But Hamilton's motive here and in the fatal duel was ideological as well as psychological and sociological. As a member of the new elite of his utopian commonwealth he must prove himself innocent of self-interest and factionalism, an attitude that Thomas Molnar has shown to be typical of collectivistic theorists from the Levellers to Rousseau and Marx.[38] In 1797 Hamilton publicly confessed to an intrigue with a married woman in order to clear himself of a charge of malfeasance as Secretary of the Treasury. The accusation was groundless, but, true to character, Hamilton sacrificed his private reputation rather than sully his honesty as a national leader.[39]

Hamilton's efforts to manipulate John Adams, once he had been elected to the highest office over his opposition, were rebuffed by Adams, who never forgave the younger man. Yet, as long as Washington lived—"an *Aegis very essential to me,*" he admitted later—Hamilton had a shield against him and others who resented his influence. It was Washington who obtained for his former aide-de-camp the rank of major general, second only to Washington himself in the provisional army raised in 1798 when war with the French seemed inevitable. So insistent was the ex-President on the choice of Hamilton, in fact, that he came close to resigning as commander-in-chief when Adams at first hesitated in favor of General Henry Knox. As it had happened before, when the scattered Whiskey insurrectionists failed to stand their ground against Hamilton's Federal troops and proved an empty threat to the national government, so the glory of leading a great army against the French in Louisiana—and, perhaps, anti-Federalists in Virginia—never materialized either. President Adams averted war with France by dramatically naming a new minister to negotiate with Tallyrand, who now promised to treat the American mission with respect. Hamilton was taken by surprise. He could neither use his army of young Federalists to seize Louisiana nor to punish Virginia and Kentucky for their resolutions against the Alien and Sedition laws.[40]

Had Hamilton been planning or considering a *coup d'état* to save the United States from its internal as well as foreign enemies? He had threatened to deploy his private army, for that is how he thought of it, "to subdue a refractory and powerful State," and he even mentioned chastening Virginia by name to one of his confederates. Jefferson may have seen through his plan when he asked:

> Can such an army under Hamilton be disbanded? Even if a H. or Repre. can be got willing & wishing to disband them? I doubt it, & therefore rest my principal hope on their inability to raise anything but officers.[41]

We can only speculate on Hamilton's intentions, but there is no question that he was desperate and ready to employ any means to stop the anti-Federalists from coming to power. Earlier, in 1783, he had urged making use of the army at Newburgh for political purposes, and while Washington lived there was hope of Hamilton's realizing his American utopia by force of arms. Then, on December 14, 1799, Washington died suddenly. It was all over for Hamilton and his dreams of military glory. The great man removed from the national scene, Hamilton must now stand alone before his enemies, both among the moderate Federalist majority in Congress and the Jeffersonian Republicans who were beginning to sense victory in the upcoming presidential election of 1800.[42]

In the spring elections of 1800, to make matters worse, one of Hamilton's many enemies, Aaron Burr, swept his Republican candidates into office in New York City, defeating Hamilton's Federalist lackies and gaining control of the state legislature. Burr's victory in the key state of New York, Hamilton knew, meant that Burr and Jefferson would soon win the highest prize of all—the national government, which was essential to the completion of Hamilton's utopian scheme for the perfectly organized Leviathan state. Hamilton, driven to extremes, wrote to Governor John Jay of New York, a staunch Federalist, anglophile, and man after his own heart, suggesting extraordinary if not illegal moves to guarantee "Public Safety" by preventing Jefferson, "an atheist in religion, and a fanatic in politics, from getting possession of the helm of state."[43] Jay would have no part of it. True, like Hamilton he had

opposed the Declaration of Independence for fear of mob rule, and dislik-
ed Jefferson and his Jacobin friends, but he had already decided to retire
from politics and was, anyway, too cautious a man to allow himself to
be manipulated by Hamilton.

Thwarted in this resort to expediency, Hamilton turned his fury
against John Adams—that "weak and perverse man"—who had stripped Hamilton of his private army and dismissed his men in the cabinet.
There was no place for Adams's vacillation, however disguised as
moderation, in the executive of a great nation. Adams and Jefferson,
Hamilton now maintained were equally bad, but, so deep was his enmity for Adams, that he would prefer Jefferson in the presidency!
Hamilton's rationalization of this *volte-face* puts one in mind of his own
precept that man is a reasoning rather than a reasonable animal:

> If we must have an *enemy* at the head of the government, let it be one
> whom we can oppose, and for whom we are not responsible, who will
> not involve our party in the disgrace of his foolish and bad measures.
> Under *Adams*, as under *Jefferson*, the government will sink. The par-
> ty in the hands of whose chief it shall sink will sink with it, and the
> advantage will be all on the side of his adversaries.[44]

The pure, the elect, the pro-Hamilton Federalists must either rule or wash
their hands of all responsibility. It was all or nothing.

Hamilton decided to attack Adams himself in a pamphlet and to compare him in the most unfavorable light with Charles Pinckney of South
Carolina, a good and innocent man who knew nothing of the intrigue.
The aspersions on "The Public Conduct and Character of John Adams,
Esq., President of the United States," which Hamilton signed, were intended for limited circulation among Federalist leaders who might be
persuaded to drop Adams and line up behind Pinckney, Hamilton's can-
didate. Burr, however, had other ideas. He got hold of a copy of the
pamphlet and had it printed in the Republican newspapers, embarrassing the Federalists by exposing their intraparty quarrels to friend and
foe alike. Hamilton's stratagem was to no avail: Adams led the Federalist
ticket with Pinckney as his running mate. As for the Republicans,
Hamilton's fears were confirmed when Jefferson and Burr were named
as standard-bearers. "There seems to be too much probability that Jef-
fersion or Burr will be President," he wrote to James Bayard. If Burr
were the victor, Hamilton went on, "he will certainly attempt to reform

the government *á la Bonaparte*. He is as unprincipled and dangerous a man as any country can boast—as true a Cataline as ever met in midnight conclave.''[45]

This man Burr now began to appear to Hamilton as a greater rival than even Jefferson, perhaps because the two New Yorkers were uncannily so much alike in character. Both were professed admirers of Caesar—''the greatest man that ever lived''—and Napoleon (despite what Hamilton wrote to Bayard). Both were given to military fantasies and lusted after the presidency, which they saw as a powerful office from which to indulge their dreams of glory and conquest and save a tottering nation. Each was a soldier of proven courage, restless for battle and ever watching for the decisive campaign, but—unlike Washington—each man's character was flawed by an unsoldierly fondness for political and sexual intrigue and insubordination. As members of Washington's staff during the Revolutionary War, the two young men did not escape the General's reprimand which, however, Hamilton overcame with that happy combination of luck and manipulative skill which caused Washington to be his patron and Aegis until the very end. Hamilton, the intimate of Washington, rose to eminence as Secretary of the Treasury in the new nation, while Burr's career, lacking this high patronage, advanced less dramatically, with Hamilton keeping a close eye on the man whose path strangely was to cross his again and again over the next twenty years. Now, in 1800, in a rehearsal for their fatal duel on the Hudson, Hamilton and Burr stood face to face. At issue was not the senate, not a governorship as in the past, but the presidency itself, which each man in his utopian plan regarded as the key to total power.[46]

The Alien and Sedition Acts, higher taxes, and other major campaign issues all favored the Republicans in the presidential election, not to mention the disarray within the ranks of the Federalists occasioned by Hamilton's abuse of Adams. When the electoral votes were counted in February 1801, Jefferson and Burr led with 73 each. Accordingly, the election was thrown into the House of Representatives, where the Federalists had a majority, and where Hamilton believed that his influence, ever weakening, was still strong enough to declare Jefferson the winner. Cataline must be stopped, he pleaded with his fellow-Federalists. ''The public good must be paramount to every private consideration . . .''[47] Burr, devoid of every principle, meant to turn ''the worst part of the community" against "the better part." Here, Burr, dangerously close to the office they both wanted, was the man of passion, driven by self-love, the man of Hobbes and Calvin against whom Hamilton had sought to organize the perfect state where true freedom not license should prevail. Here was this man about to lead the masses, the non-elect, into the nation's governing circle.

Jefferson was elected president on the 36th ballot, not so much because of Hamilton's intervention as because Burr refused to make concessions to the Federalists. In Hamilton's view, the House had chosen the lesser evil, but with Jefferson President and Burr Vice-President there was hardly cause for celebration.

The year 1801 ended with greater tragedies for Hamilton. His eldest son, nineteen-year-old Philip, whom Hamilton looked upon as his successor, was killed in a duel in November with a New York City lawyer who had assailed Hamilton's policies in a recent speech. "Never did I see a man so completely overwhelmed with grief as Hamilton," a friend of many years remembered.[48] "The scene I was present at when Mrs. Hamilton came to see her son on his deathbed (he died about a mile out of the city) and when she met her husband & son in one room beggars all description!"[49] Hamilton was crushed. His eldest daugher, lovely Angelica, never recovered from her grief, and was considered insane the rest of her long life. And Mrs. Hamilton, who was later to lose her husband in the same way, barely held herself together.

Mrs. Hamilton, the "little saint," was long known as a woman of deep religious faith. Despite many trials, some caused by Hamilton's womanizing, she had always remained loyal to her husband. Now, her husband, shaken as never before by this family catastrophe, seemed too to have glimpsed the absolute dependence of man on God's will which his wife had always cherished and he himself had written about in a youthful description of the West Indian hurricane. "What is become of thy arrogance and self-sufficiency? . . . learn to know thy best support. Despise thyself and adore thy God."[50] Hamilton began studying the Bible, a son wrote years later, and also spent many hours perusing William Paley's *Evidences of Christianity* (1794). He led the family in prayer, and was observed by relatives and friends to be more loving and friendly than ever before.

Hamilton's earlier attitude towards religion had been merely exploitative. Religion was a thought-system, a socio-political concept rather than a personal relationship to God. It was a means for organizing the state of Hamilton's ideal conception, an ideological expedient for mobilizing public opinion against the French atheists, Jefferson and other American conspirators who planned to subvert the United States by promoting skepticism and disbelief. Religious ideas, he wrote in 1797 (note the typical intellectualistic reference to religious ideas rather than beliefs), should be enlisted in the nation's preparation for war with France.

> It may be proper by some religious solemnity to impress seriously the minds of the people. . . . A politician will consider this as an important means of influencing opinion, and will think it a valuable resource in a contest with France to set the religious ideas of his countrymen in active competition with the atheistical tenets of their enemies. This is an advantage which we shall be very unskilled if we do not use to the utmost. And the impulse can not be too early given. I am persuaded a day of humiliation and prayer, beside being very proper, would be extremely useful.[51]

Hamilton's caesarism, his totalitarianism, had excluded Christ except as a servant of the state.

There were, of course, echoes of Hobbes's Erastianism and contemporary continental Josephinism in this doctrine. And it smacks of that pragmatism, elaborated in the next century by William James and John Dewey, which as a variation of 18th century utilitarianism has become the American way of life. One is inclined to agree with Molnar and others that there is a type of "American intellectual," more a creative organizer for power and a social engineer than a philosophical thinker pursuing knowledge and truth for their own sake.[52] In this phase of his life, Hamilton was an American intellectual *par excellence*.

Even as late as 1802, when his naive Enlightenment secularism was waning, Hamilton tried again to use religion to win over the American people to a defense of the Constitution. Jefferson and Burr were in office and Hamilton, knowing the former's strict constructionist view of the Constitution and states-rights philosophy and holding the latter in contempt, believed the nation's charter to be in great danger. He had struggled for so long to perfect the Constitution, only now to see his doctrine of implied powers at the mercy of anti-Federalists. There was no way for him to know that Chief Justice John Marshall, appointed ironically, by "weak and perverse" John Adams the year before, would soon in *Marbury v. Madison* (1803) enunciate the doctrine of judicial supremacy and establish the power of the court by declaring an act of Congress unconstitutional. Marshall would, in effect, achieve that centralization of power in an elite that Hamilton had failed to secure by force of arms. At any rate, Hamilton now outlined a plan for a "Christian Constitutional Society," with chapters in each state, whose members would use "all lawful means in *concert* to promote the election of *fit* men" to public office, so that Jacobin enemies of Christianity and the Constitution would never again hold high office in the nation.[53] Whether his motive here was as coarse as before, we cannot determine. But there was a moderating provision in this scheme which was new—except its harking back, in the best sense, to medieval social charity—and one that perhaps shows that Hamilton's attitude towards Christianity was somewhat less exploitative than it had been. He now urged what he called a "Christian welfare program" in which vocational schools, academies, and other free institutions would help ensure the loyalties of the "different classes of mechanics" to the Hamiltonian state by preventing their being duped by foreign ideologists like Jefferson. The plan came to nought, but it demonstrates that Hamilton himself was still a secular ideologist, to some extent, in his reductionistic, socio-political conception of religion.

Hamilton in these years repeatedly spoke of retiring from the political scene and living the new life of religion that stirred within him. Yet, like Cincinnatus, he believed he must stand ready to draw his sword in defense of the nation he had founded. In the winter of 1804, Hamilton was alarmed by word that the man he had helped keep out of the White House was conspiring to dismember the Union. Burr, it was said, was seeking election as governor of New York so that he could deliver Hamilton's home state into the hands of a junto of New England secessionists led by Senator Timothy Pickering.[54] Pickering, a die-hard Federalist, had once been loyal to Hamilton's policy of radical nationalism, but disgruntled by Jefferson's acquisition of Louisiana and its implications for New England, he was sadly playing the traitor by intriguing with the American Cataline, who was using Pickering and other extremists for his own self-aggrandisment. The Hamiltonian state, the bullwark of order against man's depraved nature, was in the gravest jeopardy ever. Burr, to Hamilton, was the very personification of that danger, the man in whom all the evils of social and personal disorder seemed concentrated. Was he also, buried at some deeper level of the unconscious, Hamilton's other self? And was the duel they would soon fight the ultimate encounter?

In the gubernatorial campaign that winter and spring, Hamilton lashed out against Burr on every occasion. The *Albany Register* and other newpapers printed letters in which Hamilton was reported to have denounced Burr as "a dangerous man, and one who ought not to be trusted with the reins of government."[55] They hinted too that Hamilton had not hesitated to vent his "despicable opinion" of Burr in language even more vituperative. Burr decided to do nothing about these insults before the election. Obviously, though, they must be answered in some way, as they were public accusations and, by the accepted code of honor at the time, required Burr to take the initiative or be branded a coward.

The vote in April, overwhelmingly rejecting Burr, marked the end of his political career. There was still the matter of his honor. On June 18, Burr wrote a letter to Hamilton demanding "a prompt and unqualified acknowledgment or denial of the use of any expressions" like those which the newspaper reports attributed to Hamilton during the recent campaign.[56] This began the exchange of letters and representations through seconds which led to the duel—or interview, as it was called—at Weehawken almost a month later.

Hamilton kept the duel a secret from Eliza. But one week before his death, he sat down at his desk and, holding back the tears, wrote a letter to be given to her in the event of his death:

> This letter, my very dear Eliza, will not be delivered to you unless I shall first have terminated my earthly career, to begin, as I humbly hope, from redeeming grace and divine mercy, a happy immortality. If it had been possible for me to have avoided the interview, my love for you and my precious children would have been alone a decisive motive. But it was not possible, without sacrifices which would have rendered me unworthy of your esteem. I need not tell you of the pangs I feel from the idea of quitting you, and exposing you to the anguish which I know you would feel. Nor could I dwell on the topic lest it should unman me. The consolations of Religion, my beloved, can alone support you; and these you have a right to enjoy. Fly to the bosom of your God and be comforted. With my last idea I shall cherish the sweet hope of meeting you in a better world. Adieu best of wives—best of women. Embrace all my darling children for me.[57]

And the night before the duel Hamilton seems to have turned as a matter of course to Theodore Sedgwick, an old friend and anti-Burrite, to explain—as he could not to his wife—why he must risk his life, even die if necessary, to stop Burr and the other secessionists from destroying the Hamiltonian empire. "I will here express but one sentiment," he condensed his political philosophy into one final testament, "which is, that dismemberment of our empire will be a clear sacrifice of great positive advantages without any counter-balancing good, administering no relief to our real disease, which is *democracy*, the poison of which, by a subdivision, will only be the more concentrated in each part, and consequently the more virulent."[58]

The dilemma for Hamilton was a new one and the most formidable of his life. He must meet Burr, pistol in hand, on the heights of Weehawken, or appear to the world not only cowardly but unworthy of the moral leadership of the great empire which was his creation. Yet, as a serious Christian, he must not kill. This dilemma of choosing between Caesar and Christ in the most personal, existential sense could be resolved in only one way. In his final letter to Eliza, written at 10:00 P.M. the eve of the fatal interview, Hamilton described what he would do:

> The scruples of a Christian have determined me to expose my own life to any extent rather than subject myself to the guilt of taking the life of another. This much increases my hazards, and redoubles my pangs for you. But you had rather I should die innocent than live guilty. Heaven can preserve me, and I humbly hope will; but in the contrary event I charge you to remember that you are a Christian. God's will be done! The will of a merciful God must be good.[59]

Then, in a tender gesture of love for his dead son, Philip, and all his children, Hamilton lay down next to twelve-year-old John and recited with him the Lord's prayer.

The next morning, July 11, 1804, Hamilton was mortally wounded by Aaron Burr as they faced each other—nationalist and disunionist—for the last time on the banks of the Hudson. The evil passions of man, which Hamilton had sought futilely to transcend mechanically in some visionary social and political system, were now overcome and transcended spiritually in Hamilton himself by an act of love for his fellow man in Christ. As he had said he would, in his letter to Eliza and in a memorandum discovered after his death, Hamilton had reserved and thrown away his first fire, even his second.

As he lay dying in the bosom of his loving family, one thing alone remained for Hamilton. He sent for Bishop Richard Moore, Episcopalian bishop of New York, and begged to be united to the church by receiving Holy Communion. "Do you sincerely repent of your sins past? Have you a lively faith in God's mercy through Christ, with a thankful remembrance of the death of Christ? And are you disposed to live in love and charity with all men?" Yes, yes, yes. "I have no ill-will against Colonel Burr. I met him with a fixed resolution to do him no harm. I forgive all that happened."[60]

## NOTES

[1]Quoted in Nathan Schachner, *Alexander Hamilton* (New York: D. Appleton-Century Company, Inc., 1946), p. 25.

[2]*Ibid.*, p. 23.

[3]*Ibid.*, pp 1-15; Harold C. Syrett and Jean G. Cooke, ed., *Interview in Weehawken: The Burr-Hamilton Duel As Told in the Original Documents*, Introduction and Conclusion by Willard M. Wallace (Middletown, Conn.: Wesleyan University Press, 1960), p. 164. Insightful on Hamilton's religious development is Douglass Adair and Marvin Harvey, "Was Alexander Hamilton a Christian Statesman," originally published in the *William & Mary Quarterly*, 3rd Series, XII (April 1955) and reprinted in Jacob E. Cooke, ed., *Alexander Hamilton; A Profile* (New York: Hill and Wang, 1967), pp. 230-255.

[4]Schachner, pp. 7. 18. 20.

[5]Quoted in *ibid.*, p. 19.

[6]*Ibid.*, p. 31.

[7]*Ibid.*, p. 34, 39-40; Charles H. Metzger, S.J., *Catholics and the American Revolution: A Study in Religious Climate* (Chicago: Loyola University Press, 1962).

[8]Quoted in Schachner, p. 19.

[9]*Ibid.*, p. 45.

[10]*Ibid.*, pp. 56, 10.

[11]Allan Nevins, "Alexander Hamilton," in the *Dictionary of American Biography*: Broadus Mitchell, "The Continentalist," in Cooke, p. 41.

[12]Schachner, pp. 144-146; Mitchell, p. 46; John A. Krout, "Philip Schuyler," in the *Dictionary of American Biography*.

[13]Quoted in Schachner, pp. 190, 187.

[14]*Ibid.*, pp. 190, 194. It is interesting to compare the two men in their social and political orientations. Hamilton, an immigrant, wanted to be one of "the better sort," as the upper-class was called in early America. He wanted to be

at the top of the deferential society and be a leader in the politics of status. Clinton, the son of an Irish immigrant, worked to replace the politics of status with one of multiple interests. See E. Wilder Spaulding, *His Excellency George Clinton* (1938), and William Chambers's "George Clinton" in John A. Garraty, ed., *Encyclopedia of American Biography* (New York: Harper & Row, Pub., 1974).

[15]Schachner, p. 196; Mitchell, p. 49.

[16]Schachner, p. 196.

[17]Claude G. Bowers, "Hamilton: A Portrait," in Cooke, p. 19; Schachner, pp. 208, 211-214. See C. Edward Merriam, *A History of American Political Theories* (New York: The Macmillan Co., 1903), pp. 100-122. For Clinton's "Cato" Letters, see Cecelia M. Kenyon, ed., *The Antifederalists* (Indianapolis: Bobbs-Merrill Co., Inc., 1966), pp. 301-322.

[18]Quoted in Adrienne Koch, "Hamilton and Power," in Cooke, p. 17. Also see *idem., Power, Morals, and the Founding Fathers; Essays in the Interpretation of the American Enlightenment* (Ithaca, New York: Cornell University Press, 1963), ch. iv., pp. 50-80. Cf. *The Federalist* No. 15 in Milton Cantor, ed., *Hamilton* (Prentice-Hall, 1971), pp. 51-53.

[19]Quoted in Koch, "Hamilton and Power," p. 217.

[20]Clinton Rossiter, "Hamilton's Political Science," Cooke, pp. 207-208.

[21]Quoted in *ibid.*, 213; Thomas Molnar, *Utopia: The Perennial Heresy* (New York: Sheed and Ward, 1967), p. 10; Cecelia M. Kenyon, "Alexander Hamilton: Rousseau of the Right," Cooke, pp. 166-184.

[22]Quoted in Rossiter, p. 213.

[23]*Ibid.*, 198.

[24]Quoted in in Kenyon, p. 173.

[25]*Ibid.*, pp. 175-182.

[26]Hamilton to James A. Bayard, January 16, 1801, Henry Cabot Lodge, ed., *The Works of Alexander Hamilton* (New York, 1904), X, p. 415.

[27]Rossiter, p. 189.

[28]Kenyon, p. 183. Miss Kenyon's essay is perceptive, but her understanding of the Middle Ages, whose social and political philosophy she likens to that of Hamilton, (pp. 178-179), is superficial.

[29]Quoted in Schachner, p. 335; Molnar, *Utopia*, p. 7.

[30]Cf. "Subsidiarity" in Walter Brugger, ed., *Philosophical Dictionary*, trans. Kenneth Baker (Spokane, Washington: Gonzaga University Press, 1972), pp. 397-398; Molnar, p. 139; Jacob E. Cooke, "The Reports of Alexander Hamilton," in Cooke, p. 74; Thomas Molnar, *The Decline of the Intellectual* (New Rochelle, New York: Arlington House, 1961), pp. 334-338.

[31]Quoted in George H. Sabine, *A History of Political Theory* (3rd. ed.; New York; Holt, Rinehart and Winston, 1966), p. 600; Molnar, *Utopia*, p. 167; Rossiter, p. 187.

[32]Sabine, pp. 603-605; Molnar, *Utopia*, p. 7; Koch, *Power, Morals, and the Founding Fathers*, p. 112.

[33]For an excellent discussion of usury, subsidiarity, and other social prin-

ciples, see Cletus Dirksen C.P.P.S., *Catholic Social Principles* (St. Louis Mo.: B. Herder Book Co., 1961), p. 186 *et passim*.

[34]Koch, "Hamilton and Power," p. 222; Nevins, "Alexander Hamilton."
[35]Dirksen, pp. 64-65; Molnar, *Decline of the Intellectual*, p. 349.
[36]Nevins, "Alexander Hamilton;" Dirksen, p. 214. John C. Miller deals with the paradoxical nature of Hamitlon's career in his *Alexander Hamilton: Portrait in Paradox* (New York, 1959)
[37]Felix Gilbert, "Hamilton and the 'Farewell Address,' " Cooke, p. 116.
[38]*Decline of the Intellectual*, p. 333; Kenyon. p. 179.
[39]Nevins, "Alexander Hamilton."
[40]On Washington as Hamilton's "Aegis," Koch, "Hamilton and Power," p. 224; Schachner, pp. 386-387; Nevins, "Alexander Hamilton."
[41]Quoted in Schachner, pp. 386, 387.
[42]Koch, "Hamilton and power," pp. 220-226.
[43]Quoted in Adair and Harvey, Cooke, p. 245; Samuel Flagg Bemis, "John Jay," *Dictionary of American Biography*.
[44]Quoted in Schachner, p. 394. For Hamilton's characterization of Adams, see Adair and Harvey, p. 243.
[45]Quoted in Schachner, pp. 396-397.
[46]Quoted in Koch, "Hamilton and Power," p. 223; Willard M. Wallace's Introduction to Syrett and Cooke, *Interview in Weehawken*, pp. 3-35; Marcus Cunliffe, "Aaron Burr," in *The Encyclopedia of American Biography*. For a less unprejudiced comparison of the two men, see Allan McLane Hamilton, *The Intimate Life of Alexander Hamilton* (New York: Charles Scribner's Sons, 1911) *et passim*.
[47]Quoted in Syrett and Cooke, p. 29; John C. Miller, *The Federalist Era 1789-1801* (New York: Harper & Row, Pub., 1963), ch. xiv, pp. 251-277.
[48]Quoted in Schachner, p. 408; Miller, *The Federalist Era*, p. 272.
[49]Quoted in Schachner, p. 408.
[50]Ibid., pp. 25, 108; Hamilton, *The Intimate Life of Alexander Hamilton*, p. 109.
[51]Hamilton to William L. Smith, April 10, 1797, William L. Smith Papers, Library of Congress, quoted by Adair and Harvey, p. 24On. *ibid*, p. 248; Molnar, *Decline of the Intellectual*, p. 336.
[52]*Ibid.*, ch. ix, pp. 260-288; Sabine, *A History of Political Theory*, pp. 303, 372.
[53]Schachner, p. 412.
[54]Adair and Harvey, p. 252.
[55]Quoted in Schachner, p. 422; Hamilton, *The Intimate Life of Alexander Hamilton*, p. 390.
[56]Quoted in Schachner, p. 423.
[57]Quoted in Hamilton, *The Intimate Life of Alexander Hamilton*, pp. 393-394.
[58]Quoted in Schachner, p. 427.
[59]Quoted in Hamilton, *The Intimate Life of Alexander Hamilton*, pp. 394-395.
[60]*Ibid.*, p. 406n.

# 7.
# Benjamin Franklin
# Poor Richard's Religion

In September 1767 Dr. Benjamin Franklin, retired printer and colonial agent, visited Paris for the first time. Like so many other tourists then and now, he visited the Cathedral of Notre Dame, but Franklin did so not for religious or aesthetic reasons but because he wanted to see the spectacular illumination presented to the city of Paris by the royal family. Later, as American commissioner and minister to the French court, Franklin would spend many years in Paris. He would never return to Notre Dame, however, a place, where he said, he could not have "any conceivable business."[1]

Of course, Franklin, like John Adams and so many other Americans of Calvinist background, could hardly be expected to admire in prayerful silence the Virgin's church, where the mother of God is glorified in magnificent portals and bas-reliefs and where the very "labors of the months are given their order in relation to her."[2] The skeptical Americans failed to see other than mariolatry in the centuries-old veneration of Theotokos. This is true; yet there is a further distinguishing characteristic of Franklin which more than any other helps explain his attitude towards Notre Dame and his life and thought in general. Benjamin Franklin was a printer, not just as a means to a competent living among the bourgeoisie of Philadelphia but in the deepest recesses of his personality; and Notre Dame de Paris like other cathedrals, so Victor Hugo observed with genius, was a book of stone—not the kind Franklin was used to. Franklin's pre-Reformation ancestors had discovered in the statues, stained glass windows, and liturgical plays of medieval cathedrals the great doctrinal truths of their Catholic faith. But while they had read the Gothic words of sculptured stone, in which medieval art presented the mind of the times, their "bookish" 18th century descendent read almost exclusively in linear print. For the printed book of Gutenberg, which Franklin and other printers could now manufacture with relative ease, was fast replacing the medieval book of stone. "The Gothic sun," Victor Hugo discerned, was setting "behind the great printing press of Mainz."[3]

Franklin was a printer and tradesman who, perhaps more than any other man, symbolized the aspirations and new dignity of labor in the early modern world. It was perfectly appropriate that in his last will and testament of 1790 he should identify himself first as "Benjamin Franklin, printer," and only then mention his high offices in the United States and Pennsylvania governments. All his life he had, so they say in the trade, the "smell of printer's ink" about him; and, appropriately enough, to this day Franklin appears in the popular imagination as a simple, honest craftsman in his plain, leather apron. Never mind his masterly diplomatic skill and intrigue among the "powdered heads of Paris." Franklin was a tradesman at heart and was proud of it. He liked nothing better than to see "good workmen handle their tools" and was ever grateful to his father, Josiah Franklin, a tallow chandler and soap boiler who taught him how to make things with his own hands.[4] It was this mechanical ability, combined with a native empirical temperament, that enabled Franklin himself to construct the apparatus for those experiments that won him recognition by the international scientific community and earned the American philosopher the admiration of men as diverse as Immanuel Kant and Sir Humphrey Davy.[5] And it was the same tradesman's outlook, albeit raised and expanded into a conscious doctrine of reality by keen intelligence, that gives Franklin's life and thought a unity of character.

Benjamin Franklin was born in Boston on January 17, 1706, one of fifteen children of Josiah and Abiah Franklin. "I remember often to have seen thirteen sitting together at his table," he wrote more than a half century later, "who all grew up to years of maturity and married."[6] Josiah was a pious man, a strict Congregationalist, and for a while intended that Benjamin, his tenth son, should go into the ministry. The boy was quick to learn almost everything, but not the doctrines of Calvinism. His father's books on religious controversies, in fact, had the opposite effect: Benjamin not only acquired a lifelong *odium theologicum*, he even stopped going to public worship whenever he could and used the time he saved for reading and writing.[7]

Josiah Franklin was realist enough to see that his son was not destined for a pulpit and that Benjamin's love of the written word and mechanical aptitude counselled the printer's trade as the next best thing. Never did a father judge his child's trade and future with more perspicacity, at least in terms of the outcome. From his printing press, Benjamin Franklin would influence millions of people in his lifetime as the author of *Poor Richard's Almanack* and other books, treatises, essays, and pamphlets on subjects ranging from electricity and demography to politics and marriage. He would exploit, as John Adams recognized, the "full power of the press."[8] And, like Erasmus of Rotterdam and the humanists of an earlier day—but without their spiritual genius, as we shall see—Franklin would use his printing press to enlighten mankind. Josiah's brilliant son, to his parents's sorrow, would be no Old Testament prophet of New England Calvinism but a herald of Enlightenment secularism.

When he wrote his autobiography late in life, Franklin recalled that in his father's library were two books that, unlike the other heavy theological reading, made a deep and favorable impression upon him. Daniel Defoe's *Essays on Projects* and Cotton Mather's *Essays to do Good* both offered the young man practical advice on how to help his fellow man. Defoe, for example, in one of his projects inspired Franklin with the idea of insurance for widows, a project which he soon advanced in print. But it was the Reverend Cotton Mather who provided the doubting Calvinist with a theology of benevolence, as it were, one that seemed to reduce personal salvation to the doing of good works. The book, Franklin noted in a letter to Mather's son in 1784, "gave me such a turn of thinking, as to have an influence on my conduct through life; for I have always set a greater value on the character of a *doer of good*, than on any other kind of reputation; and if I have been, as you seem to think, a useful citizen, the public owes the advantage of it to that book."[9] Cotton Mather was, Franklin knew, no worldly Enlightenment philosopher: the charity he urged was profoundly theological. This Christian understanding of brotherly love as a supernatural virtue, Franklin chose to ignore—indeed, throughout his long life could never appreciate—and in his characteristically practical way fastened on Mather's message as one of simple humanitarianism.

The precocious young man was at last placed in his brother James's print shop as an apprentice. Books of all sorts were now made available

to him, since he could borrow precious volumes from his fellow apprentices in the shops of Boston. Sometimes he burnt his candle into the wee
hours of the night to finish reading a book taken off the press without
permission. This was a new form of bibliolatry for a son of New England.
Printer's ink and paper became in these years so much a part of him
that, when he composed his famous epitaph in 1728, he compared "the
body of B. Franklin, Printer" to the "cover of an old book, its contents
torn out, and stript of its lettering and gilding."[10]

He read John Locke's renowned *Essay Concerning Human
Understanding*, a study which philosophically justified an empiricism
Franklin already possessed constitutionally and which his new
tradesman's life confirmed. He stole time away from his lunch periods
and Sunday religious services to mull over Shaftesbury's *Characteristics
of Men*, which attacked revealed religion, and probably, Anthony Collins's iconoclastic *Discourse on Free-Thinking*. These books, especially
those of the last-named moral philosophers, so undermined Franklin's
Calvinist faith that he remained the rest of his life a non-believer. Along
with the chatty, bourgeois *Spectator*, which brought philosophy out of
the closets and universities and into the clubs, assemblies, and print
shops—papers Franklin consumed mainly for their style—and
Xenophon's biography of Socrates, the works of Newtonians like Locke,
Shaftesbury, and Collins formed the *Weltanshauung* of the young man
who would become America's most representative Enlightenment
thinker.[11]

Locke's *Essay Concerning Human Understanding* denied the existence of innate ideas, showing in lucid prose that all knowledge and
truth were derived from experience. This could not but discredit to
Franklin's alert intelligence the Christian doctrine of Original sin, as
the burden of Locke's argument was that man's mind is *tabula rasa* at
birth and there was, consequently, no possible stain on human nature.
It was clear to Franklin then and afterwards that, despite the work of
his great contemporary, Jonathan Edwards, modern science had exploded
once and for all the myth of Adam's sin and its transmission to all men,
the characteristic "innate" idea of Calvinism.

Shaftesbury, Locke's friend, contributed a much more positive ele-
ment to Franklin's philosophy, one that the American conceived to be
truly scientific in the Age of Newton. The very harmony and perfection

of the Newtonian universe, said the Deist Shaftesbury, provided the mature thinker with the only universal religion: the love of the true, the good, and the beautiful. The religion of reason was not theology but morality, Franklin learned. Shaftesbury could be made to agree with Cotton Mather, so he discovered, by purging the *Essays to do Good* of all theological obscurantism and treating the work as an exemplary manual of Enlightenment benevolence.

If these authors contributed the substance of Franklin's philosophy of life, Xenophon's *Memorabilia* indicated the method of Socratic irony he would follow in practice. "I was charmed with it, adopted it, dropped my abrupt contradiction and positive argumentation, and put on the humble enquirer," Franklin wrote.[12] He found the method just as devastating against orthodox Calvinists in the streets of Boston as it had been against 5th century Athenians. But, as he implies, the cause he made the method serve was not always truth, for by now young Franklin was more than a little skeptical about absolutes. He had adopted Socrates's means, while failing to rise to the noble end, the vision of truth, for which the great philosopher had designed it. This divorce of means from ends was precisely what Socrates had condemned. In any case, Franklin's pragmatism, seen here and throughout his thought in general, converted the means into an end, so that he developed "the habit of expressing myself in terms of modest diffidence, never using when I advance anything that may possibly be disputed the words, 'certainly,' 'undoubtedly,' or any others that give the air of positiveness to an opinion; but rather say, 'I conceive or apprehend a thing to be so or so,' 'It appears to me.'"[13] This was the way to influence people for the good, since it avoided all opposition and dogmatism. It was also, according to John Adams, one of Franklin's severest critics, cowardly.[14] At any rate, Franklin was to make *Poor Richard* say that, if you "would persuade, speak of interest, not of reason."[15]

It was not so much that Franklin was rejecting absolute truth outright. Such nihilism was never a part of his nor the Enlightenment's character. Nor did the bourgeois philosopher feel the need to articulate a theory of knowledge beyond what Matthew Arnold hailed as "imperturbable common sense."[16] The source of knowledge for Franklin, as for Shaftesbury—another man of action—lay in nature and the empirically useful. It was this radically optimistic philosophy that motivated Franklin in all his works of benevolence, whether in explaining electricity or inventing the stove that bears his name. Although no Christian himself, at least in any recognizably theological sense, he could still accept faith, hope, and pre-eminently, charity, but as the natural virtues within man's original endowment. Leisure existed for the discovery of truth, of the useful and the good, in the sense of Shaftesbury's definition. "I have sometimes had occasion to say," the author of *Poor Richard's Almanack* made a favorite point in 1783, "that it is prodigious the quantity of good that may be done by one man, *if he will make a business of it.*"[17]

Many years later, Franklin nobly lamented the effect of his youthful Deism and iconoclastic practice in turning friends away from their traditional religious beliefs. By then he had come to realize the wisdom of Shaftesbury's and other Enlightenment moralists' teaching, so he believed, that the cultivated man of sensibility should not dispute with others those less philosophical doctrines like Christianity, which comfort and console the multitude. William James and other American thinkers of the same outlook called this in the next century the pragmatic justification of faith. It was not with the mature Franklin meant to be a condescension, rather an expression of "humility" before what he as a positivist considered the great Unknown. A disarming story Franklin liked to tell about his visit to Cotton Mather in 1723 best illustrates the ideal of humility that he aspired to in all things:

> As I was taking my leave he accompanied me through a narrow passage at which I did not enter, and which had a beam across it lower than my head. He continued talking which occasioned me to keep my face partly towards him as I retired, when he suddenly cried out, Stoop! Not immediately understanding what he meant, I hit my head hard against the beam. He then added, *Let this be a caution to you not always to hold your head so high; Stoop, young man, stoop—as you go through the world—and you'll miss many hard thumps.* This was a way of hammering instruction into one's head (Franklin always enjoyed a pun). And it was so far effectual, that I have ever since remembered it, though I have not always been able to practice it.[18]

As he grew older, Franklin would learn to "stoop" a little before other people's religious beliefs, to doubt his own "infallibility," as he put it.[19] But in his early years, the "bookish" young genius from New England was Voltairean enough in his assault on religious superstition and priestcraft.

The optimism of Shaftesbury and his followers among the English Deists, and on the Continent where Leibniz himself was influenced by his ideas, reflected the Age's Newtonian world-view. Alexander Pope, the muse of the Enlightenment and one of Franklin's favorites, sang of this optimism in his well-known couplet that "Nature and nature's laws lay hid in night; God said, let Newton be, and all was light."[20] As publisher of *Poor Richard's Almanack*, Franklin more than any other American, was to be responsible for the cult of Newton in the colonies. The same cheery Enlightenment optimism about the intelligibility of reality is found in its pages along with invocations of the great man's name. And if at last Franklin should be celebrated as the "Newton of Electricity," it was a fitting tribute for the printer-philosopher. Moreover, Newton had stopped short of trying to explain the cause of universal gravitation, "stooping" before the inner mystery of action at a distance. Franklin came to adopt the same attitude toward what he considered the nature of ultimate Being, or God.

Suffice to say the Newtonian world-machine revealed in its operations the existence of a benevolent Creator. "It sometimes is cloudy, it rains, it hails; again 'tis clear and pleasant, and the sun shines on us," Franklin echoed the Newtonian optimism and ethical ideas of Shaftesbury and the English Deists. "Take one thing with another, and the world is a pretty good sort of a world; and 'tis our duty to make the best of it and be thankful. One's true happiness depends more upon one's own judgement of one's self, on a consciousness of rectitude in action and intention, and in the approbation of those few who judge impartially, than upon the applause of the unthinking, undiscerning multitude, who are apt to cry hosanna today, and tomorrow, crucify him."[21]

Franklin left Boston in 1723. His brother James, his master in the print shop, had a wild temper which he often vented on poor Benjamin, who finally broke his indenture and fled the city. This was an object lesson in "arbitrary power" that Franklin never forgot. Besides the problems in his apprenticeship, including his brother's vindictive black-listing of the young man among the printers of Boston, there was Franklin's unpopularity with the leaders of the city's government on account of "some rubs" he had given them in the pages of the family newspaper. Benjamin knew it was time to move, too, when the "good people" in town began referring to him as the village atheist. Even his father, it seemed, had turned against him. Perhaps in New York he could find work; so he sold part of his little library and got aboard a sloop bound for the nearest city where he thought a printer might find a competence. Things would be better there.[22]

In New York, where there was not enough work for the one resident printer, William Bradford, Franklin was advised to go on to Philadelphia. Bradford's son had a press there and was looking for help. Franklin related his colorful adventures on the way to Philadephia in his autobiography. After a stormy passage from Amboy to Burlington, New Jersey, he came upon a country inn run by an "infidel" doctor. They struck up a friendship that lasted a lifetime, the two having probably been brought together by their common reading in Shaftesbury and Collins.[23]

When Franklin finally arrived in the "City of Brotherly Love" on that cold October morning, his clothes were dirty and his pockets "stuffed out with shirts and stockings." His walking up Market Street eating one "great puffy" roll while balancing one under each arm is a familiar picture from the autobiography. Every reader of Franklin's memoirs knows, too, of how the young man found work at Samuel Keimer's shop; and how soon afterwards he met Sir William Keith, Governor of Pennsylvania, through his brother-in-law's intervention. Franklin's life, like that of so many other great men, is filled with instances of such happy circumstances that smoothed the way to eminence. The man himself also had a talent for orchestrating the events of his life to advantage without the slightest hint of crass opportunism. It was Gov. Keith who promised Franklin he would set him up in the printing business, if Franklin would go to London to make arrangements for the necessary supplies. The governor proved unreliable in the end, but it was his promise of help that emboldened the eighteen-year-old printer's apprentice to leave for England in 1724. There, thrown completely on his own resources, not even possessed of the letters of introduction Keith had irresponsibly forgotten to provide, Franklin succeeded in finding work at a major printery.[24]

One of the books Palmer's London printing house was scheduled to publish was William Wollaston's *Religion of Nature*, and Franklin was asked to compose the type. As he was setting it up, he became more and more involved in many of the author's "reasonings" until he realized he must reject them; for Franklin could not simply compose type like most modern printers, he must read and understand it. The result was his first—and last—strictly philosophical essay. A *Dissertation on Liberty and Necessity, Pleasure and Pain* reveals Franklin's wide reading in Deistic literature, especially Shaftesbury. Written ostensibly to refute Wollaston's assertion that man is free, the *Dissertation* has more biographical than philosophical value, in that it clearly showed the extent to which Franklin was a disciple of Shaftesbury's cosmic utopianism. If God is omnipotent, Franklin argues, "there can be nothing either existing or acting in the universe against or without his consent; and what He consents to must be good, because He is good; therefore evil doth not exist."[25]

Franklin's youthful logic, like that of Shaftesbury—and Voltaire's Dr. Pangloss later—was simple. Only good can come from the omnipotent, all-benevolent, and omniscient God; hence, evil cannot exist. It was the old problem that, notably, St. Augustine had struggled with in his refutation of Manchaeism, but neither Shaftesbury nor Franklin and the Deists of the Enlightenment apparently knew its history. Man, Franklin continued in his Newtonian style of thought, is "a part of this great machine, the universe," and "his regular acting is requisite to the regular moving of the whole."[26] "All the heavenly bodies, the stars and planets, are regulated with the utmost wisdom! And can we suppose less care to be taken in the order of the *moral* than in the *natural* system?"[27] Assuredly not, Franklin concluded. An "all-wise Providence" governed both the moral and natural systems. There was "no such thing as free-will" and, consequently, "neither merit nor demerit." And most important, all creatures—men as well as "the beasts of the field"—were equal before the Creator. This, indeed was the best of all possible worlds!

This of course, was written long before the Lisbon earthquake, which caused grave doubts in Voltaire's mind about Shaftesbury's theodicy, and the Robespierrean Reign of Terror which the French philosopher and Franklin mercifully escaped seeing in their day. Even so, by the late 18th century Franklin had abandoned this radical optimism by his own confession. Had he lived beyond 1790, he presumably would not have been incredulous over the guillotining of his French friends, but he would have been deeply appalled.

As youthful a performance as the *Dissertation* was, it nevertheless combined with Franklin's peculiar genius the leading themes of Enlightenment thought. There was Shaftesbury's high religion of cosmic perfection, synthesized with Locke's epistemology and Newton's atomic theory. But there was also the persistence of New England Calvinism, secularized to be sure, in Franklin's belief in the absolute sovereignty of the Creator. His argument from determinism, in fact, puts one in mind of Jonathan Edwards's more subtle refutation of freedom of the will on the basis of the impossibility of a motiveless choice. Franklin, so he tells us in the autobiography, found the basic "dogmas" of Calvinism "unintelligible." Election, reprobation, and the inherited Original Sin that they presupposed, Franklin was honestly incapable of understanding. He was too much the naturalist to enter into the Edwardsian mentality. The great New England theologian would have explained this constitutional deficiency in terms of Franklin's not being a saint, i.e. of possessing only the five physical senses and not the additional higher supernatural sense that God, according to Edwards, grants to the elect. In any case, Franklin in the *Dissertation* kept the Calvinist apparatus of determinism while rejecting the orthodox theology of Original and personal sin. Other New England apostates, Ralph Waldo Emerson and Orestes Brownson, for example, would also transform orthodox Calvinism into some form of universalism under the impact of liberalism, the latter finally attaining the truth in Catholicism and Franklin and Emerson finding their resting place in more philosophical than religious doctrines.[28]

Franklin's formal break with Calvinistic and other varieties of strict determinism came some eight years later after his return to the colonies. By then, as an ambitious businessman in Philadelphia, he had established in his own mind the reality of his and other men's volitions. His essay, "On the Providence of God in the Government of the World," written for the Junto or club he founded in 1727, grapples with perhaps the major problem in Franklin's philosophical thought, and asks why the God who "has made us in some degree wise, potent and good" cannot "make us also in some degree free?"[29] Even more decisive for Franklin than this philosophical argument, harkening back at least to St. Thomas, was his awareness that man's "free agency" was necessary for those works of charity without which he believed religion was a mere sham. The essay on Providence remained Franklin's most thorough study of the question. With the passing years, he moved farther away from Calvin's deterministic logic to a position in which he seemed to regard man's freedom as almost absolute. Yet, for all this 18th century existentialism, Franklin kept to the end a confidence in God's mercy bordering on the presumptuous. Evidently, he was never terrified, as were Charles Carroll and Benjamin Rush, at the thought of losing God's friendship. His moods of pessimism, and they were deep, were fleeting, and were brought on by man's actions, not God's, e.g., British atrocities during the War for American Independence. As for evil itself, Franklin posed his humanist solution in 1763: "An answer now occurs to me," he wrote a philosophical friend, "for that question of Robinson Crusoe's man Friday, which I once thought unanswerable, *Why God no kill the Devil? It is to be found in the Scottish proverb; Ye'd do little for God an the Deel were dead.* "[30]

The mature Franklin considered the publication of the *Dissertation*, in the jargon of the printer's trade, one of the "errata" of his life. He probably meant that the essay was not only faulty in its principles but productive of that vanity which Franklin the moralist struggled to remove from his character. Mr. Palmer, the owner of the London print shop, now treated Franklin as a genius, if a mistaken one in his youthful determinism. The local Deists and free-thinkers, in which London abounded at the time, soon learned of the pamphlet, and Franklin was invited to meet a number of them, including the famous Dr. Bernard Mandeville, who had just recently published his *Fable of the Bees; or Private Vices, Public Benefits*, and Dr. Henry Pemberton, who was at the time preparing a new edition of Newton's *Principia*. The latter promised to introduce young Franklin to the greatest scientist of the age, but this never took place. Franklin did find his way into the company of Sir Hans Sloan, naturalist and future president of the Royal Society of London, who entertained the American in his home and purchased form him a New World curiosity from his elaborate collection.[31]

When he began his autobiography in 1771 and remembered these early years in London, Franklin recorded in detail what was probably his first encounter with Roman Catholicism. He was young and free—"under no religious restraint"—and had just given, willy nilly, in his *Dissertation*, a philosophical justification for moral license. His secularized Calvinism, with its naive determinism, was then just as inimical to the Catholic doctrine of freedom as the orthodox version. And the claims of Revelation, which are linked so intimately with Roman Catholicism, drew from young Franklin the ridicule that Shaftesbury, Collins, and others had proposed as the test of truth. It was with these predispositions that he took lodgings with a Roman Catholic widow on Duke Street, just across the street from the "Romanish chapel."[32]

Franklin's landlady was a convert to the faith, he noted, and "had lived much among people of distinction," of whom she had many anecdotes to tell. In the garret of the house lived another elderly Catholic woman. She had been sent abroad as a girl to become a nun, but not liking it there had returned to England and resolved to continue living as a nun in the secular world. Giving her estate to charity, and keeping only a small allowance to live on, this nameless, saintly woman ate only water gruel and dwelt in a plain, clean room with a mattress, a table surmounted by a crucifix and Bible, and a stool. Franklin was struck by these details, when he was permitted by his landlady to visit the garret, but especially by the picture of Veronica's veil which hung above the fireplace. This picture of "Christ's bleeding face" was her one great treasure, and "with great seriousness" she regaled the Deistic ex-Puritan with the story of the miracle. Franklin believed in neither saints—even though he now met one—nor in relics, he did in time come to accept particular providences or what might be called "miracles." The moralist in him, when he penned his memoirs, nevertheless discerned in the lady of the garret the same battle against vanity that he himself was waging. She was confessed daily by a priest. Why? Because, she said, "it is impossible to avoid *vain thoughts* (Franklin's italics)."[33] When Franklin returned to London in 1757, he went looking for the old "nun." He climbed to the garret room, which was exactly as he had last seen it thirty-three years ago, but the lady of the garret was gone, probably dead.

Among the passengers aboard the *Berkshire* when she sailed from London on July 21, 1726, bound for Philadelphia, were the Quaker merchant, Thomas Denham, and his new business associate, Benjamin Franklin. The two men had met coming over to England, and Denham had taken a liking to the younger printer whom he now invited to work for him in a store that he planned to open in the Pennsylvania city. The voyage took almost three months, and Franklin, as usual, occupied every moment of it with some practical purpose. He had leisure enough to examine his life so far and consider the prospects of his new mercantile career. It now occurred to him that he must have a plan to regulate his life, that he must "make some resolutions, and form some scheme of action, that, henceforth, I may live in all respects like a rational creature."[34] Franklin's "Plan of Conduct" was the result of this decision. Either he did not see that his project contradicted the deterministic philosophy he had formally adopted, or else—and more likely—Franklin was already recognizing the *Dissertation* as an "erratum." For his personal morality in London and for a while in Philadephia, he confessed in the autobiography, had been strained by "that hard-to-be-governed passion of youth," and even in Philadelphia for a while he was to continue consorting with "low women." But there is evidence that he was beginning to have some scruples about his conduct, and in his intensely practical way, Franklin could see that his sexual intrigues were dissipating his moral and physical energies. In his resolutions drawn up at sea, Franklin pledged himself to observe many of the rules of life that he would soon give to the world in *Poor Richard's Almanack.* He would try to be frugal and industrious, speaking ill of no one but only good, otherwise he "would speak truth in every instance" and "give nobody expectations that are not likely to be answered, but aim at sincerity in every word and action—the most amiable excellence in a rational being."[35] Franklin in old age claimed to have adhered "pretty faithfully" to his "Plan of Conduct," and there is every reason to believe that he did. His more ambitious "project of arriving at moral perfection," taken up a little later, is better known and is an elaboration and logical development of this typically Enlightenment exercise.

Franklin's employment with Mr. Denham in the store on Water Street was happy and instructive, but did not last long. Their almost filial relationship ended abruptly when the gentle and good Quaker died after a long illness. Strangely enough, the younger man, who lived and boarded with his mentor, also, in February 1727, became seriously ill, from pleurisy. "I suffered a great deal, gave up the point in my own mind, and was rather disappointed," Franklin wrote matter-of-factly, "when I found myself recovering, regretting in some degree that I must now sometime or other have all that disagreeable work to go over again."[36]

This passage in the autobiography, and other quotations that could be adduced, reveal an attitude towards death that can best be called naturalistic and experimental, at one with Franklin's secular, empirical *Weltanshauung*. That he formed a pact with a friend, committing the first to die to return from the other world, was perfectly in character. What a man thinks of death tells much about his philosophy, about the values around which Franklin or any other man shapes his life. Clearly, in these instances, he did not even consider the possibility of annihilation after death. "Nothingness" was an idea that Franklin as a representative Enlightenment thinker simply could not conceive. The "Great Chain of Being" ruled out its possibility in the divine scheme of things. In this vague Neo-Platonism, which he apparently never recognized as source and presupposition of his thought, there could be no void, and hence no anxiety and terror before it. But it would be unfair to expect Franklin or any other 18th century *philosophe* to be another Pascal— whom, it will be remembered, Voltaire attacked savagely. Franklin never understood anxiety in this sense, never reacted with "fear and trembling" like a Pascal or Kierkegaard because of his easy, uncritical optimism which, as we have seen, received confirmation in the writings of Shaftesbury and other 17th century utopians. Death in "the course of nature" was as "necessary to our constitution as sleep. We shall rise refreshed in the morning."[37] It was the beginning of "a party of pleasure—that is to last forever." And keeping up the physical analogy which was all Franklin the empiricist knew, death was the puling down of the old, decrepid house by the owner and the rebuilding of a new one. There was no real doubt in his mind that life began at that point men called death. In Franklin's eloquent words of consolation to his niece: "That bodies should be lent us, while they can afford us pleasure, assist us in acquiring knowledge, or doing good to our fellow creatures, is a kind and benevolent act of God—when they become unfit for these purposes and afford us pain instead of pleasure—instead of an aid, become an incumbrance and answer none of the intentions for which they were given, it is equally kind and benevolent that a way is provided by which we may get rid of them. Death is that way."[38]

Once again, Franklin's mind was working out an explanation of the nature of things along secular lines. His belief in immortality, which was consistent with some forms of Deism, preserved the substance of hope in Christianity without Christ, a position Rush, Carroll, and thoughtful Christians must dismiss as meaningless.

Mr. Denham's death left Franklin without employment, so he went back to his old job at Keimer's print shop. The old man, he wrote in his memoirs, "was an odd fish, ignorant of common life, fond of rudely opposing received opinions, slovenly to extreme dirtiness, enthusiastic in some points of religion, and a little knavish withal."[39] In him Franklin could see exactly the kind of person he did not want to be—the "enthusiast"—the very antithesis of Poor Richard. Keimer's most obnoxious trait was his religious enthusiasm. He had once, in fact, suggested to Franklin that the two men should found their own religious sect, a proposal that could not help but detract from the little respect the young Deist still had for organized religion.

Franklin stayed with Keimer only a year. Hugh Meredith, another worker in the shop, soon offered him a partnership in a new company, and it was this printery that Franklin bought out in 1729. Now, as sole proprietor, he followed his "Plan of Conduct" to the letter, taking "care not only to be in *reality* industrious and frugal, but to avoid all *appearances* of the contrary. I dressed plain and was seen at no places of idle diversion. I never went out a fishing or shooting; a book, indeed, sometimes debauched me from my work, but that was seldom, snug, and gave no scandal; and to show that I was not above my business, I sometimes brought home the paper I purchased at the stores, thro' the streets on a wheelbarrow."[40] Niether Keimer nor Andrew Bradford, the other two printers in Philadelphia, could stand up to this competition. Franklin acquired Keimer's newspaper, which he renamed the *Pennsylvania Gazette*. The old would-be prophet, deeply in debt, went off to Barbadoes; and Bradford continued to retire into the background, leaving Franklin with a virtual monopoly of the printing trade in Philadephia. In these auspicious circumstances, Franklin married Deborah Read, with whom he had exchanged promises before going to England and who had since had an unfortunate marriage. She was a resourceful and good woman, the perfect wife for Poor Richard.

Debra was not much for book-learning, but she knew how to run an efficient and frugal household. Barely literate herself, which was the case with most American women at the time, she nevertheless did not discourage her husband's literary pursuits. Franklin at twenty-four had at last come to terms with that "hard-to-be-governed passion" and could now indulge to the fullest his love of books and reading. But there were

few books in Philadelphia and not one decent shop where the titles commonplace in London could be bought. He planned to remedy this in time;
meanwhile, his earlier reading in Defoe and Cotton Mather, and his own
practical ingenuity, produced a solution: the Library Company of
Philadelphia, the first subscription library in America, which Franklin
founded in 1731. By "clubbing" their books, he and other members
of the Junto (Franklin's circle of friends which he had organized into
a brotherhood several years before) could have use of a more than ample library. Franklin prevailed upon other men to subscribe to the library,
for the most part young tradesmen like himself, and books for the ever-
growing Junto were soon being imported from England. This, he explained to his son in the autobiography, was his "university". An hour
or two of reading a day was his only "amusement", the only time he
could afford to take from his busy schedule at the printshop.[41]

Franklin's education among his books, and not in the lecture rooms
of Harvard—which he satirized in an early essay—was more significant
for his life and thought than most biographers realize. The man who
received honorary degrees from Oxford, Harvard, St. Andrew's, as well
as other institutions of higher learning, and who was selected over university men to be a member of the Royal Society of London, had all the
advantages of self-education. He also had the limitations of the man who
can select his teachers, who, in other words, reads only those books he
wants to read. Franklin never had to sit in the classroom and take
elaborate notes on metaphysics and theology, as Rush had to do as a
student at the College of New Jersey. Instead, he could study with
whomever he wanted, and he chose Renaissance and Enlightenment
authors like Montaigne, Locke, Bayle, and Voltaire, or an occasional
ancient writer like Cicero who, for all their genius, never challenged
Franklin to think transcendentally the way authors like, say, St. Augustine
and Pascal, would have done. Franklin's books reinforced his own practical nature, those traits the world acclaims in him and in the American
civilization which he personifies. Franklin, as Max Weber recognized,
was a true Calvinist, but perfectly secularized. He was not only *in* the
world, he was *of* it. He was a Calvinist without Christ. A book like St.
Augustine's *Confessions* or Thomas à Kempis's *Imitation of Christ*, a
work treasured by Carroll, Franklin would have classified as "enthusiastic." He was much more at home with Voltaire and the

*philosophes*, accepting, in the former's words, only what "our eyes and mathematics demonstrate." In short, and paradoxical as it may seem, Franklin in his experimental program of self-education may be laid open to the charge of anti-intellectualism. John Adams, who was formally educated and widely read, may have been implying just this in his attribution to Franklin of an "infantine simplicity."[42] To develop this point, we can say that Franklin made, as it were, a virtue of necessity in conducting his ingenious scientific experiments on which his lasting fame rests. Without the cultural legacy of a secondary and university background, he had few philosophical and theological presuppositions to mediate his relationship to empirical reality.

Franklin's Enlightenment trust in the power of print to better humankind is manifest in the Library Company of Philadelphia and its many imitators in America, which he believed in 1771 had made "the common tradesmen and farmers as intelligent as most gentlemen from other countries, and perhaps have contributed in some degree to the stand so generally made throughout the Colonies in defence of their privilege."[43] Books, newspapers, and almanacks could bring down tyrants. Diderot and the Encyclopedists—all *philosophes* knew this. They could also promote a party of virtue among men; for Franklin held with the liberals of the day that knowledge was virtue. And virtue could be taught to men by means of the printing press.

"It was about this time," Franklin looked back in 1784 with the same deep conviction, "I conceived the bold and arduous project of arriving at moral perfection. I wished to live without committing any fault at any time; I would conquer all that either natural inclination, custom, or company might lead me into. As I knew, or thought I knew, what was right and wrong, I did not see why I might not *always* do the one and avoid the other."[44] No project could be more Franklinian in its naivete. But lest the modern reader smile at this, he should be reminded that Franklin had repudiated the Calvinism and secular determinism of his youth and that now, as a Pelagian—disavowing any restriction on man's freedom— he had a reason to expect total, natural control of his moral life. "But I soon found," he went on, "I had undertaken a task of more difficulty than I had imagined. While my attention was taken up and care employed in guarding against one fault, I was often surprised by another."[45] Original and personal sin, the Christian explanation of this moral weakness, Franklin of course would not accept; and, in all fairness to his one-sided, practical temperament, could not understand. The true man of inquiry, he believed, could not accept such a gross idea as Original Sin simply on theological authority. It was blasphemous, common sense made clear, to think that the all-merciful "Father of the Universe" would allow disorder of this kind in His system. Grace was, therefore, a meaningless concept to Franklin. Man was free, but he was also without any supernatural blemish. Imputed guilt was a species of "demonism" nowhere found in the Bible, "every whit as ridiculous as that of imputed righteousness. 'Tis a notion invented, a bugbear set up by priests (whether *Popish* or *Presbyterian* I know not) to fright and scare an unthinking populace out of their senses, and inspire them with terror, to answer the little selfish ends of the inventors and propagators.''[46] Man was neither saint nor sinner. To prove this, Franklin, liberated from the dogmatism of the past, would devise an art of virtue by which men already good could achieve moral perfection and, organized into an international brotherhood, outlaw war and other evils and produce a veritable heaven on earth.

Franklin, always the printer, made a little book of the virtues he had come across in his reading: temperance, silence, order, resolution, frugality, industry, sincerity, justice, moderation, cleanliness, tranquility, chastity, and humility. He would concentrate on each one at a time, allowing a week to the mastery of it and then pass on to the next. At the end of each day, he would rigorously examine his conduct and mark a black dot by the virtue he had failed to observe. It was an exercise not unlike the puritan introspection of his ancestors, but it also had affinities with the ancient Stoical tradition associated with Bayle and Montaigne and which the 18th century moralists were reviving. Pierre Bayle's *Critical Dictionary* was a favorite of Franklin's, and he had seen to its early acquisition by the Library Company. More than anyone else, Bayle had popularized the notion that religion and morality were independent of each other. If this was so, and Franklin believed it, natural morality could be separated from Christianity and good would triumph over narrow sectarianism. No man of intrinsic worth, he further contended, would oppose experimental moral science like that he had described in his little book of virtues, because all Christian denominations exhorted their sectaries to be virtuous—without, however, showing them, as Franklin now proposed to do, how to acquire and practice the virtues. "Most people have naturally *some* virtues, but none have naturally *all* the virtues," he wrote Lord Kames. "To *acquire* those that are wanting, and *secure* what we acquire as well as those we have naturally, is the subject of *an art*. It is as properly an art, as painting, navigation, or architecture."[47] Just as the great Sir Isaac Newton had discovered the principles of physical phenomena, so Franklin in typical Enlightenment fashion believed he had laid the principles of moral phenomena.

Knowledge was virtue, as Socrates had taught, and virtue, Franklin added, was useful because it made men happy. "It was therefore everyone's interest to be virtuous who wished to be happy in this world."[48] That was why, Franklin alleged with David Hume and other utilitarians of the times, "certain actions" were forbidden by social convention. Their performance was forbidden because experience showed that they were bad, i.e., they did not conduce to man's happiness; they were not bad because forbidden. Revelation, in which Franklin did not believe in any case, had nothing to do with it. Christ, said Franklin, came into the world "to promote the practice of piety, goodness, virtue, and universal righteousness among mankind, or the practice of the moral duties both with respect to God and man, and by these means to make us happy here and hereafter."[49] The useful was the good, not the good the useful. *Poor Richard* noted, too, that man should be charitable, as it paid to be charitable, reverses coming sometimes even to the industrious.[50]

Discernible in this project, as in all of Franklin's benevolent schemes, was Shaftesbury's ideal of the complete moral person who lives for himself at the same time that he lives for others. Franklin modelled himself after this ideal, and at times almost attained it. For example, he refused patents for the lightning rod and the Franklin stove, which would certainly have made him a very wealthy man, because of his unselfish conviction that, as he had benefitted from other men's inventions, so they should benefit from his. His idea of "raising a united party for virtue, by forming the virtuous and good men of all nations into a regular body" was also drawn from this source.[51] His "Observations on Reading History," written for the Junto, convinced him that only by organizing an elite of virtuous men to act in history could real good in the world be achieved. This was the most elaborate of Franklin's schemes to improve mankind, although unlike his other projects—the Junto, the Library Company, the first American fire insurance company, the Philadelphia city watch, etc—it never materialized. He formulated a religious creed, Deistic in inspiration, which all members would have to accept, one that contained "the essentials of every known religion," while offending none. The Creator ruled the world by His Providence; He deserved worship by "adoration," but especially by man's doing good to his fellow man; the soul was immortal, and God would "reward virtue and punish vice, either here or hereafter."[52] Initiates, at first to be confined to young, single men, would also have to undergo Franklin's course of self-examination in the virtues before they could be admitted to the Masonic-like secret society. They would also have to swear, as in the Junto, that they loved all mankind, regardless of their religion, and wished no harm to anyone because of "mere speculative opinions," or "external way of worship." Finally, Franklin's "new man" of virtue must "love truth for truth's sake," pursue it everywhere, and share it with all mankind. Johann Gottfried Herder, another disciple of Shaftesbury, thought so well of these requirements that he adopted them in 1791 for his own use.[53]

Franklin's religious ideas at the time, condensed above in his creed for the party of virtue, can best be seen in his fuller "Articles of Belief and Acts of Religion," a private liturgy he often observed in his own home. Apparently, after his marriage to Deborah, in 1730, Franklin was induced by the local Presbyterian minister—and perhaps his wife—to attend an occasional service. He still much preferred his books to the meeting house, but he went anyway for five consecutive Sundays. Not once in that time, Franklin emphasized, did the minister preach on morality, instead he seemed intent "rather to make us Presbyterians than good citizens."[54] Thus confirmed in his original view of Presbyterian and other sects as divisive of good men, he henceforth followed his own private liturgy written sometime earlier.

"I believe there is one Supreme most perfect Being," the testament begins, "Author and Father of the Gods themselves." There were many beings superior to man, as there were many beings inferior to him. These superior beings or "Gods" were necessary in the divine economy, Franklin argued, to render the "Infinite Father" rational and glorious praise, since man himself was "an inconsiderable nothing" probably beneath the notice of the "one Supreme most perfect." Yet there was in men "something like a natural principle which inclines them to devotion or worship of some unseen power," and it was this inner consciousness of duty, along with man's faculty of reason, that prompted Franklin to praise and adore "that wise and good God, who is the author and owner of our system," and through him the Supreme Being who made all the universes. The infinite and incomprehensible, absolutely transcendent One, in Neo-Platonic language, was to be worshipped mediately, as it were, through the lesser Gods or angels. And the lesser God of "our system of planets," who might even be mortal, had passions like those he had given Franklin, cared for him, and was pleased with men when they helped their fellow man and used their divine gift of reason to observe the wisdom of his creation. "Next to the praise due to his wisdom", Franklin linked this polytheistic theology with his morality, "I believe he is pleased and delights in the happiness of those he has created; and since without virtue man can have no happiness in this world, I firmly believe he delights to see me virtuous, because he is pleased when he sees me happy."[55]

Religion, then, whether monotheistic or polytheistic—and as late as 1782 Franklin was still writing about superior beings—still meant in the last resort the practice of virtue. Franklin was not a Christian, as his Congregationalist parents suspected when they wrote to him in the spring of 1738, worried about his orthodoxy. It seems he never examined objectively the claims of Christ. The Incarnation was an idea so audacious as to be rejected out of hand by the Enlightenment to which Franklin belonged heart and soul. It was his great limitation, as we have suggested, not to be able to transcend his Age as well as the empirical phenomena of his everyday life. He remained a child of his times.

The occasion for Josiah and Abiah's troubled letter was a newspaper article in the Boston area in which Franklin was identified as a Mason. His reply of April 13, while evasive of his unbelief—a posture he always assumed out of kindness to his family members—yields a deep insight into the relativism of his mind when it came to ultimate questions: "You both seem concerned lest I have imbibed some erroneous opinions. Doubtless I have my share, and when the natural weakness and imperfection of human understanding is considered, with the unavoidable influences of education, custom, books, and company, upon our ways of thinking, I imagine a man must have a good deal of vanity who believes, and a good deal of boldness who affirms, that all the doctrines he holds, are true; and all he rejects, are false. And perhaps,'' Franklin continued in the strain of Montaigne's *Que-Sais-je?*, ''the same may be justly said of every sect, church, and society of men when they assume to themselves that infallibility which they deny to the popes and councils. I think opinions should be judged of by their influences and effects; and if a man holds none that tend to make him less virtuous or more vicious, it may be concluded he holds none that are dangerous, which I hope is the case with me.''[56] The test of an opinion, then, was not whether it conformed to objective truth, but whether it produced virtuous action. Opinions, Franklin retreated further into skepticism, varied according to the person anyway, and ''it is no more in a man's power *to think* than *to look* like another.'' Then, ending his letter to his parents with a gentle touch of his characteristic irony, which must have bruised their Christian sensibilities, he wrote: ''I think vital religion has always suffered, when orthodoxy is more regarded than virtue. And the Scripture assures me, that at the last day, we shall not be examined what we *thought*, but what we *did*; and our recommendation will not be that we said *Lord, Lord*, but that we did GOOD to our fellow creatures. See. Matt. 26''[57]

The old problem over faith versus works was very much in Franklin's mind in the 1730's, because it was then he took up his pen in the spirit of Voltaire to defend a Presbyterian minister accused of heresy. Reverend Samuel Hemphill had recently arrived in Philadelphia from Ireland and his popular sermons, unlike those of the regular preacher whom Franklin had complained about, were not filled with dogma ''but inculcated strongly the practice of virtue, or what in the religious style are called 'good works.' ''[58] Franklin, delighted, with Hemphill's almost exclusive concern with morality, was soon back in the meeting house and, when the young preacher was suspended from the ministry by his elders, Franklin as ''his zealous partisan'' wrote pamphlets in his defense. Franklin's anti-clericalism in these tracts, as in his earlier *Silence Dogood Letters*, was not that of ''*écrasez L'infâme.*'' He advocated instead, as a son of the Reformation, the removal of civil and what he regarded as other artificial supports for Christian sects. The Presbyterian elders who censured Hemphill, Franklin asserted, were no better than papists in their use of Spanish-like Inquisition against the brilliant young minister who was a loyal Protestant in upholding "the glorious cause of Christian Liberty." Deprive these un-Christlike judges of their salaries and other emoluments, make them truly dependent on God's Providence, and religious creeds, confessions, and tests would disappear along with the hypocritical, false religions based on transubstantiation, indulgences, praying to saints and angels. Again and again in Franklin's Almanack, Poor Richard asked, "What is serving God?" and answered "Tis doing good to man."[59]

True diversity of religious opinions would inevitably follow the abolition of man-made creeds and confessions, but this accorded with the ancient principle of *As many men as many minds*. Franklin, the dissenter turned liberal, explained that "there would be among Christians a full liberty of declaring their minds or opinions to one another both in public and private. And secondly heresy, that huge bugbear would no more frighten people, would no more kindle among us the hellish fires of furious zeal and party bigotry. We might peaceably, and without the least breach upon brotherly love, differ in our religious speculations as we do in astronomy or any other part of natural philosophy. Those two invaluable blessings, full liberty and universal peace would in all likelihood make the ways of truth so easy, that the greater number of Christians would even come to think alike in many cases in which they now widely differ."[60] Then people would finally see that the worst "ism" was not Arianism or Socinianism but, in an anecdote Franklin often used, rheuma*tism*.

Despite Franklin's writing talents and printing press, both of which he lent generously to Hemphill's defense, the orthodox party triumphed. The young Arian's cause was hopelessly lost when evidence was produced that he had plagiarized his sermons from the works of English rationalists. Franklin dropped out of the congregation again. Although, true to his conviction of the pragmatic value of religion, he continued paying for the support of its ministers. As for orthodoxy, well, that he later observed with his customary wit "is my doxy, and heterodoxy is your doxy."[62] Hemphill was a virtuous man, an honest heretic, Franklin insisted, even if he preferred other men's better sermons to his own. Franklin knew he was a heretic himself, and in the years to come he would become intimate with Joseph Priestley, Richard Price, and other leading nonconformists or heretics of the times. "All the heretics I have known," he wrote in 1788, "have been virtuous men. They have the virtue of fortitude, or they would not venture to own their heresy; and they cannot afford to be deficient in any of the other virtues, as that would give advantage to their many enemies; and they have not, like orthodox sinners, such a number of friends to excuse or justify them."[63] The honest man must be a heretic.

Whether the Reverend George Whitefield, another itinerant preacher who came to Philadelphia in 1739, fully qualified as a heretic in Franklin's estimation is not clear. There is no question, though, that Franklin admired and loved him. Whitefield, next to Jonathan Edwards, the most influential preacher of the Great Awakening—that religious revival that was sweeping the Colonies at mid-century—was in the Pennsylvania city to win souls for Christ and to raise money for an orphanage he planned to establish in Georgia. An Anglican priest, he was never the less a Calvinist in theology while a Methodist in church government, placing him in a strained relationship with Charles and John Wesley, the founder of the reform movement within the Church of England. Whitefield was a "Son of Thunder" who cared nothing for conservative church teaching and discipline. He wished only to promote the love of Christ in what was called, in the language of the Great Awakening, "the religion of the heart and experimental piety." The existence of the unconverted, including Franklin, as we shall see, he regarded as a scandal. Franklin loved him not for his "gloomy" theology, for Whitefield was strangely enough a predestinarian, but for his personal and social virtue and, no doubt, Whitefield's "experimental" approach to Christianity. The Methodist preacher was a "Hero of virtue," after the fashion of Shaftesbury's ideal, a man of "benevolent heart" who did not "croak" about how bad things were, but who, like Franklin, tried to improve them by doing good. His project for an orphanage in Georgia was an instance of this social charity.[64]

At first, Franklin was skeptical in his attitude toward the evangelist. Ever since his apprenticeship in Keimer's shop he had had a bad taste for wild religious enthusiasts, and he had just barely escaped with honor the debacle over Rev. Hemphill. While he liked the idea of founding an orphanage, he thought it better located in Philadelphia than in the south. When the orthodox clergy denied Whitefield the right to preach in the churches of the city, however, Franklin once again espoused the cause of a persecuted heretic. "It is a principle among printers," he wrote in his *Pennsylvania Gazette* in the midst of the controversy over Whitefield, "that when truth has fair play, it will always prevail over falsehood."[65] The revivalist went into the fields to preach. Franklin went too. "The multitudes of all sects and denominations that attended his sermons were enormous, and it was a matter of speculation to me," his rationalist bias was apparent, "to observe the extraordinary influence of his oratory on his hearers and how much they admired and respected him, notwithstanding his common abuse of them, by assuring them they were naturally 'half beasts and half devils'."[66] Over and above Whitefield's Calvinism, Franklin was pleased with the salutary effects of the revivalist's preaching. So religious, it seemed did the people of Philadelphia become, "that one could not walk thro' the town in an evening without hearing psalms sung in different families of every street."[67] Franklin himself was, of course, unaffected by Whitefield's fervent oratory on sin and the need for repentance. One evening at an outdoor revival Franklin, indifferent to the theological content of what Whitefield was saying, determined by experiment that the evangelist could be heard clearly by upwards of thirty thousand people.

Eloquence, which Franklin admired and confessed he did not possess himself, could "turn many to righteousness."[68] Whitefield possessed it in the highest degree, and Franklin, seeing him deprived of a pulpit, joined with others in providing the evangelist with a building in which to preach. Franklin paid tribute to the force of Whitefield's eloquence in his memoirs. He went to hear the great revivalist preach in the "new building,' But, as he opposed Whitefield's locating the orphanage in Georgia, determined that he would not contribute anything to the collection for that purpose. "I had in my pocket a handful of copper money, three or four silver dollars, and five pistoles in gold. As he proceeded, I began to soften and concluded to give the coppers. Another stroke of his oratory made me ashamed of that and determined me to give the silver; and he finished so admirably that I emptied my pocket wholly into the collector's dish, gold and all."[69] Whitefield was often accused by his enemies of using these funds for his own benefit, but Franklin called him "a perfectly *honest man*," a judgment which he emphasized "ought to have more weight as we had no religious connection."[70]

If the two men had no religious connection, it was not for lack of

Whitefield's efforts to convert the Deist printer. Franklin printed Whitefield's biography as well as his journals and sermons, but also ran in his newspaper other people's attacks on Whitefield's "enthusiastic ravings." They often discussed religion, agreeing with Poor Richard that "Heaven is to the virtuous," and scoffed at those Christians of "Sunday appearance" who were too good to do good. On hypocrisy among Christians, a favorite theme of Deists and Great Awakeners alike, Franklin always quoted Dean Swift that "he never knew a man who could not bear the misfortunes of another like a Christian."[71] Oddly enough, Franklin could not pierce through his own rhetoric to see that Whitefield, the man he was discussing Christianity with, was living proof that there were Christians worthy of the name. Saints, or people who came very close to being saints, did exist. But sanctity was an ideal whose meaning Franklin could not fathom, as we saw earlier in his meeting with the woman of the garret.

As a utilitarian, even more so than a Deist—Franklin was willing if necessary to sacrifice "truth" and natural law for utility—the American wanted an empirical religion of pure charity. Deism, he saw from his own experience with men, "though it might be true, was not very useful."[72] Revealed Christianity was probably not true either, but it was useful, and could be made more so if ministers like Whitefield would only play down, or remove entirely, mysticism in their doctrines and teach Jesus's ethics of brotherly love. Some mysticism was necessary in religion, especially for the young, weak, and ignorant who might not otherwise acquire habits of virtue. "If men are so wicked as we now see them *with religion*," Franklin argued with a would-be author who asked him to read a manuscript against organized religion, "what would they be if *without it?*" As Poor Richard said, "Talking against religion is unchaining a tiger; the beast let loose may worry his deliverer."[73]

Whitefield's genius was too penetrating not to see that his Philadelphia friend conceived the nature of Christianity as irrational. "I do no despair of your seeing the reasonableness of Christianity. Apply to GOD; be willing to do the divine will, and you shall know it."[74] Franklin urged against Whitefield's "reasonableness of Christianity," his Calvinism, that it was a species of theological fatalism that violated natural reason by so emphasizing faith and grace and neglecting good works as to lead to that "doctrine of devils," antinomianism. This was not the case with

Whitefield personally, but notwithstanding, Calvinist teaching discouraged moral action. "For to say that God regards men for any thing else besides goodness and virtue, is such a notion as makes all men both virtuous and vicious capable of being equally regarded by him, and consequently there is no difference between virtue and vice."[75] Voltaire had made much the same criticism of Jansenism in France. Such a pessimistic doctrine as Calvinism also made a shambles of Franklin's moral science, his art of virtue, which was designed to improve people by giving them the means to virtue. It was unscriptural, too, according to Franklin, who quoted chapter and verse, but in the secularizing manner of Jefferson.

When they differed in this way, which was often, the two men could always restore consensus by once again acknowledging the need for promoting virtue in the world. Franklin saw in his friend's charismatic preaching, apart from theology, an opportunity to win men not for Christ but for his party of virtue. (Franklin, like many scientists, was always too concerned with secondary causes to investigate the First Cause.) Franklin suggested in 1749 that Whitefield try to gain more converts to virtue among the upper classes, as was the practice of Confucius, since the multitude would copy their social betters, fearing "less the being in hell than out of fashion."[76] Perhaps Whitefield's experience preaching to great numbers of men would help Franklin or some other moral scientist discover a more precise, universal method for reforming mankind. "He that shall discover that, will, in my opinion deserve more, ten thousand times, than the inventor of the longitude."[77]

To Whitefield, his friend's art of virtue was pure and simple ethical naturalism. The Methodist evangelist, like St. Augustine centuries earlier, wanted somehow to make Franklin see that beyond the virtues which they both accepted lay the God who had made them. For Franklin, in his naive realism or positivism, was always confusing the Creator with His creation. On theology proper, there wasn't much Whitefield could do to refute Franklin's basic charge that Calvinism and Antinomianism were inseparably connected. Nor could he overcome Franklin's objection to predestinarianism, i.e., it rendered God no God at all, as "now having determined everything, he has divested himself of all further power . . . he has tied up his hands, and has now no greater power than an idol of wood or stone."[78]

Franklin shared with Whitefield, in 1749, another of his ideas for the raising up of a party of virtue. This was the Philadelphia Academy, where he proposed useful knowledge should be taught to young men, especially by requiring the study of "good history . . . to fix in the minds of youth deep impressions of the beauty and usefulness of virtue of all kinds, public spirit, fortitude, etc."[79] History was the record of man's natural experience, Franklin held with other Enlightenment thinkers, and so it could teach men many truths about themselves and the world. Some of its most valuable lessons, Franklin the social pragmatist realized, were those of "showing the necessity of a *public religion*, from its usefulness to the public; the advantage of a religious character among private persons; the mischiefs of superstition, etc. and the excellency of the CHRISTIAN RELIGION above all other ancient or modern."[80]

The *Proposals Relating to the Education of Youth in Pennsylvania*, printed and distributed gratis by Franklin, contained many other ideas designed to motivate youth to serve mankind and give them at the same time the knowledge to attain that "great aim and end of all learning."[81] Franklin asked Whitefield for his reaction. To be useful in the truest sense, answered the great preacher, the proposed academy should have more *aliquid Christi* in it. Franklin, he said, rightly conceded the excellence of the Christian religion in his proposal, but failed to integrate this supreme truth into the nature and curriculum of the academy. "The grand end of every Christian institution for forming tender minds," Whitefield inevitably returned to theology, "should be to convince them of their natural depravity, of the means of recovering out of it, and of the necessity of preparing for the enjoyment of the supreme Being in a future state. These are the grand points in which Christianity centers. Art and sciences may be built on this, and serve to embellish and set off this superstructure, but without this, I think there cannot be any good foundation."[82] The Philadelphia Academy, if uninspired by true Christianity, would be just another Babel, confusing youth rather than helping them.

Franklin was undeterred. As a trustee of the "New Building" constructed for Whitefield's revivals, one who was said to be "merely an honest man, and of *no sect* at all," he arranged for the use of the building by the proposed academy. Whitefield was a great preacher, but he was no organizer; and, moreover, there was now a decline in his following, so that the meeting house could not be maintained. The structure, already in disrepair, was transferred to the Academy. Franklin's temple of virtue would still be used, as he originally intended, "so that even if the Mufti of Constantinople were to send a missionary to preach Mahometanism to us, he would find a pulpit at his service."[83]

The citizens of Philadelphia, despite Franklin's own airy convictions, were not about to welcome a missionary of Islam into their midst. That Franklin should write this in his autobiography, though, was typical of the idealism of the liberal thinker for whom truth was to found not only in the Christian tradition but everywhere. He praised, for example, the Dunkers of Pennsylvania who were so undogmatic as to refuse to put any of their beliefs in credal form, since their doctrines progressed according to God's constant Revelation and they did not want to bind their descendents in the faith to any sacred teaching. "This modesty in a sect," he endorsed the Dunker's process theology, "is perhaps a singular instance in the history of mankind, every other sect supposing itself in possession of all truth, and that those who differ are so far in the wrong." The sects which claimed absolute truth, he went on, were like the proverbial man in the fog who, seeing others wrapped in the fog, rode on never realizing that he was enveloped in the fog too. "I cannot help imagining that multitudes of the zealously orthodox of different sects who at the last day may flock together in hopes of seeing each other damned will be disappointed and obliged to rest content with their own salvation."[84] "Different sects," the folk philosopher wrote in *Poor Richard*, "like different clocks, may be all near the matter, though they don't quite agree."[85]

Franklin's understanding of the Protestant Reformation in contrast to Whitefield's was that of a permanent, ongoing reform like that of the Dunkers. Whitefield rightly condemned "popery and arbitrary power" but dogmatized about theology like Roman Catholics and Presbyterians. He was not a man of inquiry prepared to "stoop" before the mystery of things. He was, in the final analysis, a sectarian, whose religion, Franklin implied, was like "a chedder cheese, 'tis made of the milk of one and twenty parishes."[86] Unwittingly, the Methodist preacher was one of Christianity's worst enemies, as by multiplying the formal tenets and duties of Christians beyond the simple Christ-like commandment of brotherly love, he was preventing its spread among men. Christ himself, Franklin claimed, preferred "the heretical but charitable

Samaritan to the uncharitable though orthodox priest and sanctified Levite."[87] For *doing good to men* is the *only service of God* in our power; and to *imitate his Beneficence* is to *glorify him*."[88] Confessions and creeds were obstacles to this true glorification of God.

Whitefield was a God-intoxicated man: he "must have *aliquid Christi* in all my letters," he told his American friend.[89] Franklin was an Enlightenment *philosophe*, a fallen-away New England Calvinist, scandalized by the Cross itself and the post-Reformation legacy of sectarian hatred. Christianity's "enemies are ready to say not what was said in the primitive times, *Behold how these Christians love one another*, but *Mark how these Christians HATE one another*! Indeed when religious people quarrel about religion, or hungry people about their victuals, it looks as if they had not much of either among them."[90] Franklin was, in truth, victimized by narrow sectarianism; he could not transcend the many quarreling religious sects, could not lift his perspective above historical temporalities to conceive even the possibility that there was one Catholic, apostolic Faith of which the many religious parties were only so many incomplete expressions, and that the Man-God had founded His Church on Peter. Nor could he see, as Rush did so clearly, that the peace and natural unity that he generously sought for man, could not be a reality until there was supernatural, i.e. religious, unity among men in the Augustinian City of God. So Franklin invented his own secular "churches," the Junto, the Philadelphia Academy, the American Philosophical Society for Useful Knowledge (1743), and other institutions, each designed to effect that moral revolution in the world that the Son of God centuries before accomplished for all eternity with His own blood. Franklin revealed his great difficutly in understanding this point and meant no irreverence when he invited Whitefield to stay as his house guest in Philadelphia—not for Christ's sake but for Whitefield's sake.[91]

In 1751 Franklin's name became known in England for his *Experiments and Observations on Electricity*, identifying lightning and electricity, and a year later knowledge of his work spread to the Continent. Whitefield, ever ready to help his friend in his spiritual development, took advantage of the opportunity to whet Franklin's natural curiosity about other matters. "I find that you grow more and more famous in the learned world. As you have made a pretty considerable progress in the mysteries of electricity, I would now humbly recommend to your diligent unprejudiced pursuit and study the mystery of the new-birth. It is a most important, interesting study, and when mastered, will richly answer and repay you for all your pains.''[92] And then reminding Franklin of his mortality to prod him along in this line of thinking, the evangelist quoted Our Savior that without being born again ''we cannot enter the kingdom of heaven.''[93] What Franklin's answer was to this recommendation, we do not know. Probably, he simply dismissed it as irrelevant; for the evidence suggests that the very idea of a rebirth, a conversion, a deep spiritual experience was alien to Franklin's nature. His genius was of a different kind from that of great Western souls like Whitefield, Pascal, and St. Augustine.

Whitefield continued to press Franklin to think more about death and salvation, implying that his naturalistic friend was overly confident, even presumptuous, about life after death. ''I have seen your *Epitaph*. Believe on JESUS, and get a feeling of possession of GOD in your heart, and you cannot possibly be disappointed of your expected second edition finely corrected, and infinitely amended. *Verbum sapienti sat est.*''[94] The evangelist persisted over the next ten years in this attempt to raise some salutary anxiety in Franklin's mind about what he believed to be the pagan naiveté of his friend's post-lethal expectations. Franklin's reply was predictable. ''Your frequently repeated wishes and prayers for my eternal as well as temporal happiness are very obliging. I can only thank you for them, and offer you mine in return. I have myself no doubts that I shall enjoy as much of both as is proper for me,'' he explained in words redolent of his youthful determinism.

> That Being who gave me existence, and through almost threescore years had been continually showering his favors upon me, whose very chastisements have been blessings to me, can I doubt that he loves me? And if he loves me, can I doubt that he will go on to take care of me not only here but hereafter? This to some may seem presumption; to me it appears the best grounded hope; hope of the future; built on experience of the past.[95]

''Experience of the past''—this was Franklin's professed guide in all things, including religion. The economy of nature, he pointed out as last as 1785, showed God's wisdom and frugality, as for example in the divine invention of propagation by which He ''provided for the continual peopling his world with plants and animals, without being at the trouble of repeated new creations,'' and in the ''natural reduction of compound substances to their original elements'' by which He ''prevented the necessity of creating new matter.'' ''When I see nothing annihilated,'' Franklin argued from what he considered simple empirical observations, ''and not even a drop of water wasted, I cannot suspect the annihilation of souls, or believe that he will suffer the daily waste of millions of minds ready made that now exist, and put himself to the continual trouble of making new ones.'' And extrapolating from this divine frugality in things, he concluded: ''Thus finding myself to exist in the world, I believe I shall, in some shape or other, always exist; and, with all the inconveniences human life is liable to, I shall not object to a new edition of mine; hoping, however, that the *errata* of the last may be corrected.''[96]

Franklin's ''metaphysics'' of empiricism, for that is what it was, was derived from his own experience and his reading in Locke and other Newtonians. He was not a university philosopher, but a ''man of inquiry'' who never held an academic position; this he had in common with Locke, Hume and *les philosophes* of the Enlightenment. With Hume in particular, his intimate friend, Franklin shared a remarkably similar outlook. Franklin believed with these thinkers that the method of arriving at knowledge and truth was that of directly observing the phenomena themselves in order to discover their laws. As for the causes of the laws, philosophically speaking anyway, Franklin showed Hume's influence in maintaining that it is not of

> much importance to us to know the manner in which nature executes her laws; 'tis enough if we know the laws themselves. 'Tis of real use to know that china left in the air unsupported will fall and break; but *how* it comes to fall, and *why* it breaks are matters of speculation. 'Tis a pleasure indeed to know them, but we can preserve our china without it.[97]

Franklin, who came to accept Hume's radical empiricism or positivism, even resembled the Scottish philosopher in his personality: ''A man of mild disposition,'' Hume described himself in his autobiography, ''of command of temper, of an open, social and cheerful humour, capable of attachment, but little susceptible of enmity, and of great moderation in all my passions."[98] Franklin, said Hume, was America's "first philosopher" and "first great man of letters."[99]

But if Franklin accepted the positivism of Hume, the doctrine that the only source of knowledge is perception, he did so less because of Hume himself than because of the 17th century English metaphysics of empiricists like Francis Bacon, Locke, and Newton, which Franklin never questioned as the presupposition of his own thought. The metaphysics of "common sense," formulated a century earlier, and a secular view of life also derived from the Enlightenment *Weltanschauung*, as well as his own apostasy from orthodox New England Calvinism, largely explain why Franklin could not make any sense of Whitefield's talk of *aliquid Christi* and rebirth. Franklin never seems to have had the least inkling that pure empiricism was insufficient to resolve the ultimate questions about man and reality. Immanuel Kant, who admired Franklin's work in electricity and called him the modern Prometheus, would soon offer the world a more convincing philosophical debunking of metaphysics and a justification of religious beliefs on faith alone. He would also accomplish the philosophical reduction of religion to morality. Franklin, as a popular Enlightenment philosopher like Voltaire and the Encyclopedists, never made explicit and systematic his philosophical assumptions.

Whitefield certainly had some awareness of Franklin's distinctly modern smugness on these larger philosophical issues. He even might have realized, as more critical students of physics now do, that Franklin and the Newtonians metaphysically assumed a great deal when they treated nature as uniform, since, as Hume and Kant demonstrated, this could not be established on purely empirical grounds. Franklin would have been surprised to learn that he was a metaphysician after all! In point of fact, Franklin was as victimized by the Newtonian scientific conception of the world as he was by the existence of Christian sectarianism.

Like many others of his generation, Franklin looked upon Newton's method in his *Principia Mathematica* as the standard for all sciences, physical as well as human. This method included both mathematics and experimental verification, but it was Newton's empiricism that Franklin stressed. "Hypotheses are not to be regarded in experimental philosophy," Newton had written in the third edition of the *Principia*—"I frame no hypotheses."[100] That, notwithstanding this formal rejection of hypotheses, Newton used them is seen, for example, in his *a priori* theories of atomism and the ethereal medium. But the point is that Franklin and other credulous Newtonians accepted the possibility of sciences, physical or human, without hypotheses.

In common with the great scientific thinkers of the Renaissance— Francis Bacon in particular—18th century thinkers wanted to purge natural philosophy of the occult qualities of the medieval Aristotelians, and that was understandable. Franklin, typically, was scrupulous and even obsessive about avoiding "hypotheses," not only in his studies of natural phenomena but in the areas of religion and non-empirical reality in general. He was so much on guard against framing hypotheses as to restrict severely his contact with the real (the same would be true of the 19th century American pragmatists). Of his writings on electricity, Franklin, "the Newton of Electricity," wrote to a friend in this vein, that they are "but *conjectures* and *suppositions*; which ought always to give place, when careful observation militates against them. I own I have too strong a penchant to the building of hypotheses; they indulge my natural indolence: I wish I had more of your patience and accuracy in making observations, on which, alone, true philosophy can be founded."[101] When a heated controversy arose in 1777 about the relative merits of pointed or blunt lightning rods, he, as the inventor of the rod, declined to take part in it. "I have never entered into any controversy in defence of my philosophical opinions; I leave them to take their chance in the world. If they are *right*," Franklin put his case with the felicity of Poor Richard, "truth and experience will support them; if *wrong*, they ought to be refuted and rejected."[102]

Franklin's rejection of the meta-empirical, that which lay beyond his sense experience, meant that for him as for Herbert Spencer later God and ultimate reality belonged to the realm of the unknowable. Science, on the other hand, belonged to the realm of the knowable, the phenomenal. There could be no bridging of the two, as Rush and Carroll believed there could be. Hence, when he was asked shortly before he died whether he believed in the divinity of Jesus, Franklin replied with a casualness that would otherwise be inexplicable that he had

some doubts . . . though it is a question I do not dogmatize upon, having never studied it, and think it needless to busy myself with it now, when I expect soon an opportunity of knowing the truth with less trouble. I see no harm, however, in its being believed, if that belief has the good consequence, as probably it has, of making his doctrines more respected and more observed; especially as I do not perceive, that the Supreme takes it amiss, by distinguishing the unbelievers in his government of the world with any peculiar marks of his displeasure.[103]

Franklin's characteristic scientism is implicit in this honestly given final judgment: he was again confusing science with a philosophy of science, empiricism, and universalizing the narrow experimental method by applying it to an object, the ultimate question of God, which demanded the response of the whole man.

In his openness to non-empirical reality, in his repudiation of what we have called scientism, Newton was closer to Whitefield than to Franklin. The great physicist, even though he tended to exaggerate the role of natural reason in religion—causing him to reject the mystery of the Trinity as inaccessible to man's intellect—devoted his closing years to biblical exegesis on the prophecies. But in their philanthropy, their dedication to man's welfare, Whitefield and Franklin could not have been more congenial. They prided themselves on being reformers: the Great Awakening preacher, for example, was a father of the Methodist Church, and Franklin was, among other things, a leader of the "Reformation" within the British Empire that led to the independence of the American Colonies. The two men were also often maligned by their opponents but, although savagely attacked, they maintained great respect for each other. One time Whitefield illustrated his profound regard for his friend's benevolence with an anecdote that Franklin prized. When in his travels to remote parts of the Colonies he read libels written against his friend and knew nothing of the facts themselves, he told Franklin, "they rather gave me this good opinion of you *that you continued to be useful to the public*: for when I am on the road, and see boys in a field at a distance pelting a tree, though I am too far off to know what tree it is, I conclude it has *fruit* on it."[104]

Whitefield, like most dissenters a pro-American in the constitutional crisis with Britain, applauded Franklin's defense of colonial rights before Parliament in 1766. Parliament's repeal of the Stamp Act that year, in which Franklin was highly instrumental, was accompanied by passage of a much stronger Declaratory Act, "binding the colonies in any way whatsoever." By passing this flagrantly unconstitutional act, Franklin believed Parliament was arrogating to itself absolute power, even to dictate religion to the colonists and establish that "popery" that he and Whitefield dreaded.

When the ministry dispatched several regiments to Boston, ostensibly to protect the people of Massachusetts, Franklin wrote prophetically to Whitefield comparing the reinforcements to "setting up a smith's forge in a magazine of gunpowder." It was presumably his last letter to Whitefield, as the revivalist was to die within a year. Franklin was depressed. He saw that the British Empire, "that fine and noble China vase" which he loved, was about to be shattered. As at other critical times in his life—especially when his little boy, Franky, died in 1736—Franklin now questioned that divine Providence which otherwise comforted him in a long life.

"I see with you," he shared his anxiety with his saintly friend,

> that our affairs are not well managed by our rulers here below; I wish I could *believe* with you, that they are well attended to by those above [a possible allusion to his earlier polytheistic belief]; I rather suspect, from certain circumstances, that though the general government of the universe is well administered, our particular little affairs are perhaps below notice, and left to take the chance of human prudence or imprudence, as either may happen to be uppermost. It is, however, an uncomfortable thought, and I leave it.[105]

Whitefield died before he could answer, but, in no uncertain terms, made clear in a note at the foot of Franklin's letter his unqualified trust in divine Providence. *"Uncomfortable* indeed! and, blessed be God, *unscriptural*, for we are fully assured that 'the Lord reigneth,' and are directed to cast *all* our own care on him, because he careth for us."[106]

Franklin could not long maintain doubt about particular Providence, for he had already in the 1730's concluded that the extreme form of Deism, which had God "make so glorious a universe merely to abandon it," was as absurd as the opposite doctrine of rigid predestinarianism. Not that he solved the problem of evil which, of course lay behind his anxiety. With Shaftesbury and his Age, Franklin never doubted that nature afforded "proofs of divine Providence." Indeed, his very understanding of charity towards man was bound up with his belief that the cosmic order required in its design that men help other men in the same way that the processes of nature cooperated with one another to benefit all. Some diseases were even permitted by God, he once said, in order to provide men with an opportunity to serve their fellow man, as in Franklin's active support of the Pennsylvania Hospital. The discovery of smallpox innoculation, and his own invention of the lightning rod, Franklin believed, were examples of particular Providence (Franklin always blamed himself for having hesitated to have his boy, Franky, innoculated against the disease that caused his death). Still, he was struggling with the problem of evil once again on the eve of the American Revolution.

It was irrational, mad, in a word, evil, that Britain and America should be at one another's throats. His "Rules by Which a Great Empire May be Reduced to a Small One (1773)" reflected Franklin's profound disillusionment with Britain's new imperial policy. When he received word of the Boston Tea Party, he desperately offered secretly to raise the money himself to compensate the East India Company. The bloodshed at Lexington and Concord, two years later, angered him. How could a "few blundering ministers" destroy the Britannic-American Empire that he had worked so hard to construct in almost forty years of public service. The "abounding pride and deficient wisdom," the "devilism" of the British Government, was beyond all reason. King George III was a "madman," and his ministers were no better. Britain had every reason to allow the colonists to tax themselves and grow wealthy, since the Americans were loyal to the Empire and would strengthen it over the centuries with the resources of a continent. If Parliament was so jealous of the colonist's population growth—which Franklin saw as the key to America's greatness—and wanted to stop it at any cost, why not adopt a less cruel method from the pharaohs of old, Franklin observed satirically, and pass a law requiring colonial midwives "to stifle in the birth every third or fourth child."[107] In this way the Colonies would be diminished without letting loose blood-thirsty savages and mercenaries to murder American women and children for the king's money.[108]

The crimes of George III, in any event, seemed to go unpunished, casting doubt on the reality of particular Providences. It must be, Franklin concluded, that he and other evil men who prosper in this life despite their cruelty would receive their just reward in a future state.[109]

Franklin's bitter experience in the American Revolution had a much more personal and tragic aspect. His illegitimate son, William Franklin, who had been appointed governor of New Jersey by virtue of his father's influence, remained loyal to Britain during the war years. Benjamin and Deborah had both recognized William as their son from the beginning, treating him the same as their other two children, Franky and Sarah. But when the crisis of 1776 came, William opposed American independence as treason to King and country. All through the years of the war, and afterwards, while he was minister of the United States in Paris, Franklin looked after William's own illegitimate son, William Temple, and saw to his education in Swiss and French schools. In 1784, the War over, Franklin sent the boy back to his father in England, and had him carry what was to be his last letter to William senior. "Nothing has ever hurt me so much, and affected me with such keen sensations as to find myself deserted in my old age by my only son; and not only deserted, but to find him taking up arms against me in a cause wherein my good fame, fortune, and life were all at stake."[110] The next year, on his way back to America, Franklin saw his son in England—for the last time. Nor, apparently, did they keep up any kind of relationship after that. In his last will and testament of 1790 Franklin, seemingly deficient in that Christian charity that he so fervently recommended, cited the "public notoriety" of William's role against him, and used this to justify his "leaving him no more of an estate he endeavored to deprive me of."[111]

There is no doubt that William's conduct towards his father was, in some measure, occasioned by his resentment against the elder Franklin for his alleged callous treament of Deborah Franklin, who died in 1774 while her husband was in London.[112] In any case, these and other experiences of his during the black years of the Revolution severely tested Franklin's naive Enlightenment optimism. In fact, his letter to Dr. Joseph Priestley in 1782 grimly foreshadowed 20th century nihilism in its despair and suggests how close these extremes really are. After saying that he wished for leisure to study inanimate not animate nature, he explained:

> Men I find to be a sort of beings very badly constructed, as they are generally more easily provoked than reconciled, more disposed to do mischief to each other than to make reparation, much more easily deceived than undeceived, and having more pride and even pleasure

in killing than in begetting one another; for without a blush they assemble in great armies at noonday to destroy . . . but they creep into corners, or cover themselves with the darkness of night, when they mean to beget, as being ashamed of a virtuous action. A virtuous action it would be, and a vicious one the killing of them, if the species were really worth producing or preserving; but of this I begin to doubt.

Then he must have shocked the younger dissenting minister and humanitarian with a macabre thought. "I know you have no such doubts, because, in your zeal for their welfare, you are taking a great deal of pains to save their souls. Perhaps as you grow older, you may look upon this as a hopeless project, or an idle amusement, repent of having murdered in mephitic air so many honest, harmless mice, and wish, that, to prevent mischief, you had used boys and girls instead of them."[113]

These gloomy reflections dissipated with the coming of peace in 1783, or, perhaps more likely, relegated once again to Franklin's subconscious. "There has never been, nor ever will be, any such thing as a *good* war, or a *bad* peace," he once again summoned the easy confidence and wit of Poor Richard.[114] America's victory against overwhelming odds signaled the triumph of civil and religious liberty in the world and was clearly providential. "I am too well acquainted with all the springs and levers of our machine," he wrote an estranged friend in England,

not to see that our human means were unequal to our undertaking, and that if it had not been for the justice of our cause, and the consequent interposition of Providence, in which we had faith, we must have been ruined. If I had ever before been an atheist, I should now have been convinced of the being and government of a Deity! It is he who abases the proud and favors the humble. May we never forget his goodness to us, and may our future conduct manifest our gratitude.[115]

Here was the resolution of the doubts that he had confided to Whitefield at the beginning of the trouble.

Human affairs were, after all, governed well like the universe itself. Franklin's saintly friend,George Whitefield, had prayed for his conversion while he lived, only to be disappointed. "He used, indeed, sometimes to pray for my conversion but never had the satisfaction of believing that his prayers were heard," Franklin wrote impishly in his autobiography. "Ours was a mere civil friendship, sincere on both sides, and lasted to his death.'' But, in a true sense, Whitefield's influence on him continued long after the holy man's death. In Franklin's new and strong conviction of the reality of particular Providences there was marked evidence of a kind of conversion. So Whitefield's prayers were answered. It was Franklin who was to make the motion at the Federal Constitutional Convention in 1786 to begin the deliberations with a prayer, for "GOD *governs in the affairs of men*. And, if a sparrow cannot fall to the ground without his notice, is it probable that an empire can rise without his aid?''[116]

The American Revolution was the overpowering event in Franklin's life as it was in the lives of Jefferson, Adams, Washington, and others. Ultimately, he justified the War and the founding of the United States in terms of the greater virtue of the American people. How else was a *philosophe* like Franklin, pledged to Enlightenment cosmopolitanism, to resolve the paradox of being an American nationalist? Even so, the paradox was a glaring one not only for Franklin but for Jefferson, the two outstanding *philosophes* of the American Revolution. Of course, this is easier to see in the perspective of two hundred years, and after the slaughter of millions upon millions of men, women, and children in the name of nationalism. Had Franklin and Jefferson been able to stand apart from their Age, to resist the great temptation of being children of their times (as Pascal counselled), they might have seen that the very Christianity that they rejected alone offered in its metahistorical values the unity of mankind that they professed.

But what of Franklin, the man himself, swept along like most of us in the ebb and flow of history? The Federal Constitutional Convention, inexplicably to Franklin, voted down his motion for prayer to "the Father of Lights to illuminate our understandings.''[117] Franklin laid aside his old scheme of purging Christianity of all creeds, confessions, and rituals and retaining only "the Christian doctrine of forgiveness of injuries and doing good to enemies.''[118] He had too little time left for that. But he did oppose the clause in the Pennsylvania Constitution requiring an oath that the whole of the Old Testament was divinely inspired. "There are several things in the Old Testament,'' he wrote with a rare peremptoriness, "impossible to be given by *divine* inspiration; such as the approbation ascribed to the angel of the Lord, of that abominably wicked and detestable action of Jael, the wife of Heber, the Kenite.''[119] To David

Hartley, who had earned his respect as Britain's representative at the peace negotiations, Franklin proposed with ironic seriousness in 1783 a compact between Britain, France, and America.

> How many excellent things might have been done to promote the internal welfare of each country; what bridges, roads, canals, and other useful public works and institutions, tending to the common felicity, might have been made and established with the money and men foolishly spent during the last seven centuries by our mad wars in doing one another mischief. . . . You are all Christians. One is *The Most Christian King*, and the other *Defender of the Faith*. Manifest the propriety of these titles by your future conduct. 'By this,' says Christ, 'shall all men know that ye are my disciples, if ye love one another.[120]

Thus, Franklin persisted in his vain attempt, as Rush, Carroll, and Whitefield would have seen, to build Christendom without Christ, to expect men to overcome sin and love one another without supernatural grace.

Benjamin Franklin's motto was "Exemplum adest ipse homo"—the example presents the man himself.[121] We could have no better criterion for judging his or anyone else's life. We might even adopt his method of what he called "moral algebra," and draw up two columns of merits and demerits and arrive at a "judgment" about his character in this way.[122] Certainly, his acknowledgement and loving care of his illegitimate son, William—who was not left on the doorstep of a foundling home, as were Rousseau's children, or destroyed in the womb by abortion—would rank high among his merits. His neglect of Deborah assuredly would have to be placed in the negative column. But this, clearly, is not the way to proceed with Franklin, although, its Benthamite crudity aside, it would decidedly result in a favorable "judgment" of the man. Perhaps it is truer and more accurate to say that, while Franklin was not a Christian, apparently never having the grace of belief in Christ's divinity and redemptive sacrifice, he tried very hard and did not fail by much in loving God and man as a true Christian should. His many works of charity bear witness to this.

But it is in the natural order, the world of the Enlightenment, that Franklin belongs and in which his life and character should be assessed. Here again, John Adams was brilliantly insightful when he maintained that perhaps the only way of understanding "so singular a phenomenon" as Franklin's reputation, which was "more universal than that of Leibnitz or Newton, Frederick or Voltaire," was by reconstructing "a complete history of the philosophy and politics of the eighteenth century."[123] Franklin, in other words, was more than any other man the personification of the Enlightenment, revealing in his life and thought all its strengths and weaknesses. In an age known for its lack of alienation, Franklin was *par excellence* the unalienated man.

The people of Europe and America were right in seeing him as the greatest, noblest character of the 18th century Enlightenment. "As he has wrested the lightning from heaven," said Turgot, the French *philosophe*, speaking for all men, "so he would soon wrest the sceptre from tyrants."[124] No one, including Voltaire, had a purer conception of man's duty to his fellow man than Franklin, and no one in the secular order was more consistent in practicing what he preached than "Old Ben Lightning Rod."[125] His benevolence, his love for man, was more comprehensive than that of Voltaire, Adams, and Jefferson, who were, in large part, prevented from attaining Franklin's moral stature by their narrow, lifelong anti-clericalism and the Manichean spirit that occasioned it; although, like them, Franklin never realized that Christianity alone perfects human life and love.

As so often happens with those rare men who are both great and good, Franklin has left us an epitaph on the life of a friend which, in its integrity and humility, could serve well as his own. "His departure is a loss, not to his family and friends only, but to his nation, and to the world, for he was intent on doing good, had wisdom to devise the means, and talents to promote them."[126] The judgment, seriously given, applies as well to no other Founding Father. Moreover, it provides us with what Franklin conceived as the ideal of the new nation he had helped establish, an ideal he aspired to throughout his lifetime and one that was proclaimed.in his natural morality of duty to God and man. This ideal, spiritualized and perfected in Christian love, remains the best ideal for Americans and all people of the world.

## NOTES

[1]BF to Charles de Weissentein, July 1, 1778, John Bigelow, ed., *The Life of Benjamin Franklin Written By Himself* (3 vols.; Philadelphia: J. B. Lippincott & Co., 1875) 2: p. 441, hereafter cited as *Life*; BF to Mary Stevenson,

September 14, 1767, Leonard W. Labaree, *et al.*, eds., *The Papers of Benjamin Franklin* (40 vols.; New Haven: Yale University Press, 1959-) 14: p. 254, cited below as *Papers*.

[2]Émile Mâle, *Religious Art From the Twelfth to the Eighteenth Century* (Noonday Press, 1949), p. 94.

[3]*Ibid.*, pp. 96, 93; Frank L. Mott, ed., *Benjamin Franklin; Representative Selections, with Introduction, Bibliography, and Notes* (New York: American Book Company, 1936), Introduction, p. lvii. See BF's "Apology for Printers," *Papers*, 1: pp. 194-199; Clinton Rossiter, "The Political Theory of Benjamin Franklin," in Esmond Wright, ed., *Benjamin Franklin; A Profile* (New York: Hill and Wang, 1970), p. 167.

[4]BF's autobiography in L. Jesse Lemisch, ed., *Benjamin Franklin; The Autobiography and Other Writings* (New York: The New American Library, 1961), p. 26; Mott, p. lviii.

[5]*Ibid.*, p. lvi; I. Bernard Cohen, "The Empirical Temper" in Charles L. Sanford, ed., *Benjamin Franklin and the American Character* (Boston: D. C. Heath and Co., 1955), pp. 83-93.

[6]Autobiography, p. 21. An excellent biography is Carl Van Doren *Benjamin Franklin* (New York: The Viking Press, 1938).

[7]Autobiography, pp. 29, 22, 26.

[8]Quoted in Sanford, p. 23. Autobiography, p. 26.

[9]*Life*, 3: p. 261, Van Doren, p. 28.

[10]*Papers* 1: p. 111; Autobiography, p. 27.

[11]Autobiography, p. 30.

[12]*Ibid.* Mott, p. xvii.

[13]Autobiography, pp. 31, 35.

[14]Van Doren, p. 600.

[15]*An Almanack For the Year of Christ 1734* . . . By Richard Saunders, Philom. Philadelphia: Printed and sold by B. Franklin, in *Papers*, 1: p. 355.

[16]Mott, p. v.

[17]BF to Thomas B. Hollis, October 5, 1783, *Life* 3: p. 238; Mott, p. xviii; Wilhelm Windelband, *A History of Philosophy* (2 vols.; New York: Harper & Brothers, Pub., 1958) 2: p. 509, BF to Jane Mecom, September 16, 1758, *Papers* 8: p. 154. On Jane Mecom, see *The Letters of Benjamin Franklin & Jane Mecom*, edited with an introduction by Carl Van Doren, Mem. Amer. Philos. Soc 27 (Philadelphia, 1950).

[18]BF to Samuel Mather, July 7; 1773, *Papers*, 20: p. 287, Autobiography, pp. 50, 69-70.

[19]BF to the Federal Constitutional Convention, *Life* 3: p. 395.

[20]Quoted in *Poor Richard's Almanack, 1748, Papers*, 3: p. 251: Autobiography, pp. 35, 45.

[21]BF to Jane Mecom, March 1, 1766, *Papers* 13: p. 188.

[22]Autobiography, pp. 33-35.

[23]*Ibid.*, p. 37.

[24]*Ibid.*, pp. 38-40.

[25]Papers 1:59. Autobiography, p. 56. Cf. Alfred O. Aldridge, *Benjamin Franklin and Nature's God* (Durham, N. Carolina: Duke University Press, 1967), pp. 17-24.

[26]*Liberty and Necessity, Papers*, 1: p. 62.

[27]*Ibid*.

[28]*Ibid*., p. 63. *Life*, 3: p. 469n. Autobiography, p. 92. For a brief discussion of Edward's theology, see Joseph L. Blau, *Men and Movements in American Philosophy* (New York: Prentice-Hall, Inc., 1952), pp. 17-27.

[29]*Papers*, 1: p. 269.

[30]BF to John Whitehurst, June 27, 1763, *Papers*, 10: p. 303.

[31]Autobiography, pp. 56-57; BF to Thomas Hopkinson? October 16, 1746? *Papers*, 3: pp. 88-89.

[32]Autobiography, pp. 58-60; W. R. Sorley, *History of English Philosophy* (Cambridge: Cambridge University Press, 1937), p. 160.

[33]Autobiography, pp. 60-61; "On the Providence of God in the Government of the World," *Papers*, 1: p. 269. Hereafter, all italics are original.

[34]BF, "Plan of Conduct," *Papers*, 1: pp. 99-100; Autobiography, p. 62.

[35]"Plan of Conduct," *Papers*, 1: pp. 99-100; BF to Thomas Hopkinson? October 16, 1746? *Papers* 3: pp. 88-89; Autobiography, p. 81.

[36]*Ibid*, pp. 64-65, on Thomas Denham's influence, see Frederick B. Tolles, "Quaker business Mentors: the Philadelphia Merchants," in Wright ed., pp. 7-18.

[37]BF to George Whatley, August 21, 1784, *Life* 3: p. 288.

[38]BF to Elizabeth Hubbart, February 22, 1756, *Papers*, 6: p. 407; BF to Mrs. Mary Hewson, March 19, 1784, *Life*, 3: p. 258.

[39]Autobiography, p. 69.

[40]*Ibid*., pp. 78-79, 49.

[41]*Ibid*., pp. 53, 64, 80-82, 89-91; Van Doren, p. 94.

[42]Quoted in Sanford, p. 25, BF, "Silence Dogood, No. 4," *Papers*, 1: pp. 14-18 (The Silence Dogood letters, 14 in all, were printed in 1722 in *The New England Courant*, James Franklin's newspaper); Autobiography, p. 140; the quotation from Voltaire is in Crane Brinton's article on the *philosophe* in the *International Encyclopedia of the Social Sciences*, ed., by David L. Sills, (The Macmillan Co., 1968) 16: p. 357.

[43]Autobiography, p. 82.

[44]*Ibid*., p. 94.

[45]*Ibid*.

[46]Bf, "A Defense of Rev. Hemphill's Observations," *Papers*, 2: p. 114; *ibid*., p. 115

[47]May 3, 1760, *ibid*., 9: p. 105; *ibid*., October 21, 1761, p. 375; BF to Jonathan Williams, February 24, 1764, *ibid*., 11: p. 89 and n. Van Doren, p. 105; Autobiography, p. 96; on Montaigne's "moral hygiene" or art of virtue, see John S. Spink, *French Free Thought from Gassendi to Voltaire* (New York: Greenwood Press, 1969), p. 7.

[48]Autobiography, p. 103. "A Defense of Rev. Hemphill's Observations,"

p. 105.

[49]Ibid.; Autobiography, pp. 70, 103.

[50]1758, *Papers* 7: p. 349; Max Weber's views on Franklin's utilitarianism are well known. See Brian M. Barbour, *Benjamin Franklin: A Collection of Critical Essays* (Englewood, N.J.:Prentice Hall, 1979), pp. 14-19.

[51]Autobiography, p. 106; Lemisch, p. 239, Windelband, 2: p. 508.

[52]Autobiography, pp. 92-93; "Observations on Reading History," *Papers*, 1: pp. 192-193.

[53]*Ibid.*, p. 259 and note.

[54]Autobiography, p. 93.

[55]BF, "Articles of Belief and Acts of Religion," *Papers*, 1: pp. 102-103.

[56]*Ibid.*, 2: pp. 202-203, and headnote, pp. 198-199; *ibid.*, p. 204n. Van Doren, pp. 132-136.

[57]*Ibid.*, p. 204. Franklin meant to cite Matt. 25; *ibid.*, p. 203. Franklin often quoted the Bible in his family correspondence.

[58]Autobiography, p. 110.

[59]1747, *Papers*, 3: p. 105, BF to "A Friend in the Country," 1735, *ibid.*, 2: pp. 66, 67, 82-85; Autobiography, pp. 20-21; BF to Richard Price, October 9, 1780, *Life*, 2; p. 542.

[60]"A Friend in the Country," p. 85.

[61]BF to Anthony Tissington, January 28, 1772, *ibid.*, 19: p. 46.

[62]BF to Henry Laurens, March 12, 1784, *Life* 3: n. to p. 257, Van Doren, p. 132. Autobiography, pp. 90, 110-111.

[63]BF to M. Le Veillard, October 24, 1788, *Life*, 3: p. 418.

[64]Autobiography, pp. 117, 71; BF, *Pennsylvania Gazette*; 1740, *Papers*, 2: n. to p. 290, BF to John Franklin, August 6, 1747, *ibid.*, 3, p. 169.

[65]BF, "Statement of Editorial Policy," July 24, 1740, *ibid.*, 2: p. 260; Autobiography, p. 116.

[66]*Ibid.*

[67]*Ibid.*, p. 117.

[68]BF to Mr. Coombe, July 22, 1774, *Life*, 2: p. 243.

[69]Autobiography, pp. 118, 119.

[70]*Ibid.*, p. 118.

[71]BF to Alexander Smith, Nov. 5, 1789, *Life*, 3: p. 447, n; "Statement of Editorial Policy," headnote, pp. 259-260, *Poor Richard*, 1751, *Papers* 4: p. 95.

[72]Autobiography, p. 70 On what might be called Franklin's political utilitarianism, see, e.g.: BF to the Federal Constitutional Convention, *Life*, 3: p. 395; BF's preface to the "Declaration of the Boston Town Meeting" (1773), *Papers* 20: pp. 82-87; Mott, p. lxxviii; Rossiter, "The Political Theory of Benjamin Franklin," pp. 149-150, 156, 158-159; Gerald Stourzh, "Reason and Power in Benjamin Franklin's Political Thought," in Esmond Wright, ed., *Benjamin Franklin: A Profile*, p. 220, *et passim*.

[73]1751, *Papers*, 4: p. 96; BF to ?, December 13, 1757, *Papers*, 7: p. 295. *ibid.*, p. 294.

[74]George Whitefield to Benjamin Franklin, Nov. 26, 1740, *ibid.*, 2: p. 270.

[75]BF, "Observations on the Proceedings Against Mr. Hemphill," ibid., 2: p. 59.

[76]BF to George Whitefield, July 6, 1749, *ibid.*, 3: p. 383; "A Defense of Rev. Hemphill's Observations," p. 116; BF to Lord Kames, May 3, 1760, *ibid.* 9: p. 105.

[77]BF to George Whitefield, July 6, 1749, *ibid.*, 3: p. 383.

[78]"On the Providence of God in the Government of the World," *ibid* 1: p. 267.

[79]BF, "Proposals Relating to the Education of Youth in Pennsylvania," *ibid.*, 3: p. 412.

[80]*Ibid.*, p. 413.

[81]*Ibid.*, p. 419.

[82]George Whitefield to Benjamin Franklin, February 26, 1750, *ibid.*, pp. 467-468.

[83]Autobiography, pp. 117. 130; BF, "Proposals for Preparing the Academy Building," *Papers* 3: p. 435, headnote.

[84]BF to Elizabeth Partridge, Nov. 25, 1788, *Life* 3: pp. 418-419; Autobiography, p. 127.

[85]1749, *Papers*, 3: p. 341.

[86]1734, *ibid.*, 1: p. 356.

[87]BF to Joseph Huey, June 6, 1753, *ibid.*, 4: p. 506.

[88]Proposals Relating to the Education of Youth in Pennsylvania," 3: p. 419n.

[89]George Whitefield to Benjamin Franklin, August 17, 1752, *ibid.*, 4: p. 343.

[90]BF to Jane Mecom, February 23, 1769, *ibid.*, 16: p. 51.

[91]Autobiography, p. 119.

[92]George Whitefield to Benjamin Franklin, August 17, 1752, *Papers*, 4: p. 343.

[93]*Ibid.*

[94]*Ibid.*, January 17, 1755, 5: pp. 475-476.

[95]BF to George Whitefield, June 19, 1764, *ibid.*, 11: p. 231-232.

[96]BF to George Whateley, May 23, 1785, *Life*, 3: p. 305.

[97]Quoted in Mott, pp. xxxix-xl; Frederick Copleston, S.J., *A History of Philosophy* (8 vols., Westminster, Md.: The Newman Press) 6: pt. i, pp. 15-16.

[98]Quoted in *ibid.*, 5: p. 260.

[99]Quoted in Van Doren, p. 290.

[100]Quoted in Copleston, 5: p. 151, *ibid.*, 4: p. 72.

[101]BF to John Perkins, August 13, 1752, *Papers*, 4: p. 341.

[102]BF to a Friend, October 14, 1777, *Life*, 2: p. 407.

[103]BF to Ezra Stiles, March 9, 1790, *ibid.*, 3: pp. 459-460.

[104]Quoted in BF to Jane Mecom, March 2, 1767, *Papers*, 14: p. 73.

[105]September 2, 1769, *ibid.*, 16: p. 192. BF to Lord Howe, July 20, 1776, *Life*, 2: p. 364; BF to George Whitefield, September 2, 1769, *Papers* 16: p. 192; BF to Samuel Mather, July 7, 1773, *ibid.*, 20: p. 288; Aldridge, pp. 41-42.

[106]BF to George Whitefield, September 2, 1769, 16: 192n.

[107]BF, "The Interest of Great Britain Considered," (1760), *Papers* 9: p. 94; BF, "On a Proposed Act to Prevent Emigration," (1773) *ibid*. 20: pp. 527-528, 526; BF to Francis Maseres, June 26, 1785, *Life*, 3: p. 316; BF to Lord Howe, July 20, 1776, *ibid*, 2: p. 364, BF to the Marquis de Lafayette, August 19, 1779, *ibid*., pp. 483-484; BF to a Friend, October 3, 1775, *ibid*., p. 348, BF "Rules by Which a Great Empire May be Reduced to a Small One," *Papers*, 20: pp. 389-399; *Life*, 3: p. 423.

[108]BF to David Hartley, February 12, 1778, *Life*, 2: p. 412, BF to John Winthrop, May 1, 1777, *ibid*., pp. 393-394.

[109]BF to James Hutton, July 7, 1782, *ibid*., 3: pp. 179-180.

[110]August 16, 1784, *ibid*., pp. 279-280. On William Temple, see Van Doren, *et passim*.

[111]*Life*, 3: p. 470. This consisted of BF's lands in Nova Scotia, books and papers that William already possessed from his father, and certain debts that BF had incurred in favor of his son, Van Doren, p. 761.

[112]William Franklin to Benjamin Franklin, December 24, 1774, *Life*, 2: n. to p. 244.

[113]BF to Joseph Priestley, June 7, 1782, *ibid*. 3: pp. 59-60.

[114]BF to Jonathan Shipley, June 10, 1782, *ibid*., p. 62.

[115]BF to William Strahan, August 19, 1784, *ibid*., p. 285, BF to Samuel Mather, July 7, 1773, *Papers*, 20: p. 287.

[116]BF to the Federal Constitutional Convention, *Life*, 3: p. 388; Autobiography, p. 118.

[117]BF to the Federal Constitutional Convention, *Life*, 3: n. to p. 389. on virtue, e.g., see BF to Joseph Priestley, July 7, 1775, *ibid*., 2: pp. 344-345.

[118]BF to Granville Sharp, July 5, 1785, *ibid*., 3: pp. 319-320.

[119]BF to a Friend in England, August 21; 1784, *ibid*., p. 289. The OT reference is to Judges, ch. iv. For BF's not having enough time for religious reformations, BF to Alexander Small, September 28, 1787, *ibid*., p. 398.

[120]BF to David Hartley, October 16, 1783, *ibid* 3: p. 240.

[121]*Papers*, 2, illustration facing p. 230.

[122]BF to Joseph Priestley, February 8, 1780, *Life*, 2: p. 501.

[123]Quoted in Sanford, p. 23.

[124]*Ibid*., p. 24.

[125]"What means that flash, the thunder's awful roar," Thomas Willing eulogized Franklin on his death in 1790,
"The Blazing sky—unseen, unheard before?
Sage Smith replies, 'Our Franklin is no more.'
The clouds, long subject to his magic chain,
Exulting now their liberty regain," Horace W. Smith, *Life and Correspondence of the Rev. William Smith, D.D.* (Phila. 1880), 2: pp. 324-325, 344, cited in *Papers* 4: 469n.

[126]BF to Miss Catherine Louisa Shipley, April 27, 1789, *Life* 3: p. 435.

# Conclusion

The history of our Revolution," John Adams complained with some justice, "will be one continued lie from one end to the other. The essence of the whole will be that Dr. Franklin's electric rod smote the earth and out sprang General Washington. That Franklin electrified him with his rod, and thenceforward these two conducted all the policy negotiations, legislatures, and wars."[1]

For all his cynicism, Adams's words were prophetic. Today Franklin and Washington are best remembered as heroes of the American Revolution, Jefferson ranking next in popularity. Adams himself, Hamilton, and Rush are known only to the historically literate public. Carroll is forgotten.

Not only is this sadly the case, but, as if dictated by some historical law of modesty, even those who are idolized by the people—Franklin, Washington, Jefferson—remain hidden in their real character. Perhaps this is as it should be, for as Rush and Carroll would forewarn us in their Christian perspective, man is ultimately a mystery whose real "name" is known only to God. But it is also true that Adams, Franklin, Washington, Jefferson, Hamilton, Carroll, and Rush lived in the flux of time, as we do, and the exigencies of history required that they make judgments about men, sometimes hasty ones like that of Adams above and deeper judgments like that of Hamilton who, in his final Christian conviction, preferred death to killing another man in a senseless duel. What did the Founding Fathers think of man—themselves and others? Analyzing their ideas on man and his culture, while fully realizing that we too are subject to all the limitations of temporality, what judgments can we offer in conclusion to explain these men and, possibly, the meaning of the nation that they founded?

On the nature of man, the anthropologies of the Founding Fathers reflect their positions *vis-à-vis* Christianity. Adams, as we have seen, in his secularized Calvinism conceived man as depraved. His Manichaenism, rejecting the Incarnation and the Redemption of mankind, predisposed him not only to jaundiced views of Franklin, Washington, and Hamilton, and man in general, but to an acceptance of the very finality of man's imperfection and misery. There could be, for Adams, no hope of personal salvation in the Christian sense, an attitude he shared with Jefferson, Franklin, and Washington. Like these men too, Adams denied the need for, and reality of, supernatural grace to perfect man's nature in this world. Revelation, it seems, made no sense to Adams; and without Christ, God and man, revealed and revealer, man must be understood exclusively in natural terms. Adams retained, however, his New England Calvinistic heritage in that he continued to divide men into sinners and saints or, at the very least, maintained a deep suspicion of those he encountered in life. With Jefferson, Franklin, and Washington, Adams failed to see that man's ultimate and only real happiness lies in the spiritual enjoyment of the Beatific vision of God which in Christian teaching is reserved for the blessed in life after death. In short, as Enlightenment thinkers, these men confined man's vocation to happiness in the dimension of this world only. This was their understanding of Jefferson's "right to the pursuit of happiness" enshrined in the Declaration of Independence.

Adams's obsessive fear of corporate authority, especially in the Roman Catholic Church, was consistent with his pessimism about man and his motives. Indeed, in his opposition to the universal papacy and the canon and feudal systems sanctioned by the medieval Church, Adams lends himself to classification as a reformer like Martin Luther in Friedrich Engels's famous thesis about the Protestant Reformation as the first bourgeois revolution to deny the Church's authority in the interest of the new class.[2] Of course this could be said, more or less, of the other Founding Fathers as well. Hamilton, however, his articulate capitalism notwithstanding, never attacked medieval civilization with the ideological sophistication of Adams; and Carroll and Rush were, unlike the others, essentially too Christocentric and universalistic to be bourgeois spokesmen.

Adams was a permanent dissenter. His orthodoxy was negative, reducing in the end the Protestant principle of individualism to a form of historical nihilism, consequences Jefferson and Franklin were spared chiefly on account of their Pelagianism. They more typically subscribed to Renaissance and Enlightenment humanism and welcomed the triumph of reason over what they considered the blind, irrational forces of history; Adams, on the other hand, true to his Manichaen outlook, found only conspiratorial lust for power in his own and past generations. Paradoxically, Adams looked more deeply into history than any of the others, but his historical perspective was narrowed by a coarse secularism and distorted by a radical, uncompromising naturalism which left out man's spiritual and transcendent dimension altogether. Had the others read more widely in history, philosophy, and literature—in what Oswald Spengler called modern *buch und lesen kultur*—they might have shared Adams's extreme pessimism about man and his works. As it was, Jefferson and Franklin were, in spite of themselves, less antagonistic to medieval conceptions of man and history, at least to the extent that they saw much good in man and had hope for the future.

Adams, Washington, and Hamilton were all Federalists in politics and, not surprisingly, possessed in common (before Hamilton's conversion) a view of man as "a reasoning rather than reasonable animal."[3] Elitist and pessimistic in their solution of the problem of man, each of them placed his hope in new institutions rather than spiritual reform of man himself. Adams urged the separation and balance of powers in government. Washington, severe with ordinary men who lacked his virtues, must curb the excesses of human nature and promote civic duty through Roman-like discipline by the state. Soldiers, Washington and Hamilton exalted the will, not the intellect, and conceived of the American nation as its embodiment.

Franklin's anthropology, while very close to Jefferson's, in the last resort seems to have foundered in skepticism—derived as much from classical as from Renaissance and Reformation sources—and had its political counterpart in his doctrine of utilitarianism. The state for Franklin was neither a delicately balanced machine, as with Adams, nor the Leviathan of Hamilton and Washington. It must be, like all things in Franklin's scientism, merely empirical. Early America's greatest scientist believed that natural law and natural rights were, at best, only hypotheses; and, as the great Newton had said, the careful philosopher must not just reduce hypotheses in the manner of Ockham but eliminate them altogether. Hence, for Franklin as for Hume and Bentham, legal, political, and other norms were nothing but conventions, the result of agreements among men for the sake of utility. In the 19th and 20th centuries, Justice Oliver Wendell Holmes, Hans Kelsen, and the various schools of legal relativism have drawn the consequences of this voluntaristic denial of "meta-juridical norms" in asserting that positive (statutory) law is absolute.[4] As we have suggested above, Jefferson's humanism, his nominalistic and subjective emphasis on the natural rights of the individual to the detriment of the older Aristotelian-Thomistic concept of natural law and community, leads to the same anarchic individualism—inevitably, the *anomie* of Durkheim—the collectivization of man and the absolutization of the state.

The post-medieval differentiation of *regnum* and *sacerdotium*, the Renaissance and Reformation atomization of Gospel, Church, and public order, and of man himself is seen in all the Protestant Founding Fathers, with the exception of Rush.[5] The nominalistic, Lutheran separation of Church and state, held by all these men—although in qualified senses by Adams, Carroll, and Rush—marked the beginning of the autonomous and now omnicompetent state. Hobbes saw the implications of this in the 16th century. Once the Church was privatized and divorced from social and political life, a vacuum was created which the state was quick to fill. The Church was absorbed by the secular power, as in Anglican Erastianism, and in those submissive "civic" religions that today barter away the kerygma for bourgeois respectability in the nation-state. "Once the 'autonomous state' has broken all bonds," Romano Guardini has written in words that perhaps only Rush and Carroll would have understood, "it will be able to deliver the last *coup de grace* to human nature itself."[6]

Rush and Carroll would have fathomed Guardini's warning, because their anthropology was Christian. They were not limited in their thinking about man to the one-dimensional, secular conception of man that the others presupposed in their bourgeois Enlightenment *Weltanschauung*. Jeffersonian man was the "natural man" of modern liberalism, turned inward to himself and not to God. Forgetful of his being made in the image of God, man hypostatized his own nature and existence, severing himself from the One in whom he "lives and breathes." There could be no autonomous state for Rush and Carroll. Their only hope for man was in Christ the Redeemer, not in the absolutized natural reason of Jefferson and Franklin, the mechanized distribution of power in Adams, or the Caesarism of Hamilton and Washington. Charity was their only absolute, the divine order of love proclaimed by Jesus in the New Testament kerygma. If Jefferson and Franklin as Enlightenment humanists believed that man's nature was its own perfection, and that all that was necessary in order to liberate man was to reform society, the two Christian signers of the Declaration realized that man's nature must first be perfected by grace. The law that Jefferson and Adams extolled in a "government of laws not men," Rush and Carroll knew, must be radicalized in love, or else, as demonstrated over and over again in history, the law—as Guardini and others have warned—would be turned against man himself as in Jesus's time. Jefferson, Adams, and Franklin were, like the positivists and Marxists of our day, enslaved to the phenomenological, the temporal, the historical, in their attitude towards man. Rush and Carroll—and later Hamilton—saw with St. Augustine that the Incarnation and Redemption had freed man from his bondage to time and culture. The *unum necessarium*, they realized in their faith, was Christ.

Within the secular city that they hoped to build as *philosophes*, Jefferson, Adams, Washington, and Franklin naively trusted in science and right reason. The natural, they maintained with Rousseau, who was teaching this neo-humanism in a more open way, was good and desirable, although Adams as a Calvinist *manqué* was inconsistent on this point. Once again, Rush and Carroll were saved from this error by their Thomistic appreciation of the relationship between faith and reason. Rush, who was greatly influenced by Franklin's personal qualities and achievements, was never even tempted to accept the much older man's scientism. His conception of nature was essentially medieval rather than modern, recognizing that nature is not autonomous and treating the empirical as only one of its aspects. Rush and Carroll were Pascalian in their affirmation of the "real" as including, but not restricted to, the empirical and the mathematical. The autonomous, secular city in this more universal Christian perspective must be as fictitious as the self-subsisting "nature" of Bruno, Spinoza, and other modern pantheists. Neither nature, man, nor culture was autonomous. Rush's ideal of the *res publica christiana* which he proposed as a civilization of love for the new United States reflected this truth. Its conception lay in his and

Carroll's truly revolutionary awareness that man is called to respond to God's absolute commandment by imitating Christ and transforming sin and law into humility and love. Indeed, this was the message of Carroll's breviary, Thomas à Kempis's *Imitation of Christ.*

The finite, neo-pagan values implicit in the Enlightenment doctrine of self-creating nature, man, and culture remained for the most part dormant until the French Revolution. For reasons still not clear there was, to the great credit of the Founding Fathers, no Reign of Terror. Hamilton, Adams, and Washington were fearful of Jacobinism, but Jefferson was no Robespierre, although he wrote hyperbolically about the necessity of watering the tree of liberty with blood every 20 years. At any rate, Adams, Hamilton, Washington and the American secular conservatives were incapable of rising to the challenge of these new, post-Christian ideas; if they lashed out at French atheism in the late 1790's, as did Hamilton and Adams, they nevertheless failed to offer any constructive alternative programs. Hamilton's idea for Christian Constitutional Societies might have been advanced as part of a larger scheme to counter modern atheism, yet the evidence, such as it is, does not suggest anything more than a palliative measure. Adams, having lost his faith, could only react to the philosophy he had once fostered—now unmasked and lurid in its evil—and retreat in despair into a private world of gloom. In his final years, he was still riding his favorite hobby horse: the danger the Roman Catholic Church posed to the world. He even lent credence to wild reports of disguised Jesuits invading the country to seize it for Rome, calumnies widely printed in the nativist newspapers of the time.[7] Washington was dead by 1799. In any case, his Stoical remoteness made him appear cold and aristocratic. A man whose own exacting self-discipline caused him to hang rather than shoot men for desertion, because the former means of death had a more terrifying effect on soldiers, could hardly lead the nation back to Christendom.

As secular conservatives, Adams, Hamilton, and Washington were, as we have suggested, so philosophically close to Jefferson, Franklin, and the French thinkers that they operated within what was, in effect, the same world-view and, like it or not, were reduced to a reactionary role. They were all what Metternich called "presumptuous men," pretending to an independence from the divine order of things. Rush and Carroll were different. Their more searching analysis of the meaning of man allowed them to transcend their age and its historical categories, as Pascal had urged, and solve the problem of culture by recognizing man's true essence as the adopted son of God. They were not "presumptuous men," for they discerned in man the need for legitimate authority; Rush as a mature Protestant thinker discovering it in the Bible and Carroll finding it there and in the Magisterium of the Roman Catholic Church. Hence, the alternative they offered to atheism in the modern world was the New Testament kerygma, which Rush in particular tried to apply in detail to American society in the post-Revolutionary period. This was his ideal of the Christian Republic, an evangelical community of love, that would integrate man, nature, and culture in Christ, restoring the wholeness of things by doing away with the false autonomies of the modern age.[8]

Rush and Carroll realized at a deeper level than Jefferson, Adams, and Franklin could in their secular humanism that politics and economics were moral sciences, that they existed only for man and like all things stood in a new relationship to man because of the Word made flesh. Their *recherches de l'esprit*, and that of the Christian Hamilton, revealed the ontological mystery of man as greater than any merely natural explanation. They would have none of the subjectivism that lurked in the thinking of the others. Value and reality were not separate, as Jefferson, Franklin, Washington, and other modern thinkers maintained in a tradition that went back beyond Descartes to the nominalism of Ockham and Luther. The rights of man, so celebrated by Jefferson and the Enlightenment, must be balanced by the duties of man. Most of all, Rush and Carroll argued, the rights of God should be acknowledged not only in private but in the public order as well. Even Kant had said that the hallmark of the *Aufklärung* was making "public use" of one's faculty of reason.[9] So, it was clear the truths of the Incarnation and the Redemption, along with the natural truths of reason—natural law, for example—should be institutionalized in post-Revolutionary America, offering the world a lesson in the necessary objective conditions for that just society that St. Augustine had called for at the beginning of the Christian era. This was no pale reflection of finite Enlightenment values, no reactionary conservatism, but a daring program which transcended history and culture themselves in proclaiming with Jesus a kingdom of absolute love in which all men would be gathered to live in peace and await the Millennium.

Rush's conception of the ideal Christian society, which Carroll would have accepted in essence but which was nowhere developed in his writings, was radically different from Jeffersonian society in not being what Max Scheler called a *Gesellshaft*.[10] The society of the *philosophes* was merely contractual and for that reason superficial, diametrically opposed to the community of love. It was bourgeois insofar as it was the social and political counterpart to the new class's nominalization and mechanization of reality in which higher, supra-individual values were denied or treated as secondary. The social contract theory of Hobbes, Locke, and Rousseau was its political expression. It was unhistorical as Enlightenment thought was in general, a point Edmund Burke later was to make with telling effect. Closely interrelated with Newtonian mechanics, the atomistic *Gesellshaft* type of society presupposed a cold world of objects homogeneous in space and time. Jefferson's abstract individualism and his weakened regard for the "social" were both cause and effect of his acceptance of this modern psuedo-theory, as was Rousseau's collectivism.

Jefferson liked to say that his "trinity" of genius was Francis Bacon, Sir Isaac Newton, and John Locke, each of whom we now recognize with Descartes as creators of the secular, bourgeois world-view of the Enlightenment. Jefferson, Adams, and Franklin—even Washington, although he read little by comparison—were exponents of the new "book culture" which Marshall McLuhan has written about with such insight. If one would know the thinking of these men, one must read the books they read, and they have left a good record of what those books were. Franklin in his bibliomania went so far as to identify himself with a book in his epitaph. They left impressive libraries: Franklin, like Andrew Carnegie years later, remembered the difficulty he had had as a young man obtaining good books and sought to help others with their self-education by promoting lending libraries. Jefferson and Adams were, of course, lawyers and their training for the bar as apprentices consisted almost wholly of reading. But the "*buch und lesen Kultur*" of modern men like these, now coming to an end in the electronic age, ultimately derived from profound changes in Western man's consciousness of himself, of reality, and of the nature of the Godhead which first began to agitate European thought during the late Middle Ages. Gutenberg's introduction of moveable print, providing the new, emerging consciousness with a technology, was only an effect of this revolution in Western man's spirit. But Protestantism and "book culture" were intimately, if not causally related. Luther's and Calvin's strong tendency to reduce the Gospel to the Bible, the written word alone, without recognition of the Church's authority as guarantor of the Scriptures, greatly encouraged an almost absolute respect for books of all kinds. Moreover, the Reformation, in turn, by weakening the Church removed from her discipline writers and artists—members of the rising bourgeois intelligentsia—who could now express all manner of ideas and produce their books and art free of restraint. The dissolution of the medieval guilds in favor of individual competition was likewise related to the "marketing" and consumption of ideas along the same proto-capitalistic lines.[11]

Rush, it is true, centered his faith exclusively on one book—the Bible—and to that extent he too was representative of modern culture. The book, however, was *sui generis*. And, in his evangelical Protestant Christianity, Rush drew absolute supernatural truths from the inspired text which Franklin and Jefferson treated as though it were just another, if grand, product of human folly and intelligence. The point is that Rush transcended book culture in recognizing the kerygma, as Carroll did too in his Catholicism. In the pages of Locke's *Second Treatise of Government* all the Founders read about the state of nature, natural rights, and the social contract which, according to Locke, are the means by which men form political society. Jefferson and the others stopped there, with Locke's natural explanation of the origin of government. Rush and Carroll elevated Locke's classical discussion, as it were, to a spiritual plane by replacing the minimal, liberal concept of natural law with the divine commandment of brotherly love. This was a Christian perfection of social contract theory, reminiscent of the best medieval thought. The tragedy is that America followed the Lockean, Jeffersonian, i.e. liberal-bourgeois, model of society as the collection of individuals and gave little attention to the common good until recent times.

Just as Rush and Carroll disagreed with modern ideas of autonomous man and culture, so they maintained the older view of nature. Against the naturalism of Jefferson, Franklin, and Washington, which repudiated belief in the supernatural and explained nature in its own terms, Rush and Carroll held that the material world was not the sole reality, but, on the contrary, was fully intelligible only to the spirit. In medicine for example, Dr. Rush's field, Jefferson, naively rejecting hypotheses as did Franklin, believed in the *vis medicatrix naturae*—the curative power of nature—which, Rush argued, the Christian physician must reject as theologically as well as scientifically unsound. The Deistic "nature" which Jefferson endowed with perfect, self-existing medical qualities could not be, since nature had fallen with man in his Original Sin and was in need of redemption through Christ.[12] The same was true of the natural rights that Jefferson had written about so eloquently in the Declaration of Independence. They did not exist as essences in some absolute Deistic Nature: like nature itself the precious natural rights found their source in the one living God. Nature, its laws and the rights it conferred, was not an end but only a means to lead man to Christ, the Truth Himself. Jefferson confused immanent, secondary causes, those revealed by Bacon, Newton, and Locke, with God, the primary, transcendent cause. This could only result in the 19th century in the practical atheism of William James, John Dewey, and those other modern American philosophers who with a more rigorous logic than Jefferson not only absolutized nature but derived all truth from praxis. Rush and Carroll, the latter protected from the error by his Jesuit education in Thomism, tried to stop this post-Enlightenment development of American thought by attacking the modern idea of the autonomy of nature.

As Rush and Carroll realized so clearly, modern thinkers like Jefferson, Adams, Franklin, and Washington were utopian in their stubborn refusal to see the reality of sin, Original and personal. And without an acknowledgment of sin as the curse of mankind, Jefferson and the others could not understand the need for Christ's redemptive sacrifice. Their Enlightenment faith in reason, which ultimately failed to come to grips with evil, was their justification for a naturalistic belief in progress. This secularized version of the Judaeo-Christian idea of progress, first developed systematically by St. Augustine, had been winning credence among the intelligentsia ever since the Renaissance. In its medieval formulation, the belief in the inevitable advance of mankind rested on the certain knowledge that Christ, the Son of God, had entered into history at the Incarnation to reconcile man and God in the Atonement. Not only were God and man restored to their proper relationship by the Man-God, but man, who had been alienated from the Creation, i.e. nature, because of Adam's sin, was now reconciled with nature, and hence nature could no longer be considered an absolute as in pre-

Christian, pagan thinking. In the light of the Incarnation and Redemption, then, the naturalistic Enlightenment belief in progress can be seen, and was seen, if only dimly, by Rush, Carroll, and other Christian thinkers as a neo-pagan myth. (It was also, as Georges Sorel argued, a bourgeois myth devoted essentially to the laying up of material goods; moreover, as Michelle Sciacca has asserted, this American naturalism has strong philosophical ties with Marxism,[13] as both ignore the central Christian teaching on man and his nature.)

When they signed the Declaration of Independence, Rush and Carroll knew that the Jeffersonian "Creator" mentioned in it must be specified as the God of the Judaeo-Christian tradition in order for the new nation to be conceived in truth and prosper. They were convinced of this truth, humanly speaking, as a result of their excellent formation in Protestant and Catholic schools here and abroad. Perhaps we can best summarize what Rush learned at the Great Awakening schools of Nottingham and Princeton, and Carroll at the Jesuit-run Bohemia Manor at St. Omer, as essentially what Pascal had discovered years before them. "The knowledge of God without that of our wretchedness produces pride," he wrote in words that go straight to the human condition ."The knowledge of our wretchedness without the knowledge of God produces despair. The knowledge of Jesus Christ forms the middle point; for there we find both God and our wretchedness."[14] If we were to apply Pascal's existential analysis to Jefferson, Franklin, and Hamilton before his conversion, we could say that they had learned about God but had never confronted their own wretchedness and, hence, never rose above natural theology and its pride of intellect. Adams and Washington, on the other hand, tended in their fatalism to see man wretched beyond hope. Jefferson and Franklin, Rush and Carroll agreed with Pascal, had "knowledge of God without Christ." This was nothing but Deism, which the teachers at Nottingham, Princeton, Bohemia Manor, and St. Omer had exposed as only a new form of paganism.

The teachers of Jefferson at William and Mary were Enlightenment *philosophes* who, in and out of the lecture hall, formed his thinking along modern bourgeois lines. In his autobiography he tells us that William Small, George Fauquier, and George Wythe—later, a signer of the Declaration of Independence—introduced him to the Baconian philosophy of empiricism which, in opposition to the Aristotelian-Thomistic deductive method of science, was accepted doctrine in the Enlightenment. Jefferson's ideal from then on was what he called the "expansion of science," a nominalistic program which did violence to what was left of the medieval unity of being by isolating nature, man, and culture and treating them as autonomous.[15] Franklin, as we noted earlier, came around to the same naturalistic conclusion, as did Adams, Washington, and Hamilton before his *metanoia*.

This modern, Renaissance-Enlightenment *Weltanschauung* of Jefferson, Franklin, Washington, and Hamilton was bourgeois, by which we mean that it was an ideology of the new social class whose ruling interest was exploitation of the material world. Francis Bacon, of course, was a leading spokesman for this ideology in which knowledge was narrowly conceived as power. Newton, too, for all his examination of the prophecies late in life, accepted the Baconian ideal and as president of the Royal Society—after which Franklin's American Philosophical Society was modelled—subscribed to the new, exploitative attitude towards nature. Locke, another of Jefferson's "gods," completed in his psychology the work of Descartes in reducing the soul of man to a mere machine for ideas, and in his likewise distorted naturalistic social and political philosophy made use of the same crude, mechanical analogy in treating men as monads in a nominalistic commonwealth. These and other thinkers whose names are well-known as shapers of the modern age conceived man essentially as a machine to exploit nature's wealth. Hamilton's *homo economicus* and the Industrial Revolution itself, about which Jefferson had grave doubts, were paradoxically the logical outcome of this instrumentalist, Baconian view of nature which the Virginian accepted and which he learned from his teachers at William and Mary. This bourgeois conception of man as naturally acquisitive, free, and self-determined in his relationship to nature (and culture) was emphatically not that held by Rush, Carroll and Pascal who, true to the older, Judaeo-Christian tradition, recognized man's essence as more than economic, political, and social—but as universal.

Rush and Carroll, then, were unique among the Founding Fathers as serious Christians whose faith in transcendent, metahistorical values enabled them to escape from the confining temporalities of the modern age and discover man in his permanent, universal condition. This said, however, we need to look further at the two men in terms of how they differed within the Christian tradition, noting their strengths and weaknesses and what relevance their lives have for us today. Rush, as we have implied, although he had man's theocentric essence firmly in mind, was more prone than Carroll to accommodate his Christian faith to the relative norms of the 18th century. Rush did not with Franklin and Jefferson reduce the kerygma to secular humanism, but he did try to force Christ's timeless message of love into what must be, in the very nature of the case, an impossible alliance with a mere political doctrine—republicanism. He even attempted, more generally, to synthesize the New Testament kerygma with the temporal culture of the 18th century, hoping to forestall in this way the Jeffersonian absolutization of culture by penetrating history with Christ's eternal commandment of love. This, of course, had been done many times before, especially by St. Thomas Aquinas. Rush possessed, although certainly not in the same degree of genius, the "will to synthesis" of such Christian thinkers as St. Thomas and St. Augustine. Central to this will, however, was his Great Awakening millennialism, an error that St. Augustine had warned against. And we have suggested in our necessarily brief discussion of Rush's medical ideas the fact that here also he tried to prevent the growing acceptance of the modern idea of the autonomy of nature by attempting a synthesis of evangelical Protestant Christianity and science.

In any case, by relativizing the essential Christian message (kerygma)—which must be the effect of even Rush's moderate form of historicism—by trying to relate it directly to, or embodying it in, the political, social, scientific, and other circumstances of his time, Rush was limiting its scope. Historical man is not, strictly speaking, universal man. The kerygma is a timeless message of love to man's essence whatever his period. It must judge history rather than be judged by it; but because Rush and other Christian thinkers of all ages have tended to make the kerygma dependent on the historical moment, other men like Marx and Feuerbach later could argue with devastating effect that Christianity was a mere social or historical phenomenon. Rush as "theologian" of the American Revolution, in other words, forgot that Christ came not to change the world but to redeem it. These are not necessarily the same things in the divine economy. And so today, when many 18th century forms of thought and human behavior are recognized as so many contingencies in man's development, the kerygma—God's proclamation of absolute love, which transcended Rush's time as it does ours—is confused with the anachronistic past and tragically rejected.[16]

Charles Carroll, who was not formed in the tradition of Great Awakening piety as was Rush, developed his thinking about the American Revolution more cautiously. He was not a millennialist. He did not belong like Rush to what Ernst Troeltsch called the "sectarian tradition," which required the political order either radically to accept Christ's new law of love or be abandoned.[17] Carroll was too well educated in Thomism, e.g., in the rights of the spiritual and temporal orders, by the Jesuits of Bohemia Manor and St. Omer to be an Enlightenment *philosophe* or a millennialist. As a Roman Catholic, he accepted legitimate authority in a way that even Rush could not. Republicanism, which Rush conceived as a divine vehicle of grace, Carroll knew as one of many forms of government, each with strengths and weaknesses, and each deriving its authority not from the sovereignty of the people but from God. Every nation, whatever its form of government, rested on natural law, civil law, and the law of nations—all ultimately finding their source in divine law. Together with the other nations, Carroll realized, the United States belonged to the community of nations, which was in the secular order the complement of the universal Church established by Christ for the salvation of all nations.

If Rush in his audacity conferred on the American Revolution that dramatic theoretical clarity that Hannah Arendt and others have found lacking, Carroll, as a member of a persecuted minority, gave to it a measure of realism that has endured to our own day. It was most fitting—symbolic of truth—that Carroll, the Roman Catholic Signer, should be the last surviving Founding Father. It is even more fitting that he, unlike disillusioned Rush, Jefferson, and Adams, should retain to the end his common-sense optimism about the American Revolution.

Christianity, then, was in one sense the stone these builders of the American nation rejected, except for Benjamin Rush and Charles Carroll. Yet the other Founding Fathers, even as modern men, still held fast to much that was good from the Judaeo-Christian tradition. Jefferson's enthusiasm for the defense of reason, natural law, and the principle of subsidiarity is worthy of the best Christian thinkers. And there could be no better advice (properly understood) for any age than Franklin's "Imitation of Jesus and Socrates,"[18] for man needs humbly to live both the life of the spirit and the intellect. But it was the most unlikely of all of them, the Caesarist Alexander Hamilton, who, laying down his life for an enemy, proved that the lives and thought of the Founding Fathers—even in the heady days of the American Revolution—could be completely transformed. Obedient to Christ's command of absolute love, Hamilton died very much in the manner of those other and greater figures of destiny, those who build the futures of two worlds, the only true revolutionaries—the saints.

## NOTES

[1]Quoted in Cunliffe, p. 16.

[2]*The Peasant War in Germany* (1850), cited in Abraham Friesen, "The Reformation," in C. D. Kernig, ed., *Marxism, Communism and Western Society* (8 vols.; Herder and Herder, 1973) 7: p. 150.

[3]Supra, p. 98.

[4]Michel Villey, "Philosophy of Law," in Kernig, 5: pp. 136-147.

[5]Talcott Parsons, "Christianity," in David L. Sills, ed., *International Encyclopedia of the Social Sciences* (17 vols.; New York: Macmillan Col., 1968) 2: pp. 425-446.

[6]*The End of the Modern World*, ed. with an Introduction by Frederick Wilhelmsen (Henry Regnery, 1968), p. 74.

[7]Ray Allen Billington, *The Protestant Crusade 1800-1860; A Study of the Origins of American Nativism* (New York: The Macmillan Co., 1938), p. 120.

[8]D'Elia, *Benjamin Rush: Philosopher of the American Revolution* (Philadelphia: Transactions of the American Philosophical Society, 1974).

[9]Cited in Iring Fescher and Eberhard Muller, "Enlightenment", Kernig, 3: p. 171.

[10]Lewis A. Coster, "Max Scheler," in Sills, 14: pp. 39-42. C.B. Macpherson, *The Political Theory of Possessive Individualism, Hobbes to Locke* (Oxford University Press, 1962).

[11]Klaus von Beyme, "Intellectuals, intelligentsia," in Kernig, 4: pp. 301-312.

[12]D'Elia, "Jefferson, Rush, and the Limits of Philosophical Friendship," *Proceedings of the American Philosophical Society* 117, no. 5 (October 1973), p. 336.

[13]*Les Grands Courants de la Penseé Mondiale Contemporaine* (1958). On "The Religious Atheism of Anglo-American Empiricism," see Cornelio Fabro, *God in Exile, Modern Atheism: A Study of the Internal Dynamic of Modern Atheism, From its Roots in the Cartesian Cogito to the Present Day* (Westminster, Md.: Newman Press, 1968), Part VI. Trans. and edited by Arthur Gibson.

[14]*Pensées de Blaise Pascal*, edited by Léon Brunschvicg (new ed., Paris,

1904), 7, 527, p. 420.

[15]"Autobiography" in H. A. Washington, ed., *Writings of Thomas Jefferson* (9 vols.; Washington, D.C., 1853) 1: p. 2; Jefferson to Mr. Louis H. Girardin, January 15, 1815, *ibid.*, 6: p. 411.

[16]Ingrid Maisch, Anton Vögtle, George Spitzlberger, Claus D. Kernig "Jesus Christ," in Kernig, 4: pp. 398-418.

[17]Kenneth W. Underwood, "Protestant Political Thought," in Sills, 12: pp. 598-603.

[18]Benjamin Franklin, *Autobiography*, p. 95 in L. J. Lemish, ed. *Benjamin Franklin: The Autobiography and Other Writings* (N.Y.: The New American Library, 1961).

# Index